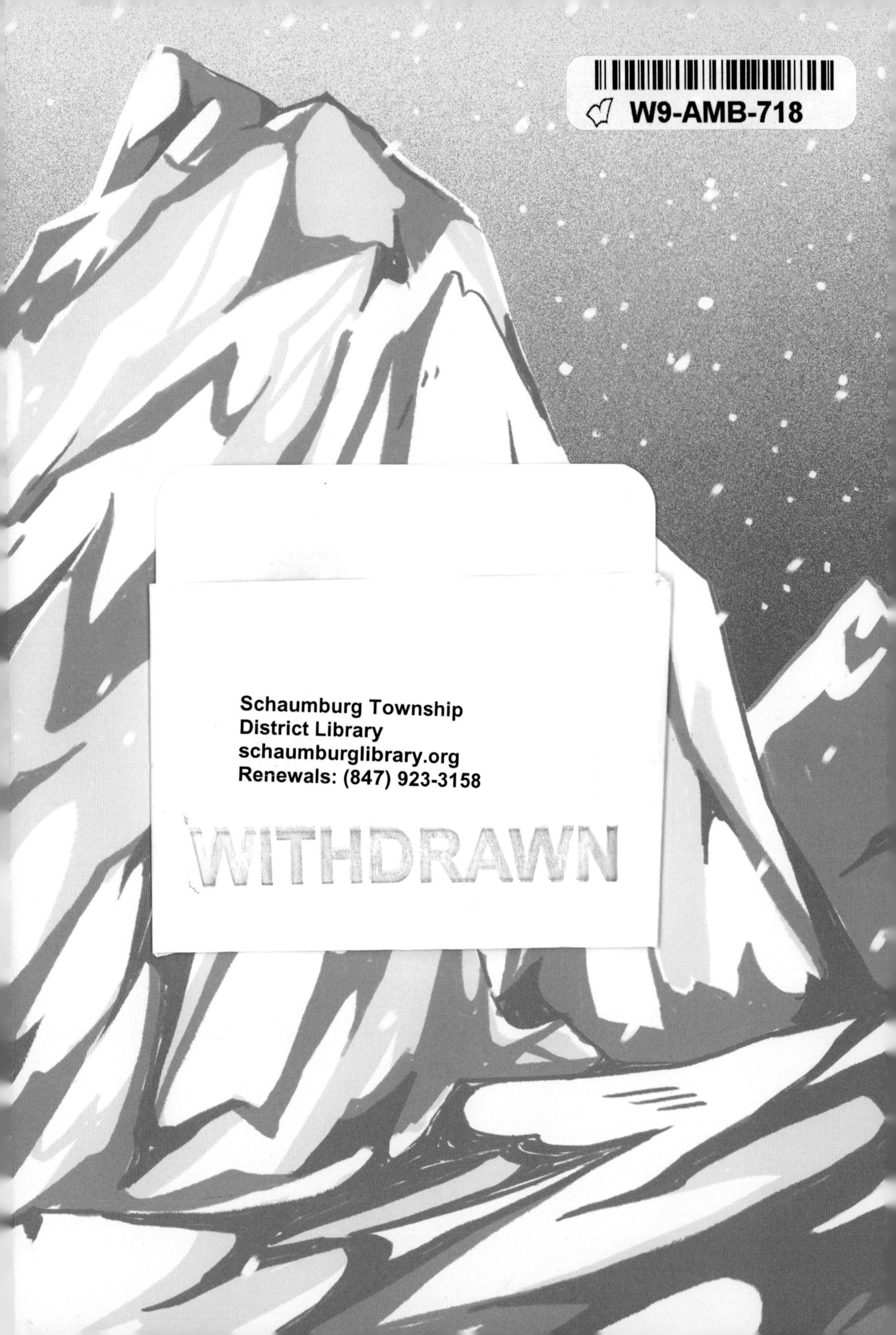

BLACK STAR

ERIC ANTHONY GLOVER : ARIELLE JOVELLANOS

ABRAMS COMICARTS MEGASCOPE, NEW YORK

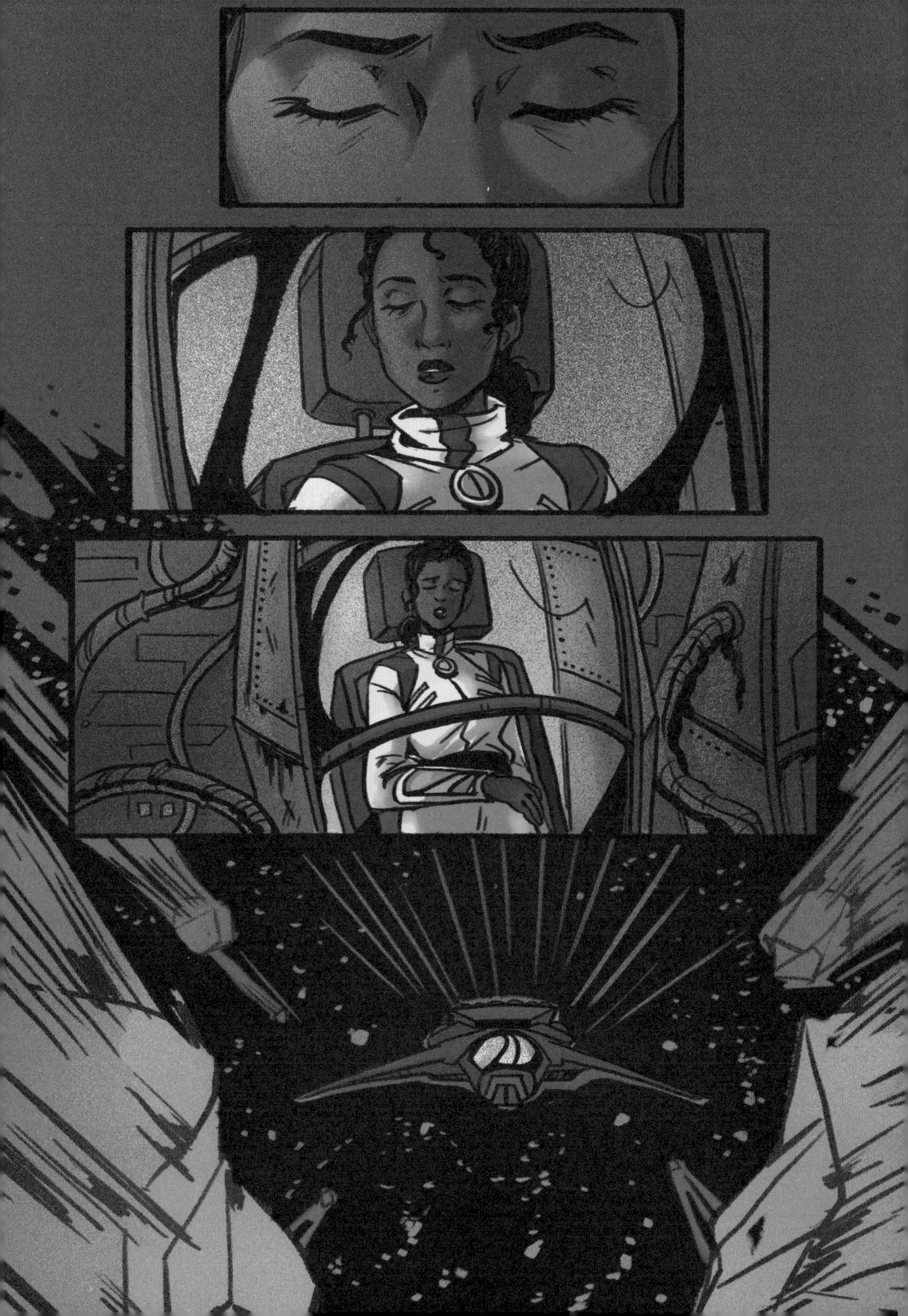

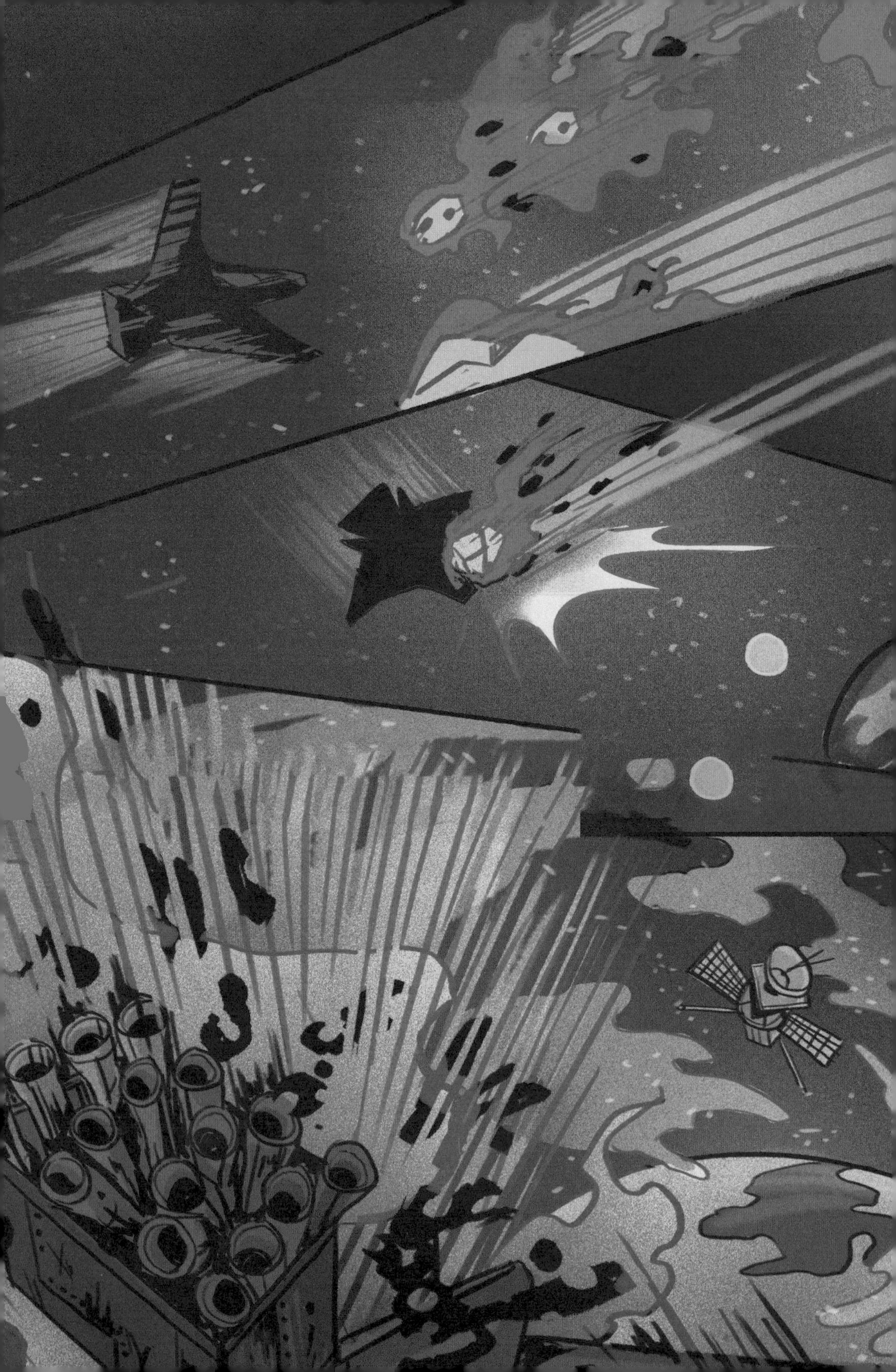

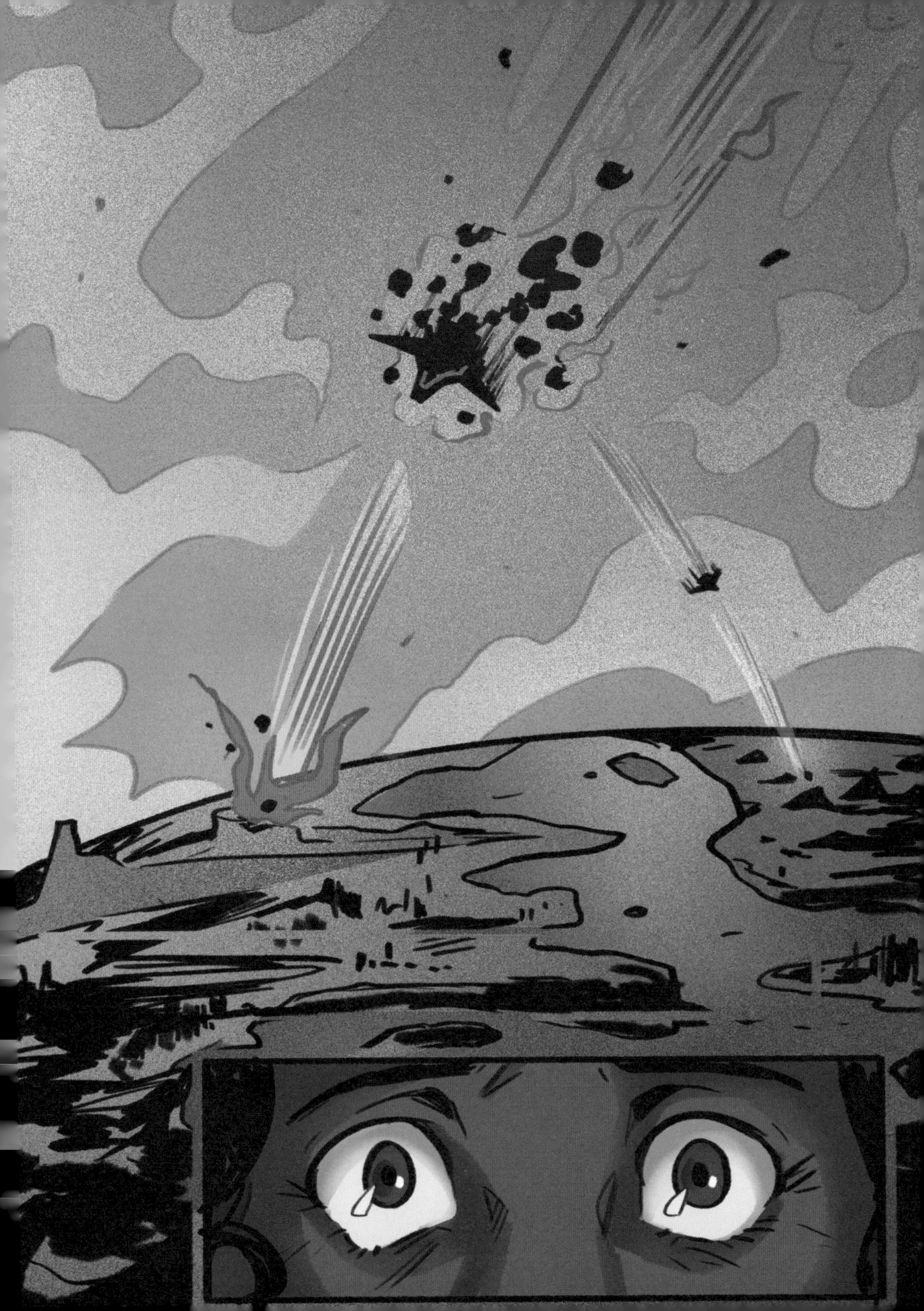

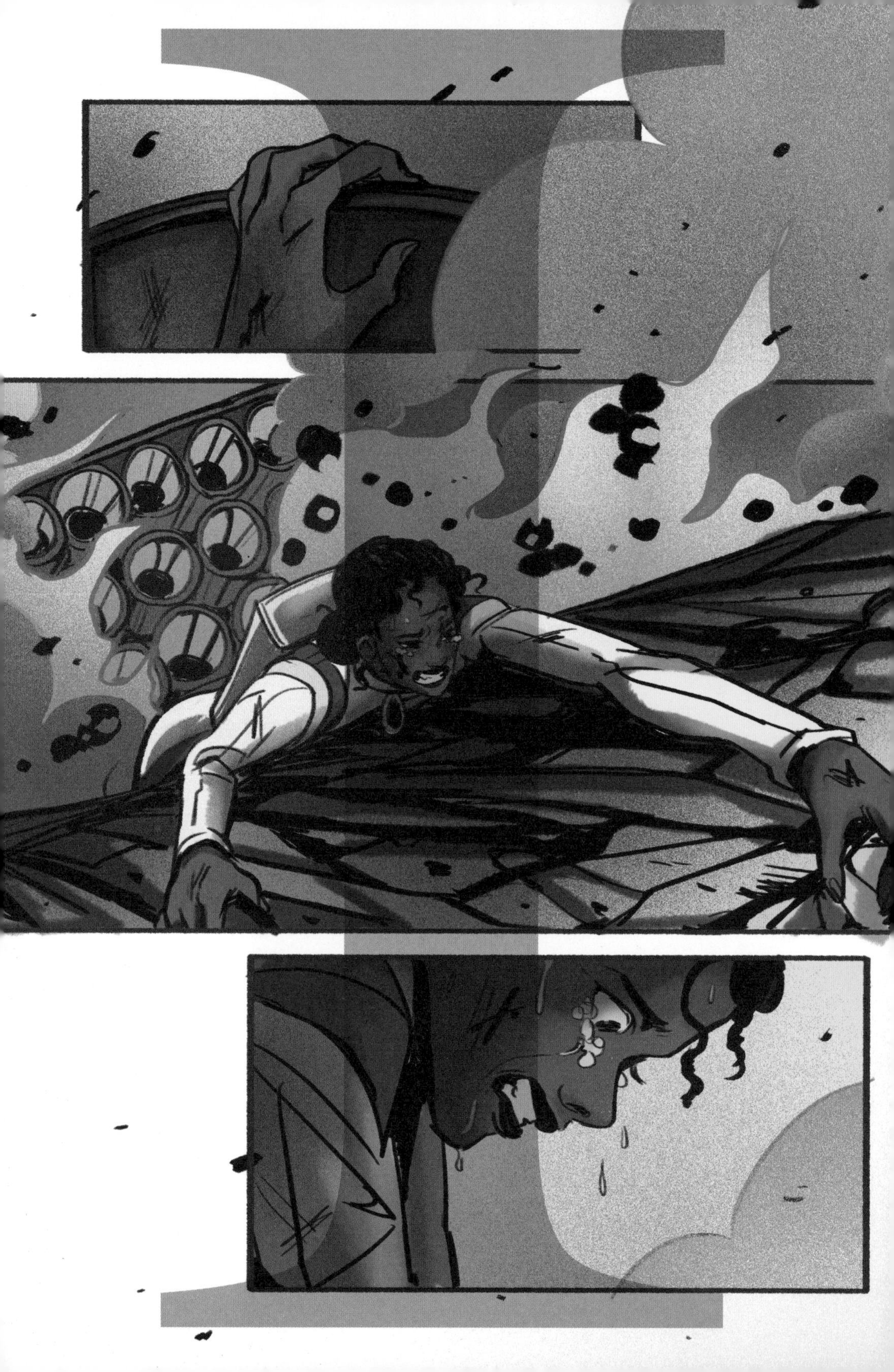

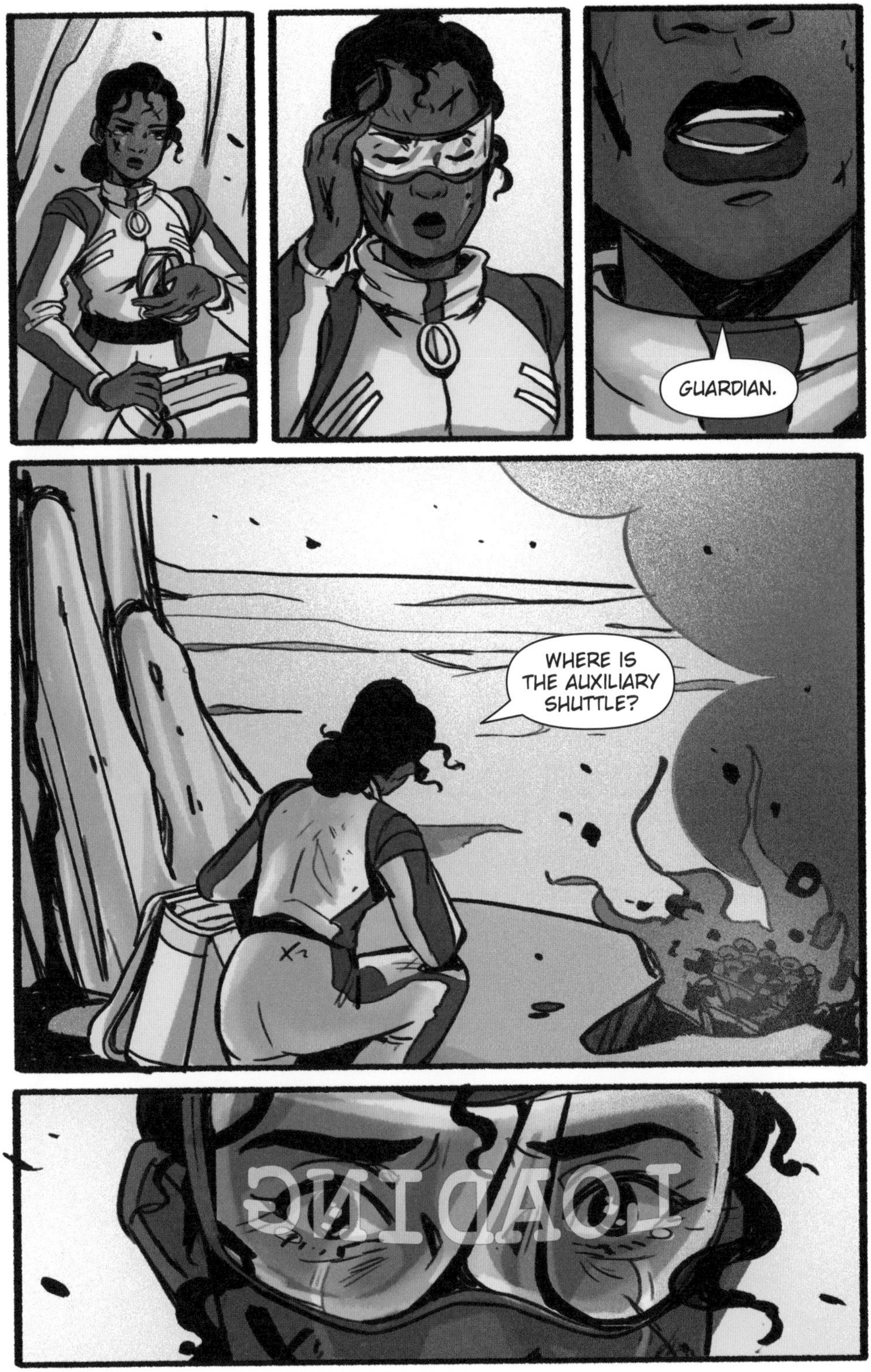
GUARDIAN.
WHERE IS THE AUXILIARY SHUTTLE?
LOADING

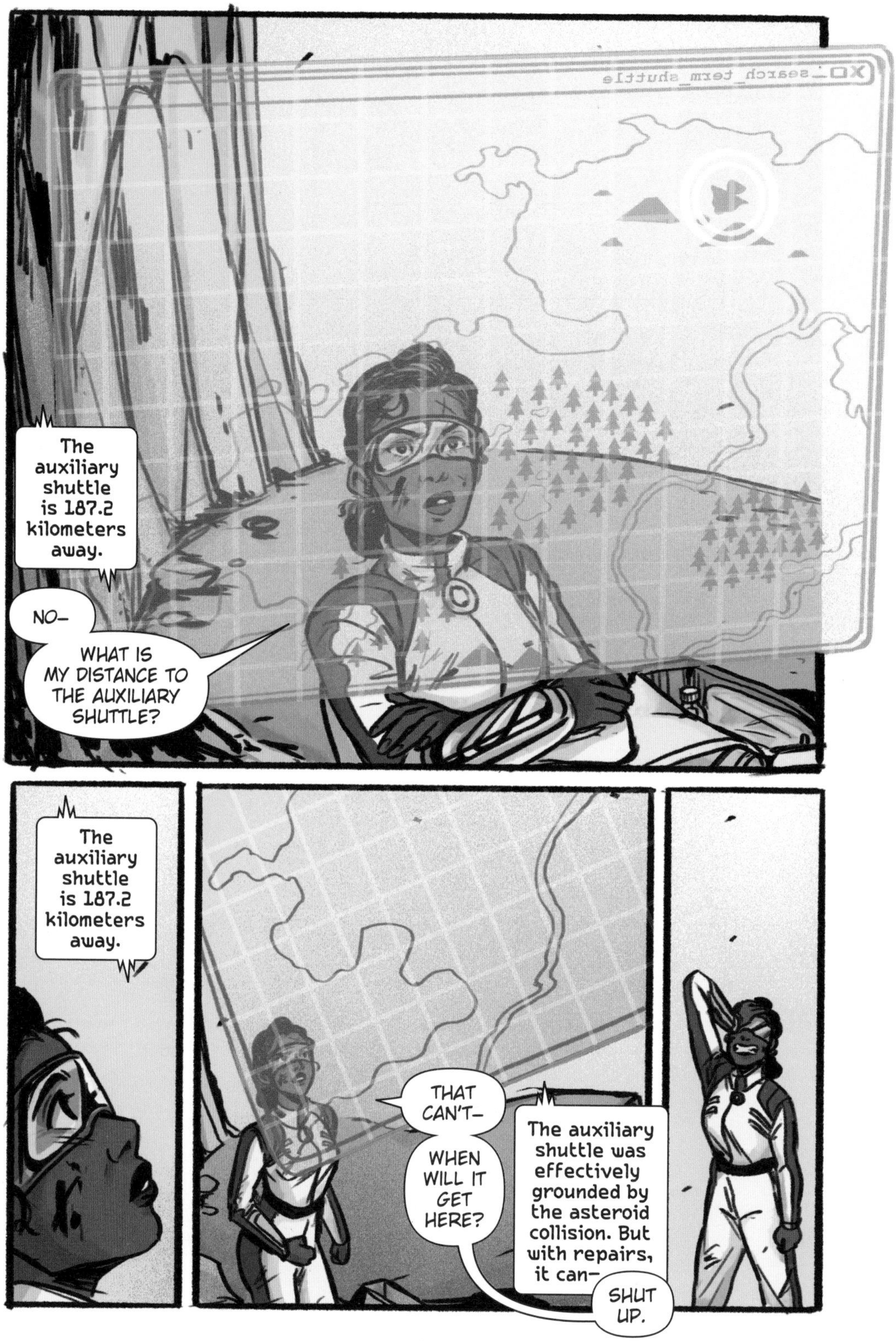
The auxiliary shuttle is 187.2 kilometers away.
NO–
WHAT IS MY DISTANCE TO THE AUXILIARY SHUTTLE?
The auxiliary shuttle is 187.2 kilometers away.
THAT CAN'T–
WHEN WILL IT GET HERE?
The auxiliary shuttle was effectively grounded by the asteroid collision. But with repairs, it can–
SHUT UP.

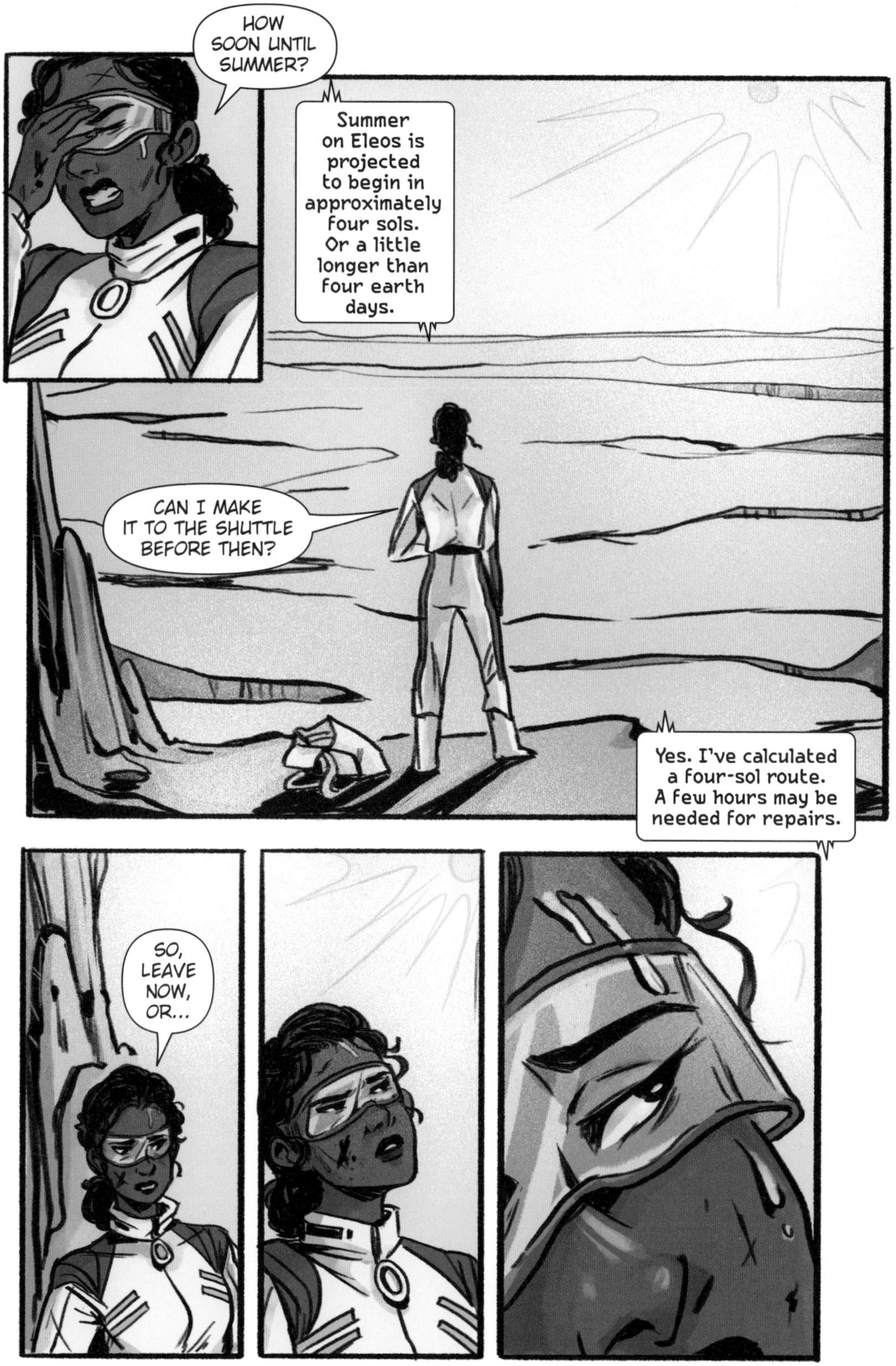
HOW SOON UNTIL SUMMER?
Summer on Eleos is projected to begin in approximately four sols. Or a little longer than four earth days.
CAN I MAKE IT TO THE SHUTTLE BEFORE THEN?
Yes. I've calculated a four-sol route. A few hours may be needed for repairs.
SO, LEAVE NOW, OR...

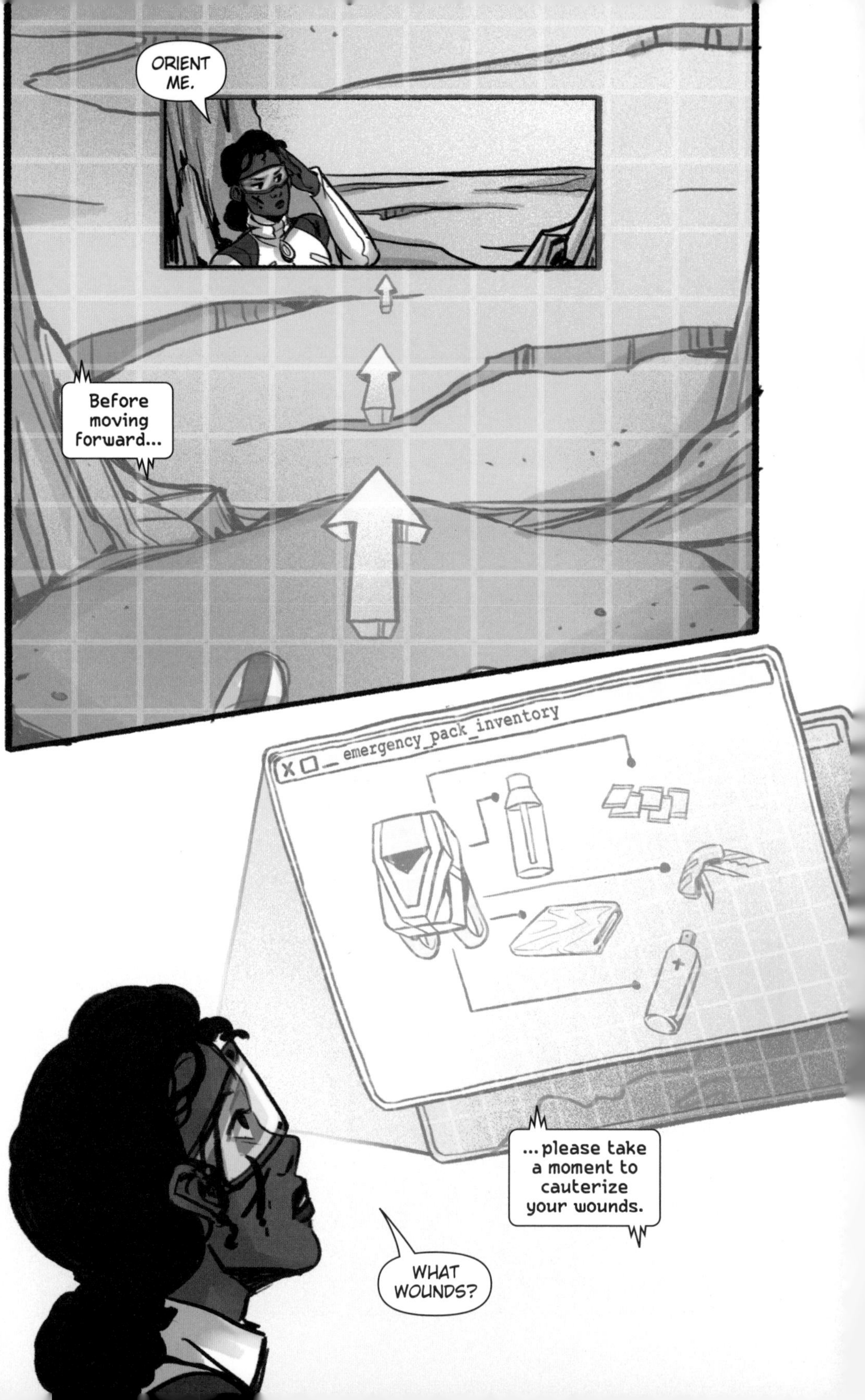
ORIENT ME.
Before moving forward...
emergency_pack_inventory
...please take a moment to cauterize your wounds.
WHAT WOUNDS?

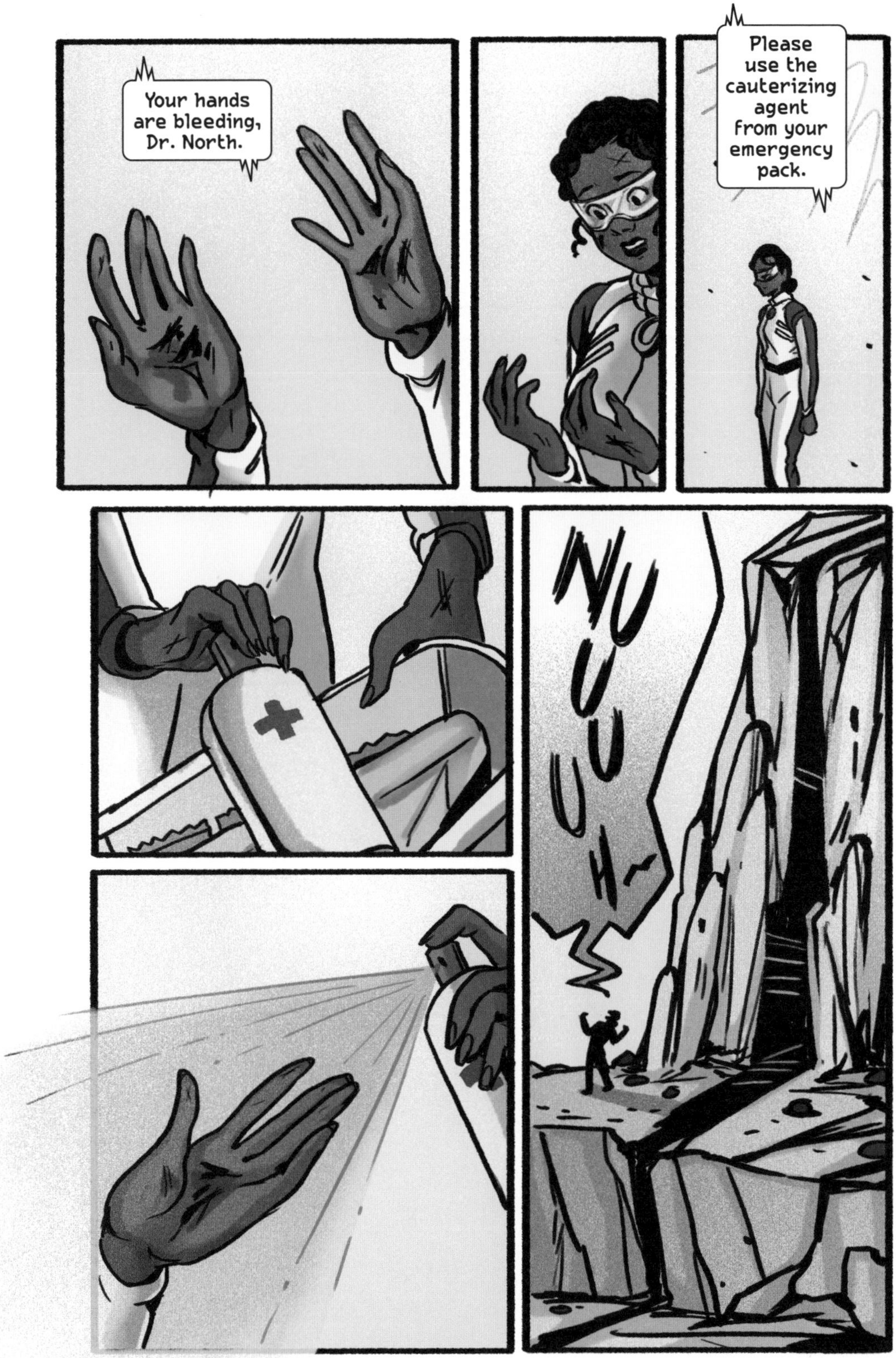
Your hands are bleeding, Dr. North.
Please use the cauterizing agent from your emergency pack.
NUUUUUH

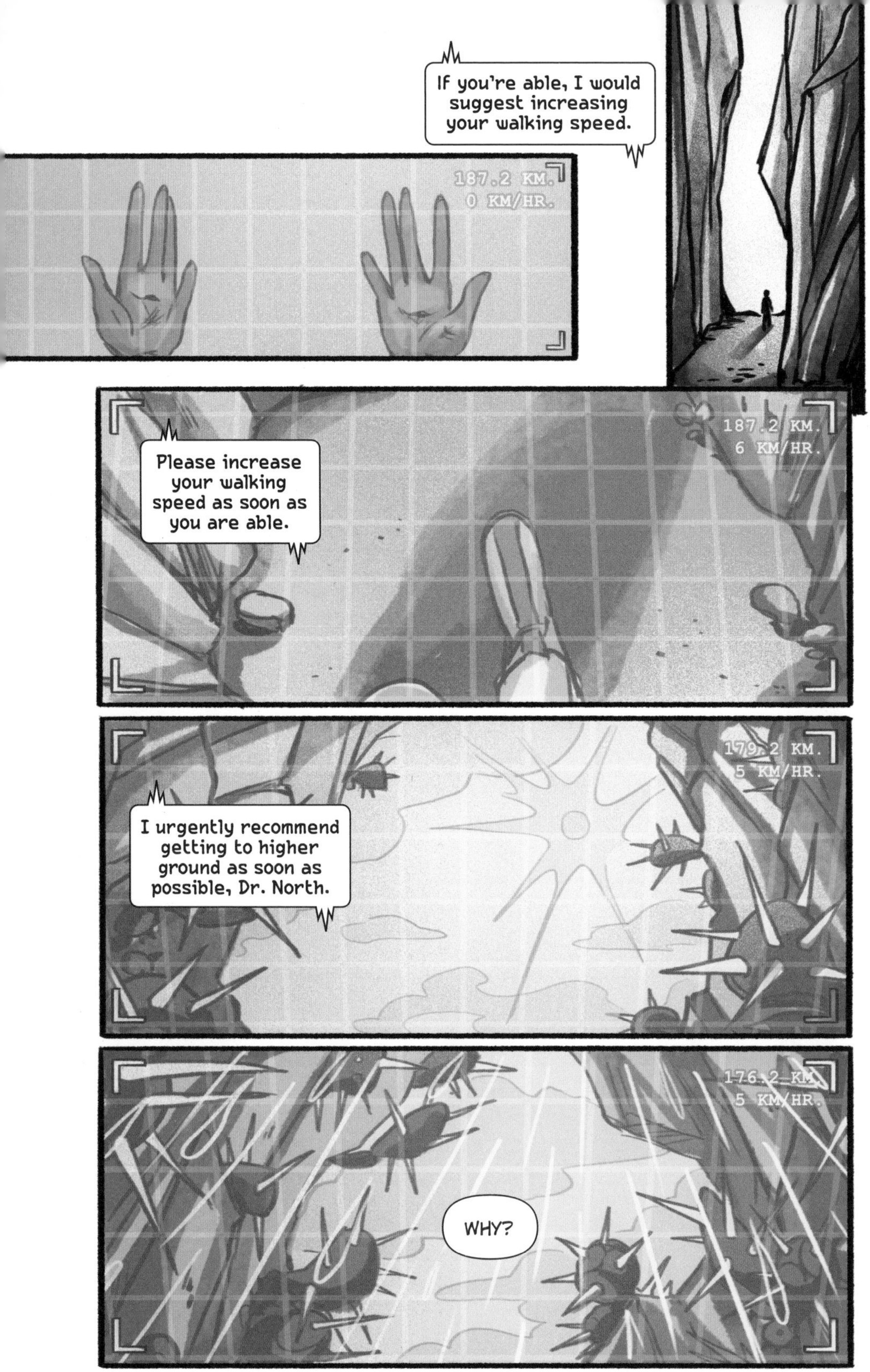
187.2 KM.
0 KM/HR.
If you're able, I would suggest increasing your walking speed.
187.2 KM.
6 KM/HR.
Please increase your walking speed as soon as you are able.
179.2 KM.
5 KM/HR.
I urgently recommend getting to higher ground as soon as possible, Dr. North.
176.2 KM.
5 KM/HR.
WHY?

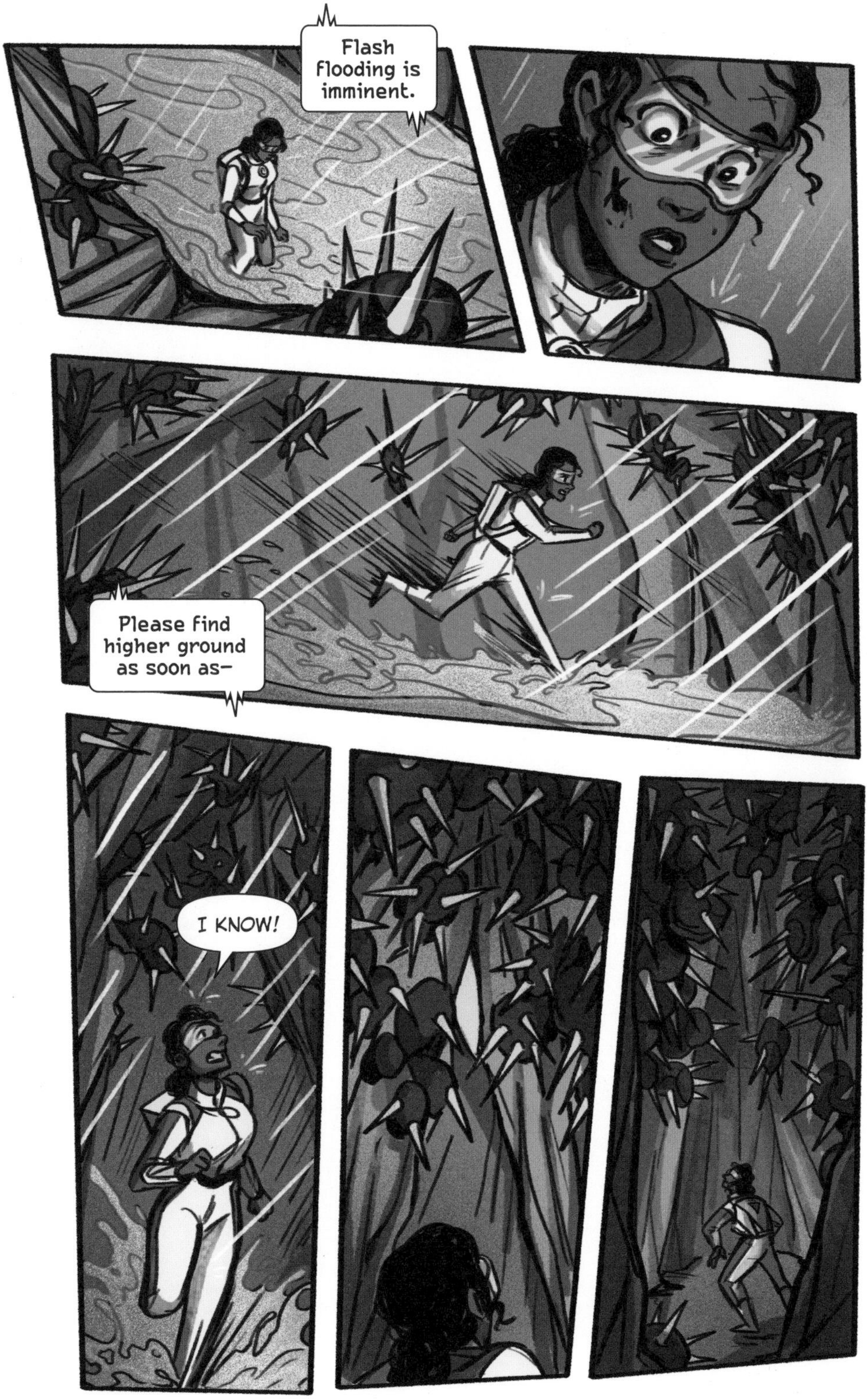
Flash flooding is imminent.
Please find higher ground as soon as–
I KNOW!

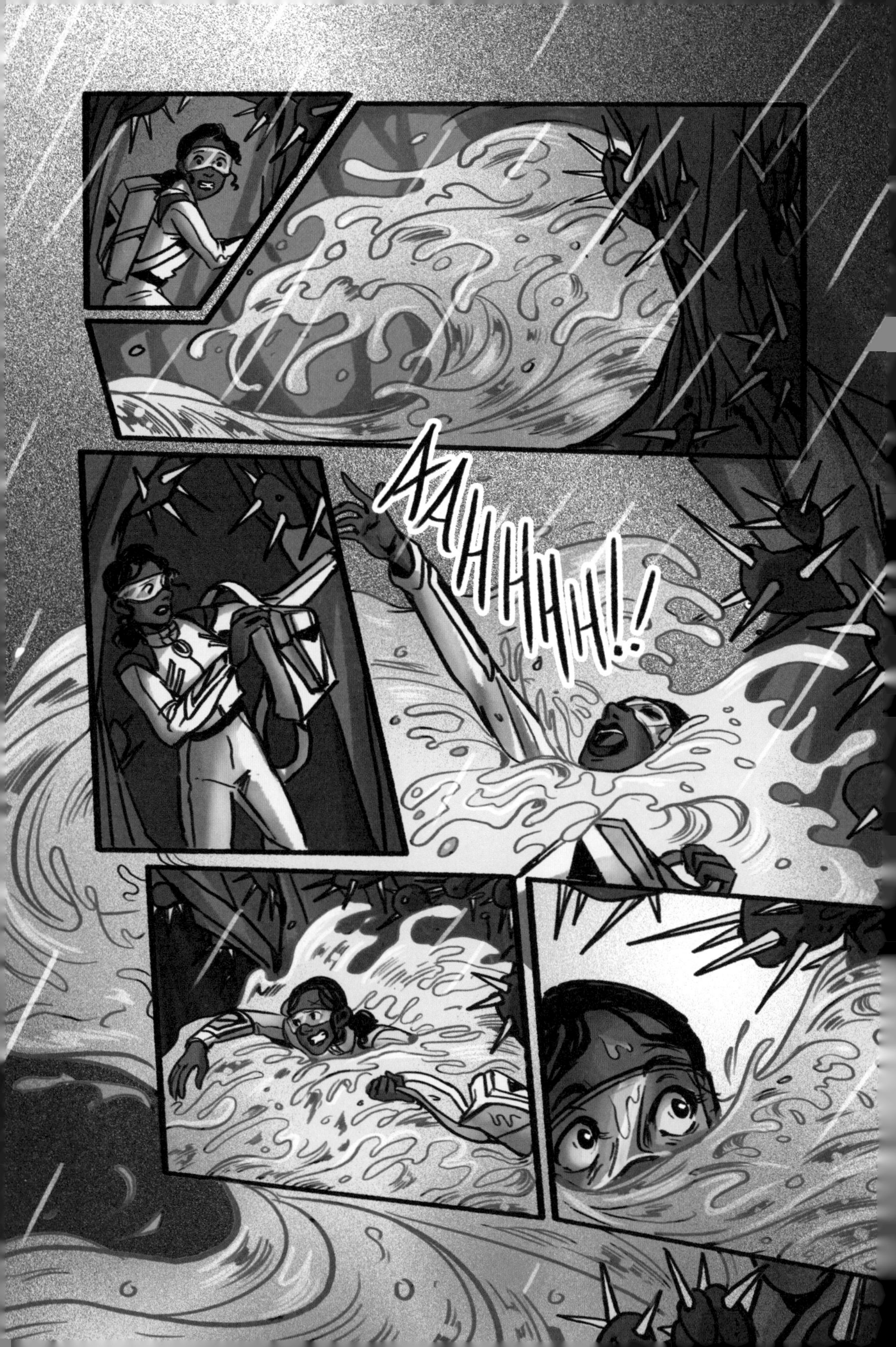
AAHHHHH!!

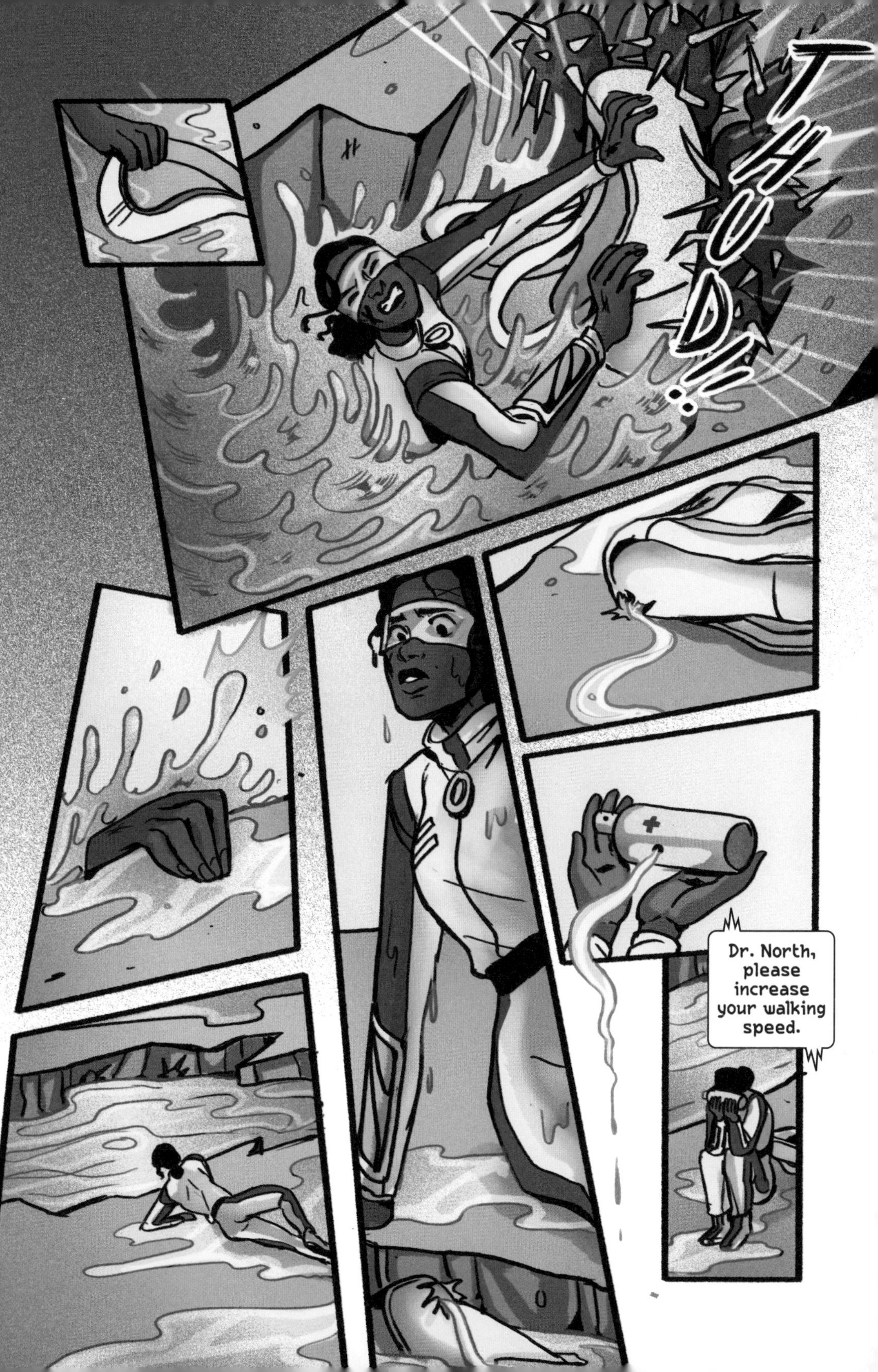
THUD!!
Dr. North, please increase your walking speed.

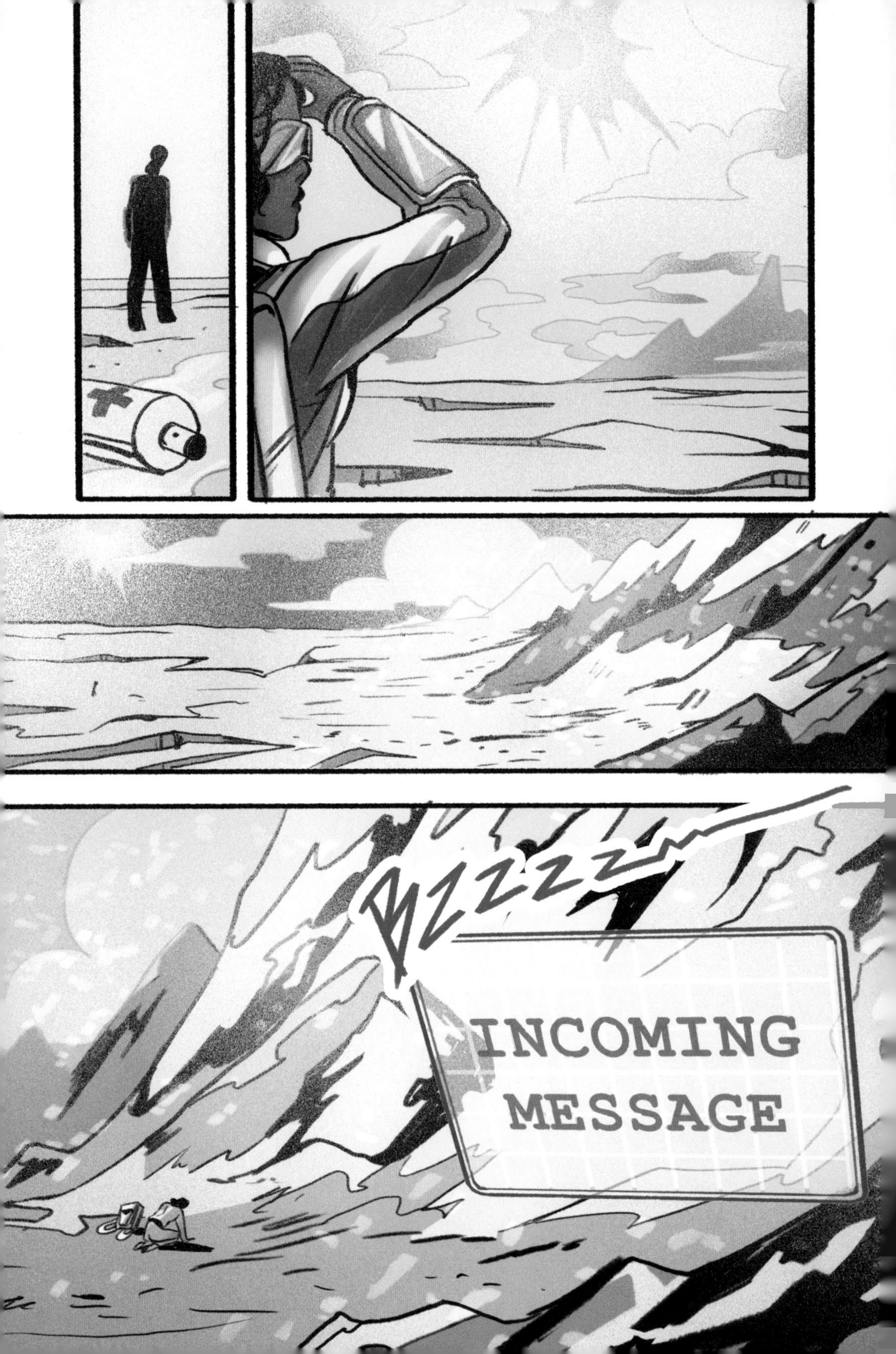
BZZZZ
INCOMING
MESSAGE

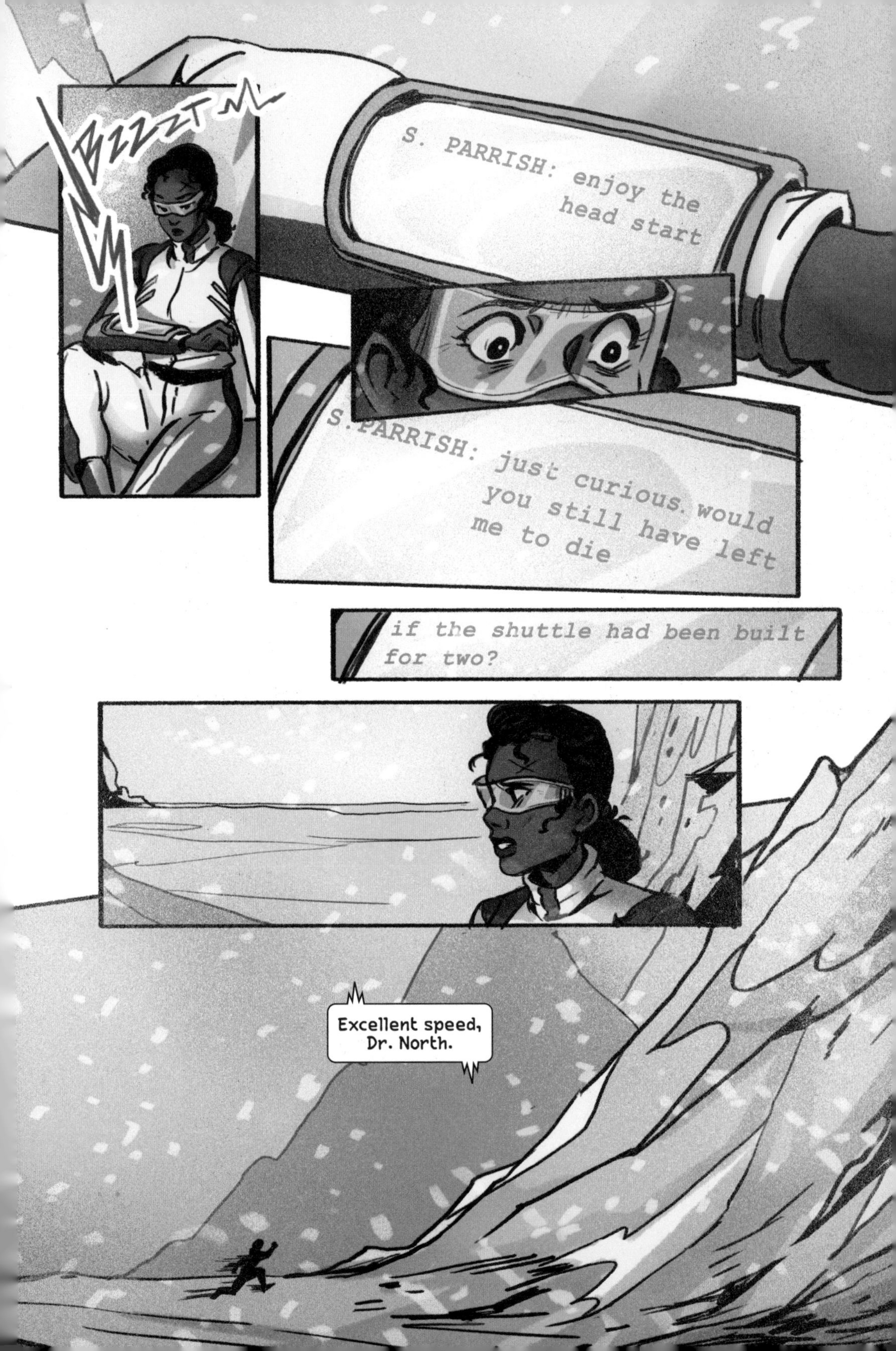
BZZZT
S. PARRISH: enjoy the head start
S.PARRISH: just curious. would you still have left me to die
if the shuttle had been built for two?
Excellent speed, Dr. North.

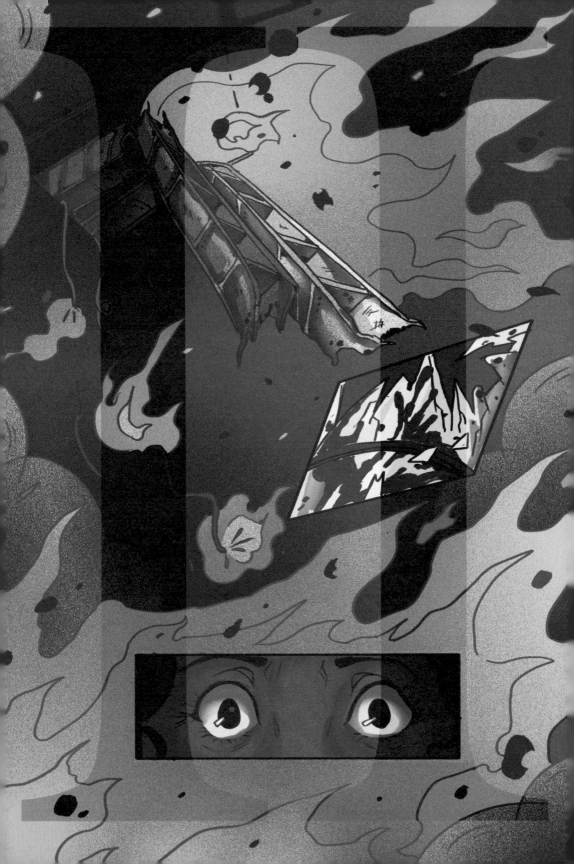

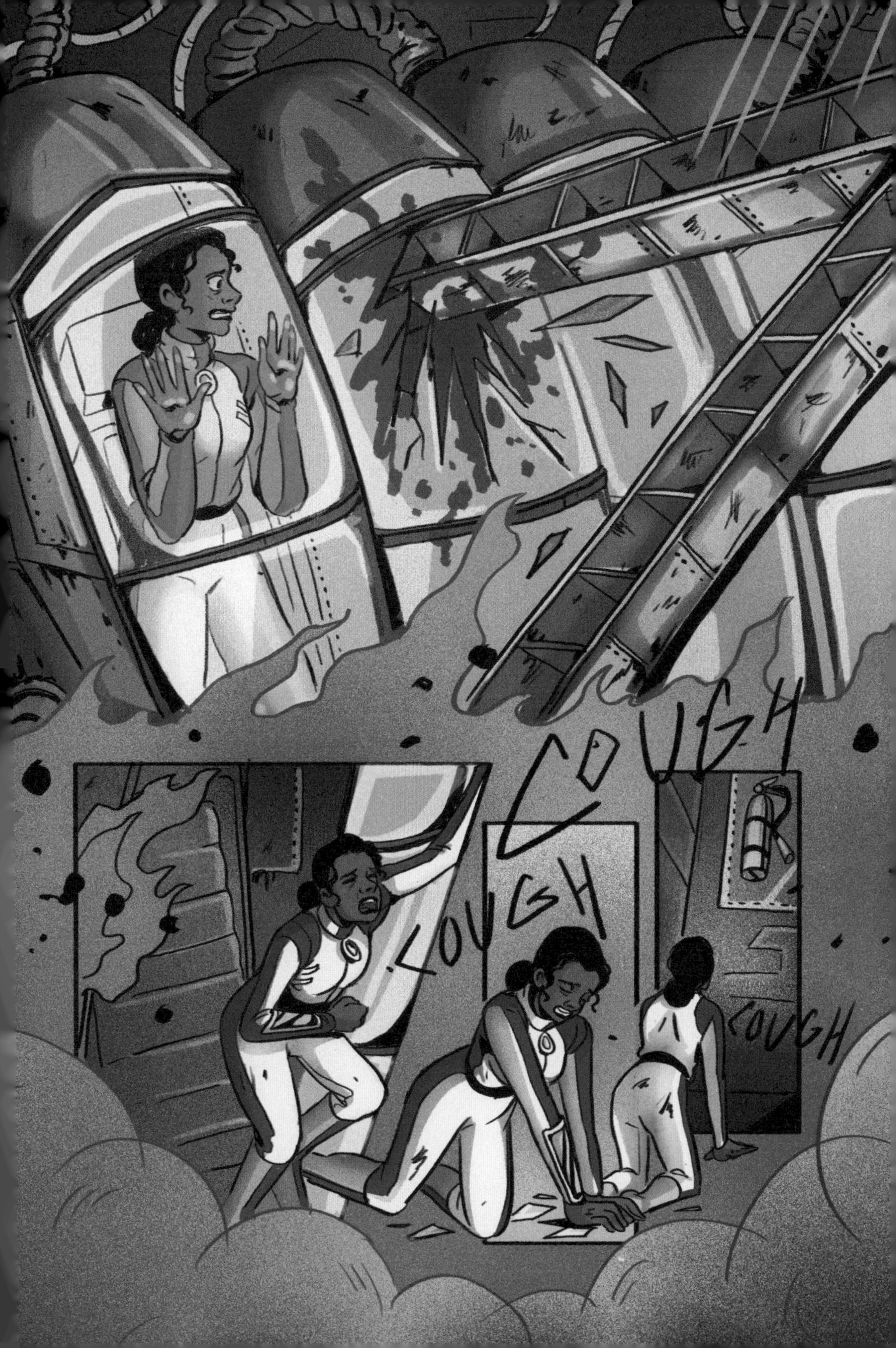
COUGH
COUGH
COUGH

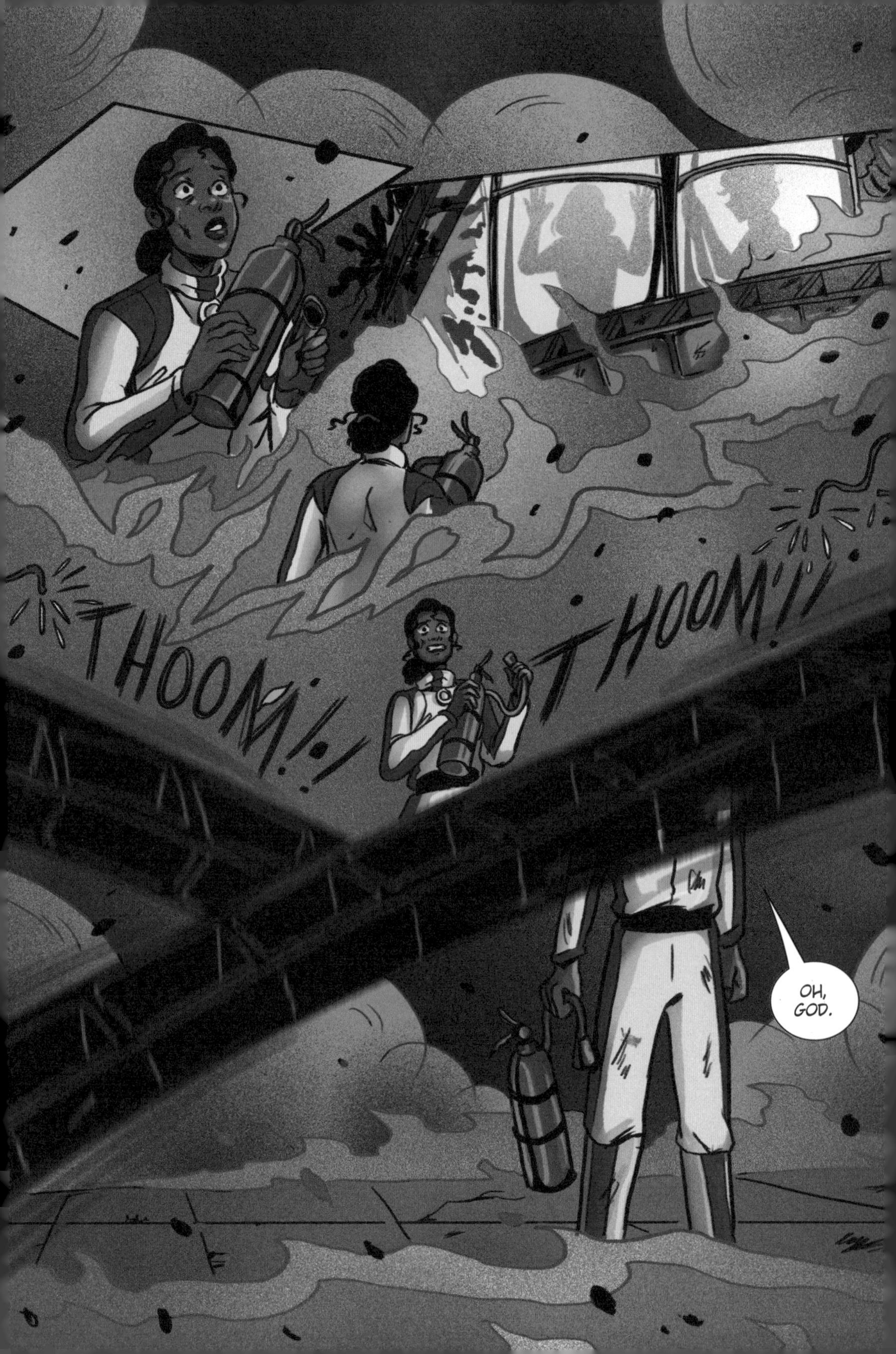
THOOM!!
THOOM!!
OH, GOD.

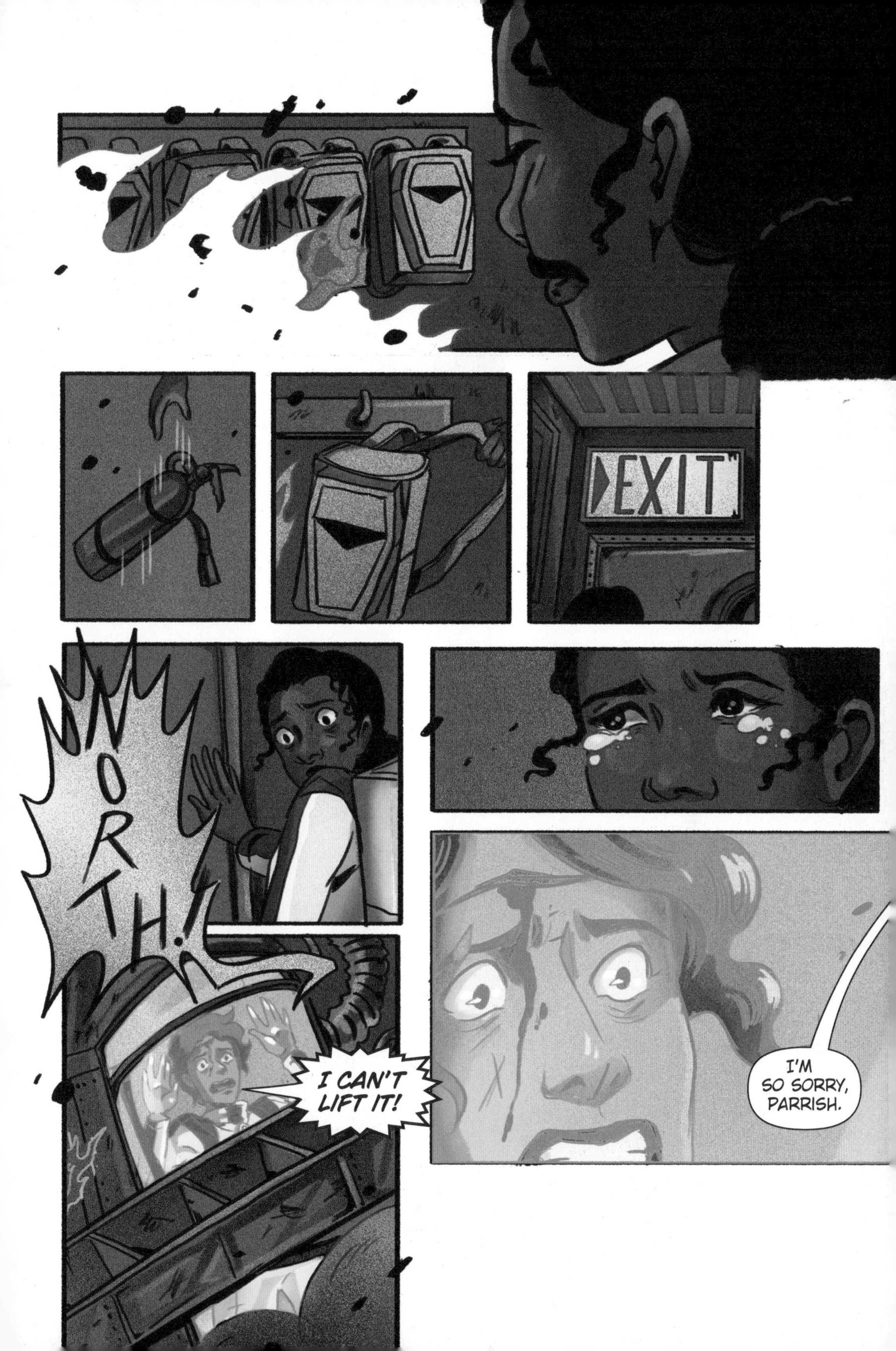
EXIT
NORTH!
I CAN'T LIFT IT!
I'M SO SORRY, PARRISH.

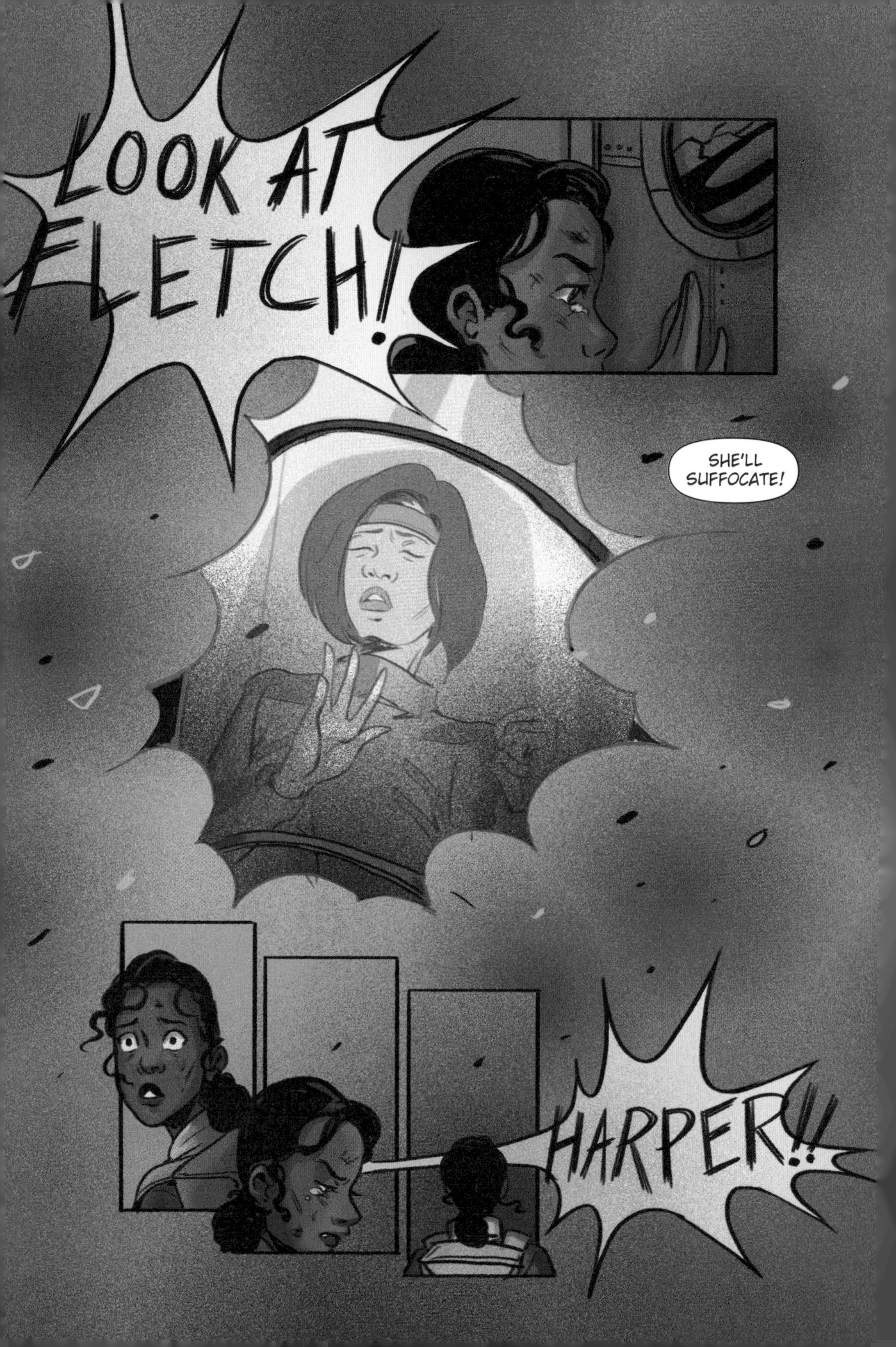
LOOK AT FLETCH!
SHE'LL SUFFOCATE!
HARPER!!

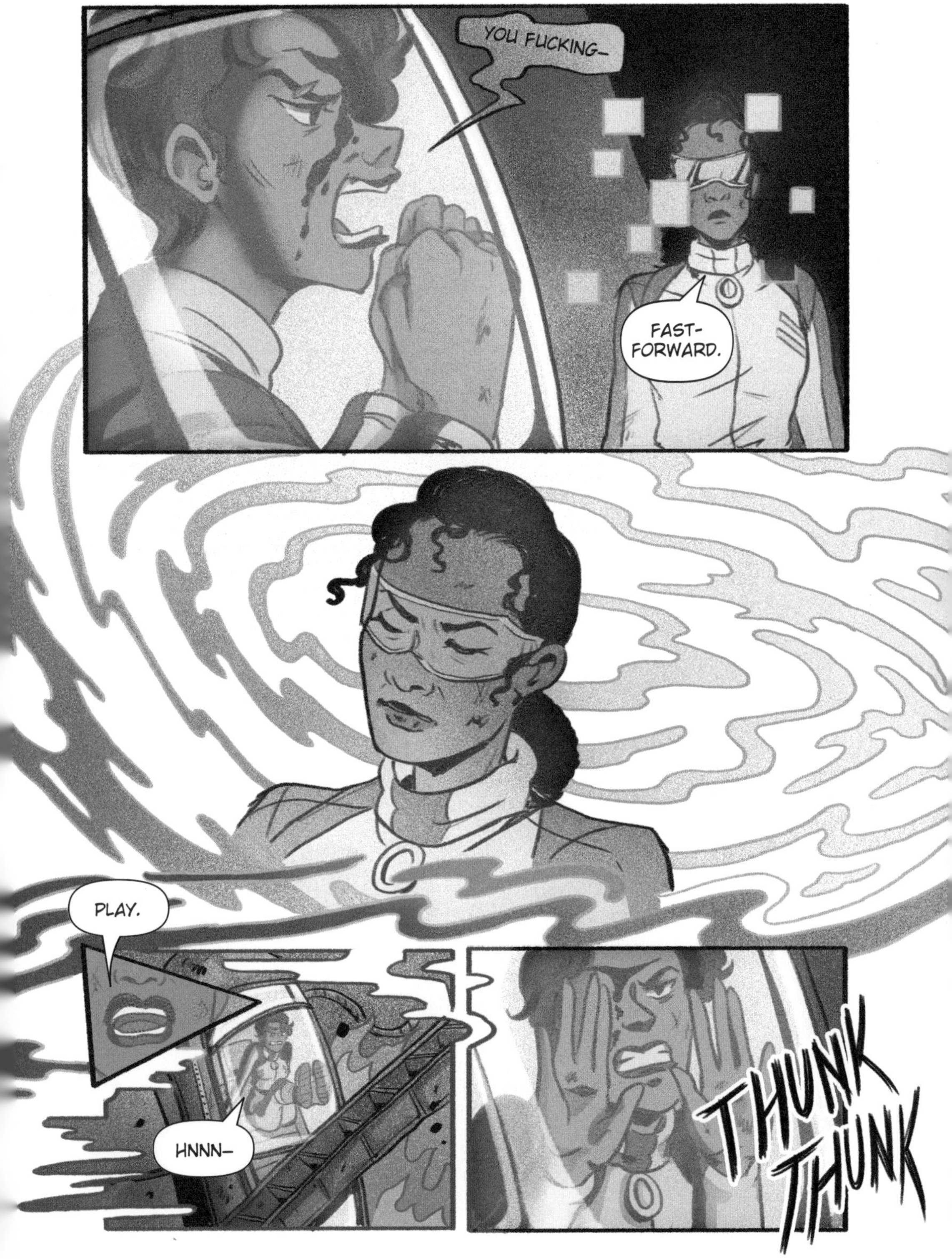
YOU FUCKING—
FAST-FORWARD.
PLAY.
HNNN—
THUNK THUNK

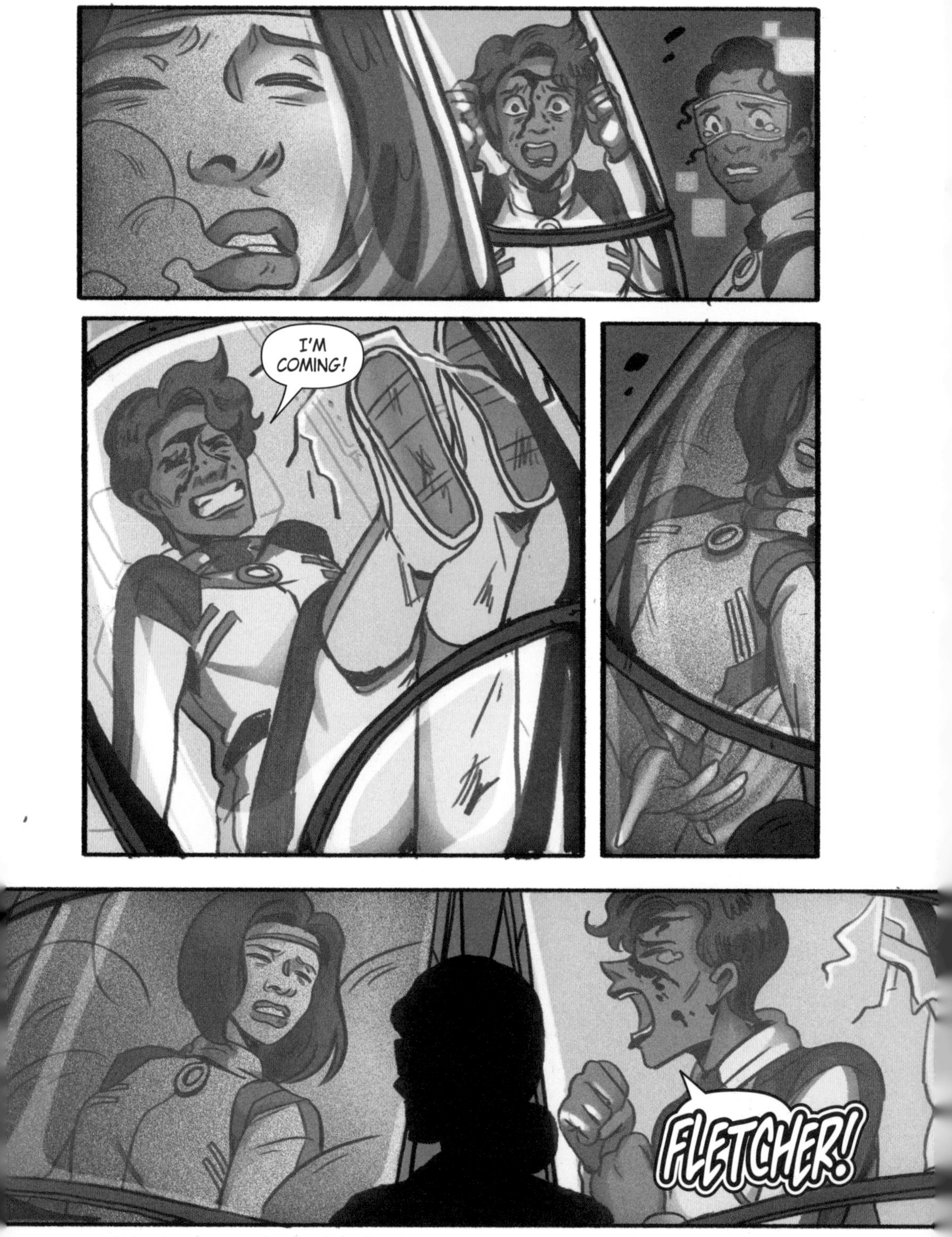
I'M COMING!
FLETCHER!

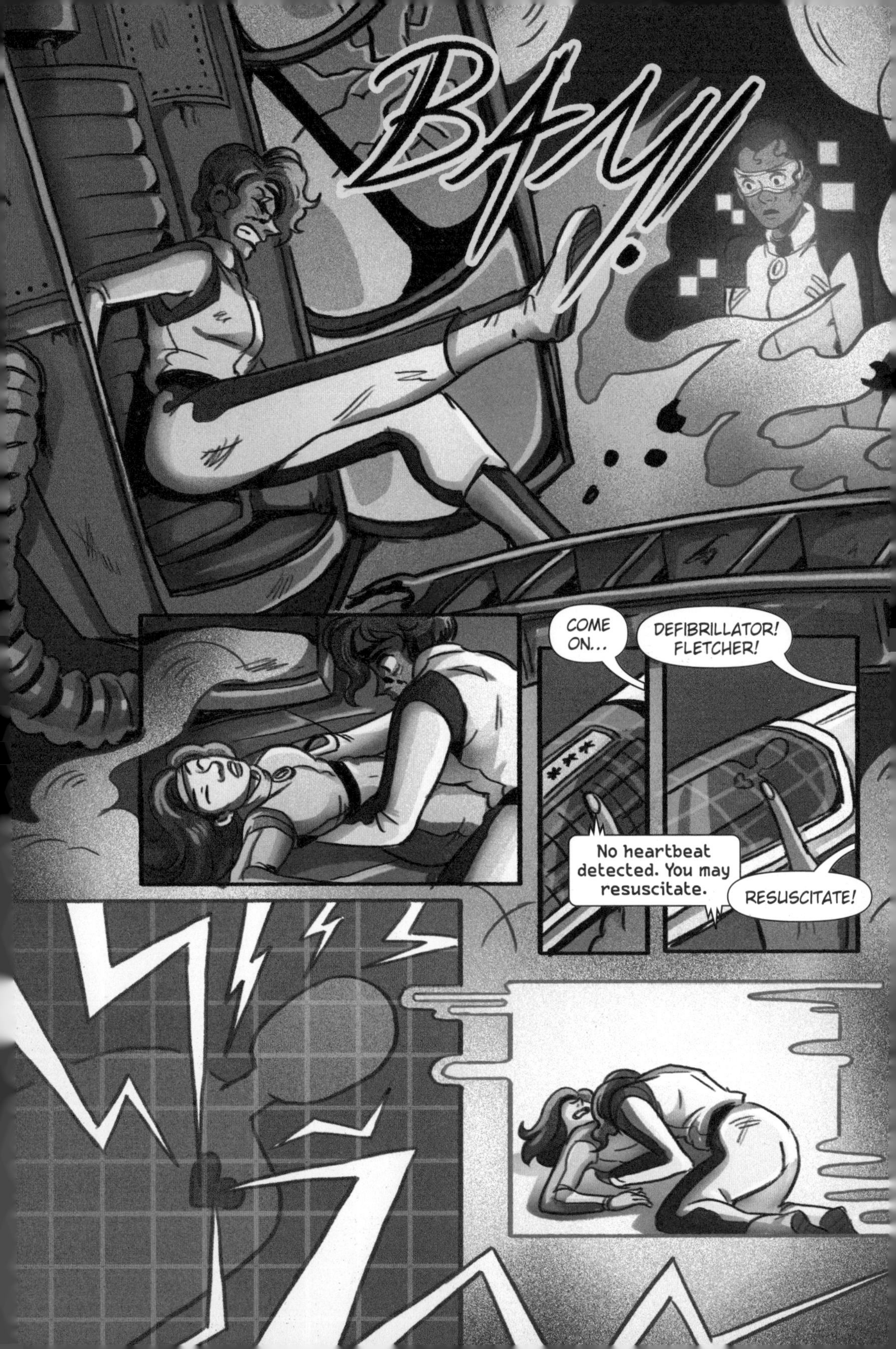
BAM!
COME ON...
DEFIBRILLATOR! FLETCHER!
No heartbeat detected. You may resuscitate.
RESUSCITATE!

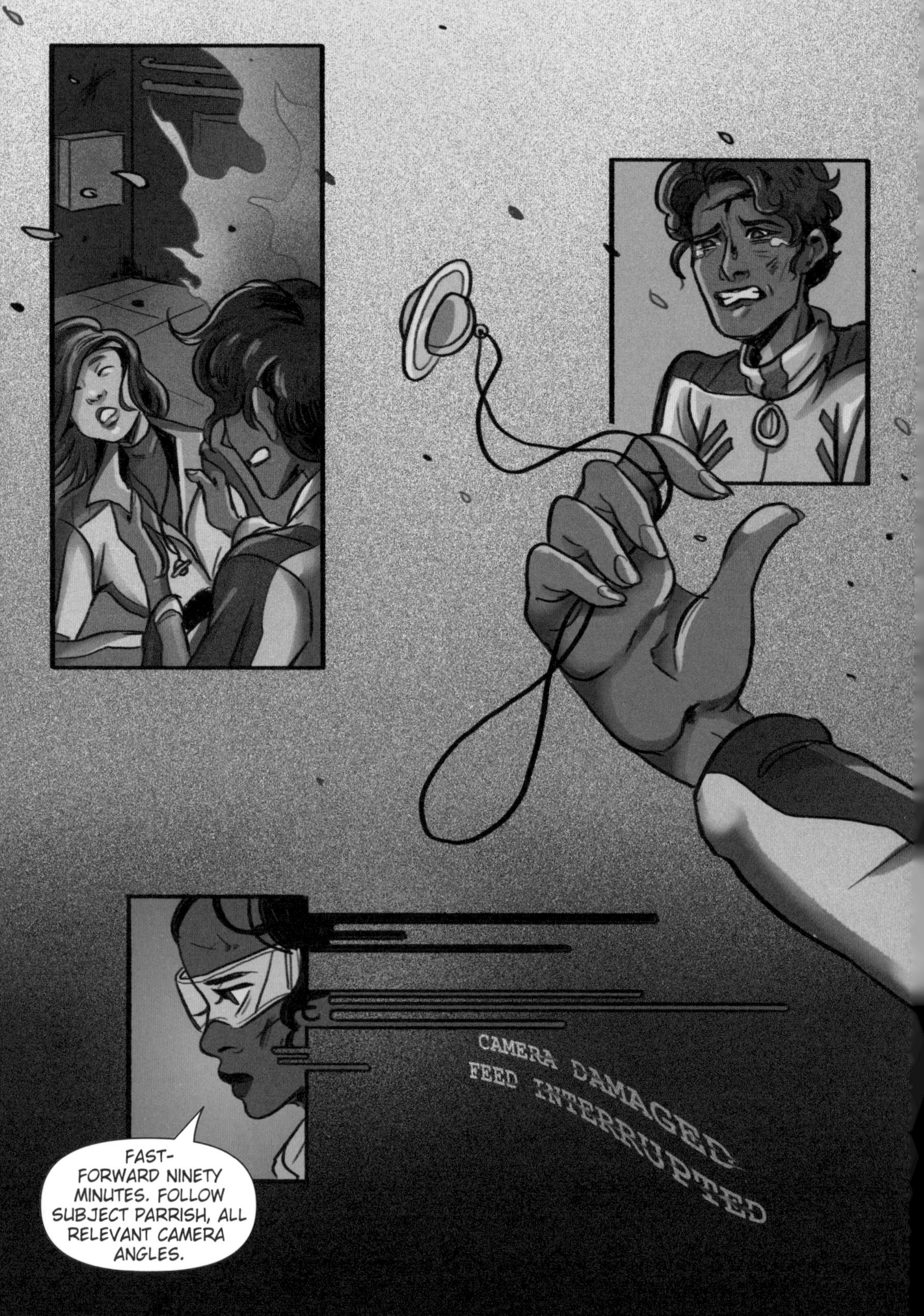
CAMERA DAMAGED
FEED INTERRUPTED
FAST-FORWARD NINETY MINUTES. FOLLOW SUBJECT PARRISH, ALL RELEVANT CAMERA ANGLES.

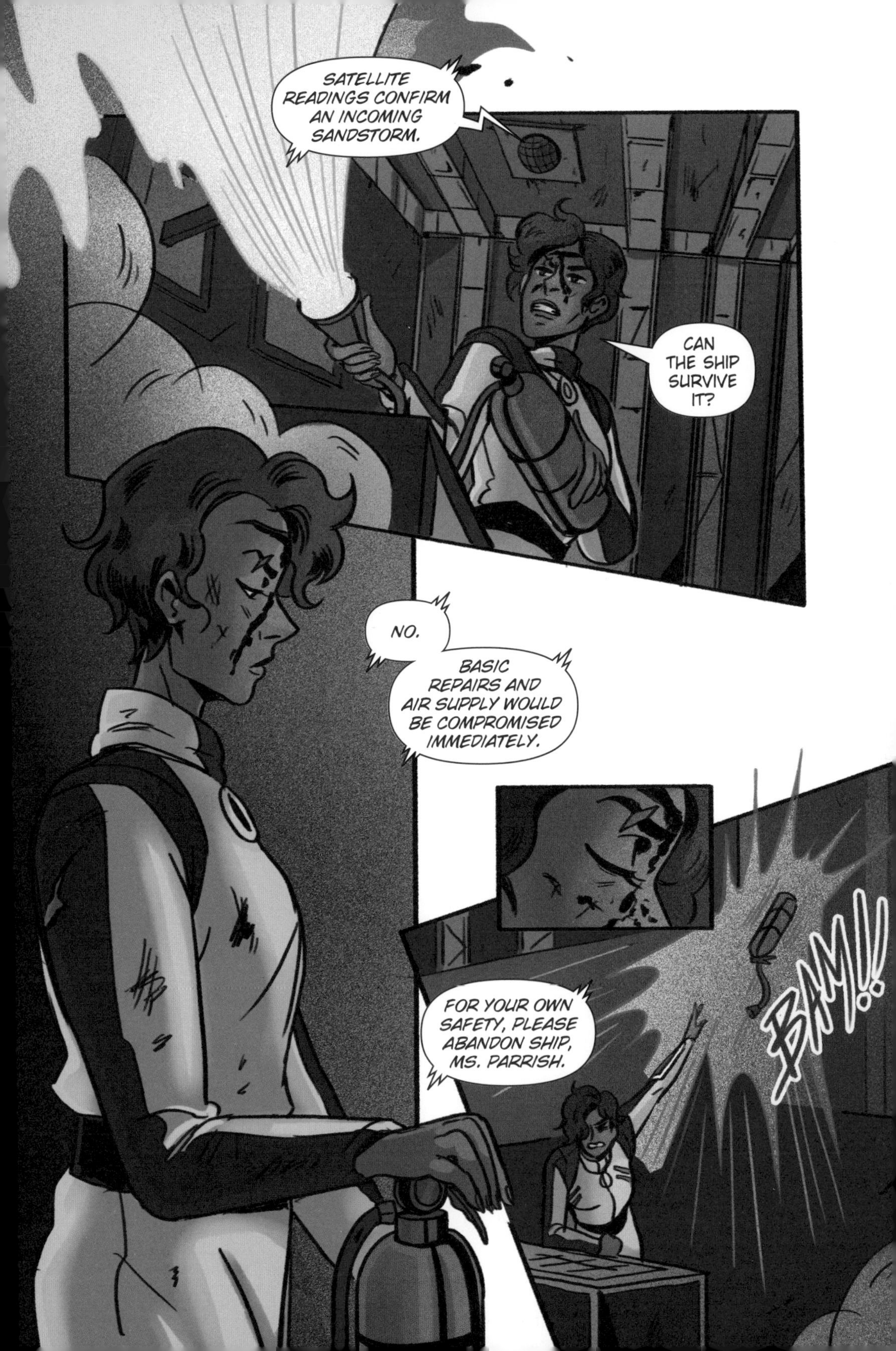
SATELLITE READINGS CONFIRM AN INCOMING SANDSTORM.
CAN THE SHIP SURVIVE IT?
NO.
BASIC REPAIRS AND AIR SUPPLY WOULD BE COMPROMISED IMMEDIATELY.
FOR YOUR OWN SAFETY, PLEASE ABANDON SHIP, MS. PARRISH.
BAM!!

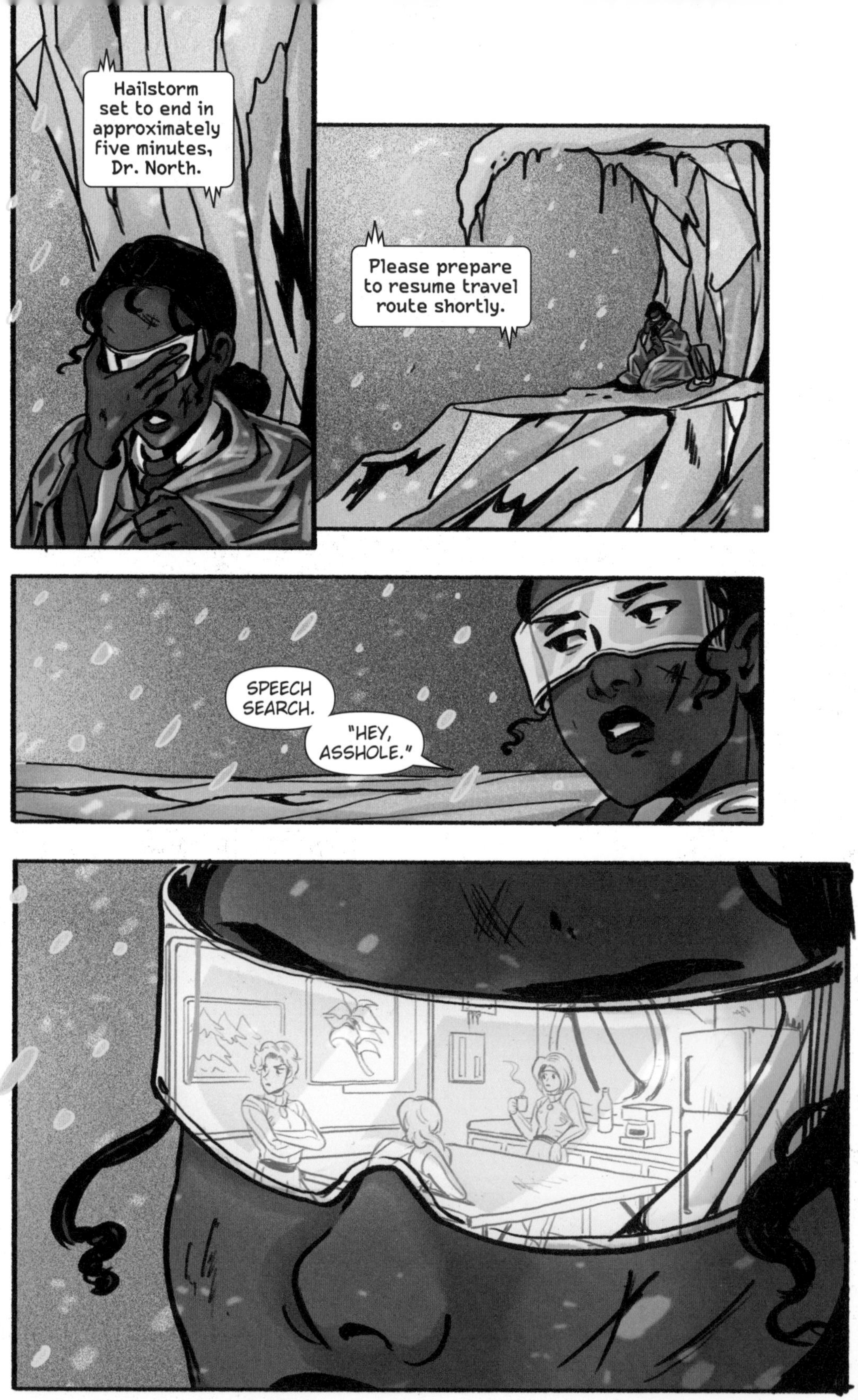
Hailstorm set to end in approximately five minutes, Dr. North.
Please prepare to resume travel route shortly.
SPEECH SEARCH.
"HEY, ASSHOLE."

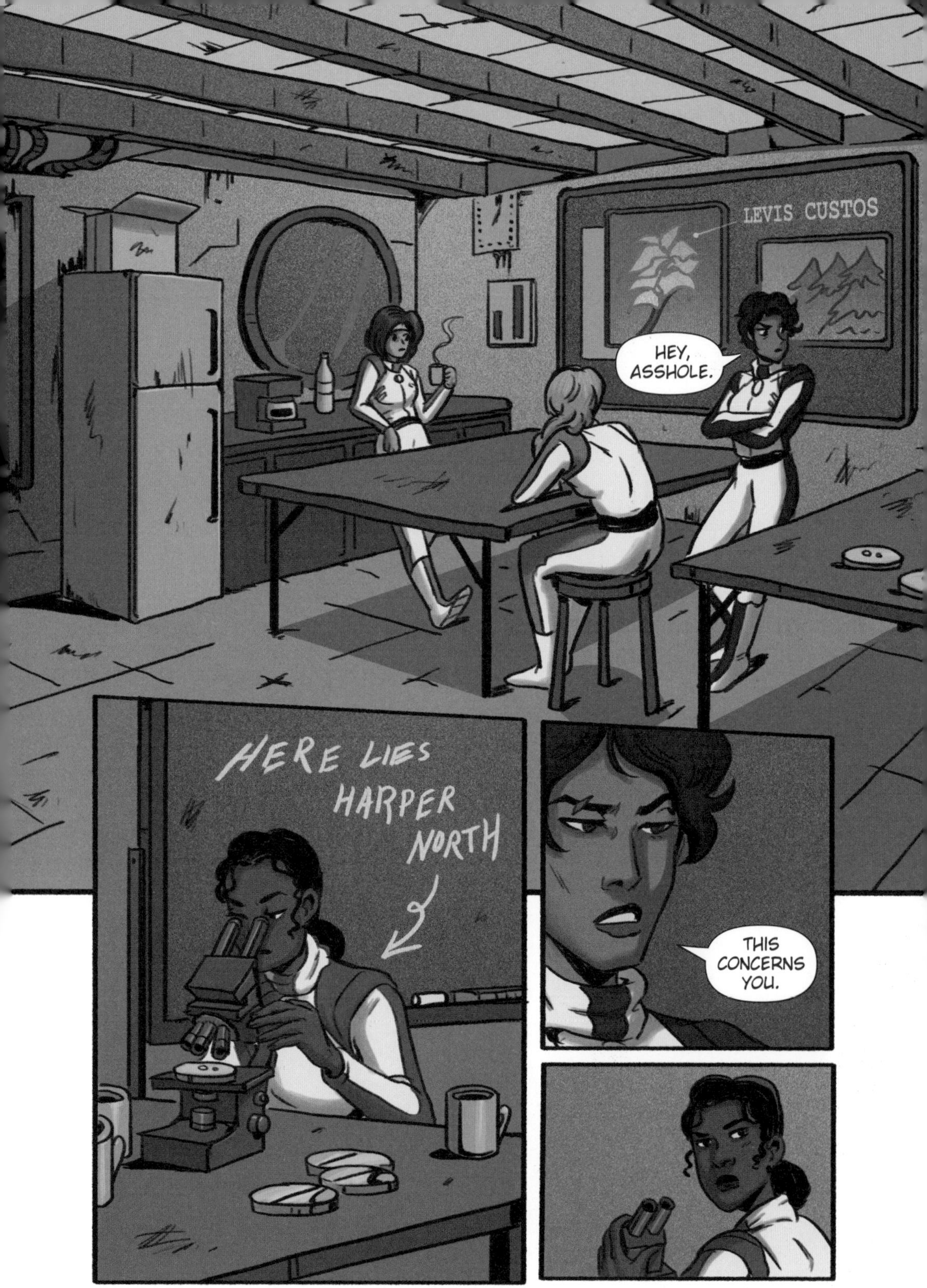
LEVIS CUSTOS
HEY, ASSHOLE.
HERE LIES HARPER NORTH
THIS CONCERNS YOU.

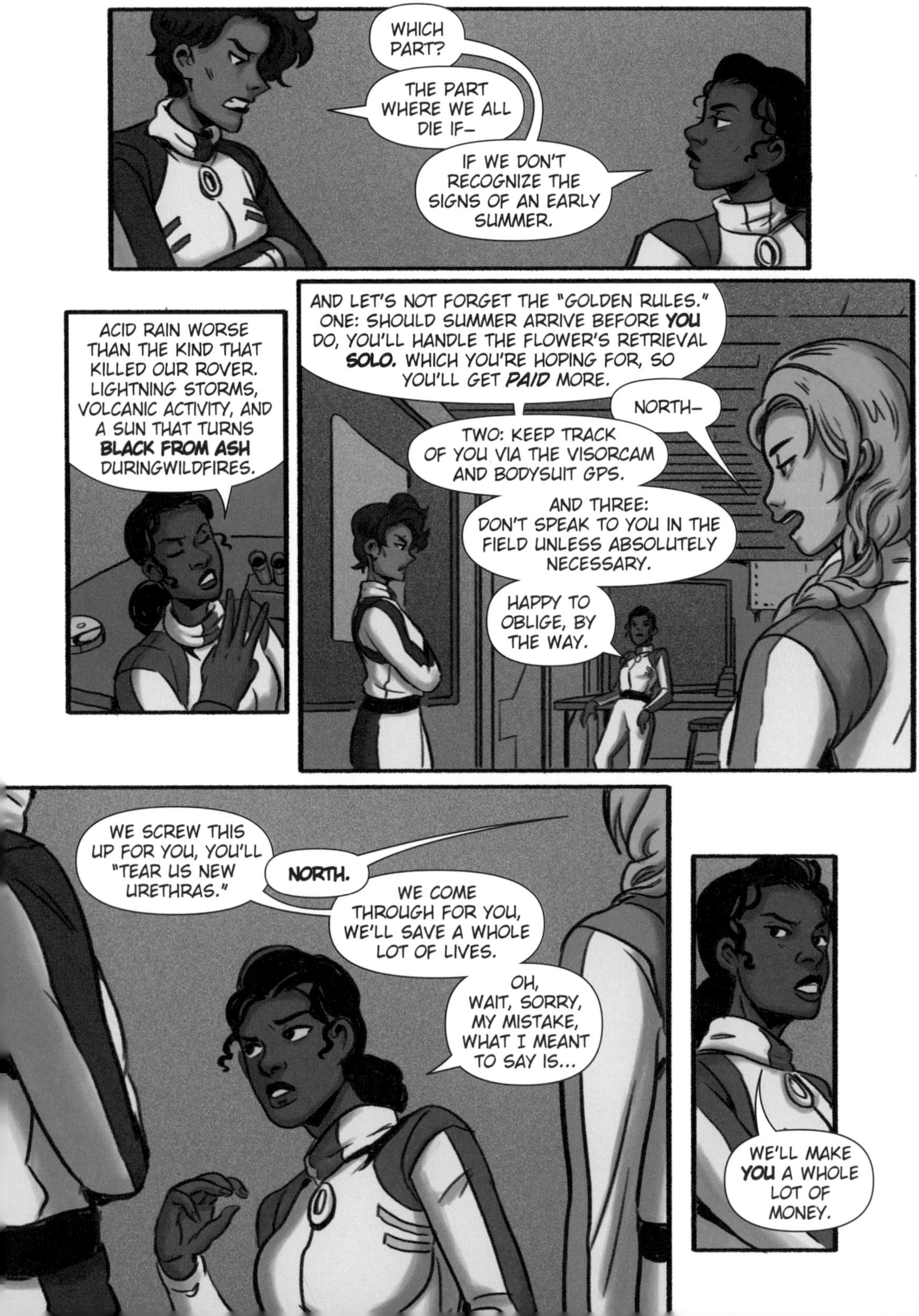
WHICH PART?
THE PART WHERE WE ALL DIE IF–
IF WE DON'T RECOGNIZE THE SIGNS OF AN EARLY SUMMER.
ACID RAIN WORSE THAN THE KIND THAT KILLED OUR ROVER. LIGHTNING STORMS, VOLCANIC ACTIVITY, AND A SUN THAT TURNS **BLACK FROM ASH** DURINGWILDFIRES.
AND LET'S NOT FORGET THE "GOLDEN RULES." ONE: SHOULD SUMMER ARRIVE BEFORE **YOU** DO, YOU'LL HANDLE THE FLOWER'S RETRIEVAL **SOLO.** WHICH YOU'RE HOPING FOR, SO YOU'LL GET ***PAID*** MORE.
NORTH–
TWO: KEEP TRACK OF YOU VIA THE VISORCAM AND BODYSUIT GPS.
AND THREE: DON'T SPEAK TO YOU IN THE FIELD UNLESS ABSOLUTELY NECESSARY.
HAPPY TO OBLIGE, BY THE WAY.
WE SCREW THIS UP FOR YOU, YOU'LL "TEAR US NEW URETHRAS."
NORTH.
WE COME THROUGH FOR YOU, WE'LL SAVE A WHOLE LOT OF LIVES.
OH, WAIT, SORRY, MY MISTAKE, WHAT I MEANT TO SAY IS...
WE'LL MAKE **YOU** A WHOLE LOT OF MONEY.

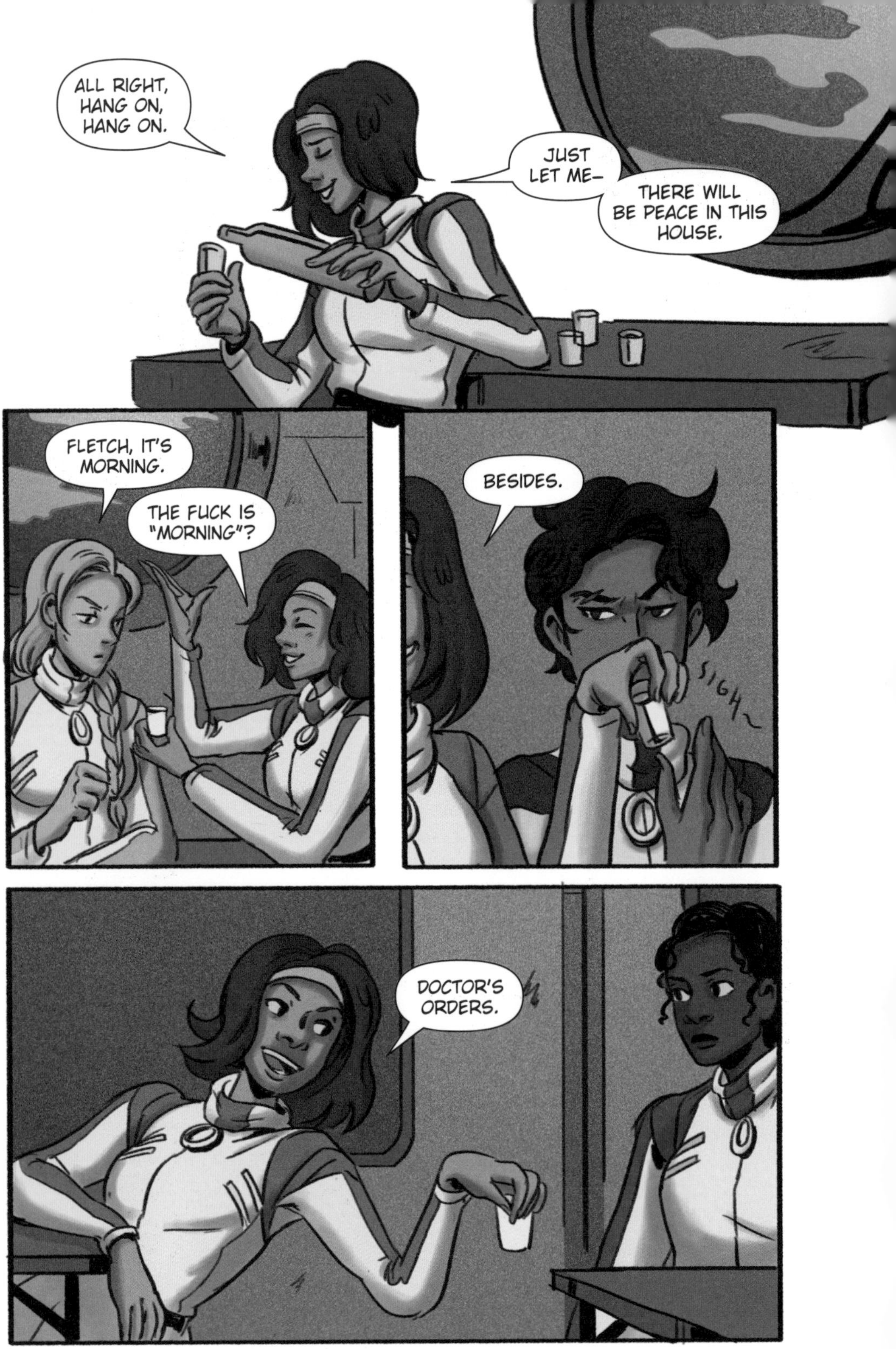
ALL RIGHT, HANG ON, HANG ON.
JUST LET ME–
THERE WILL BE PEACE IN THIS HOUSE.
FLETCH, IT'S MORNING.
THE FUCK IS "MORNING"?
BESIDES.
SIGH~
DOCTOR'S ORDERS.

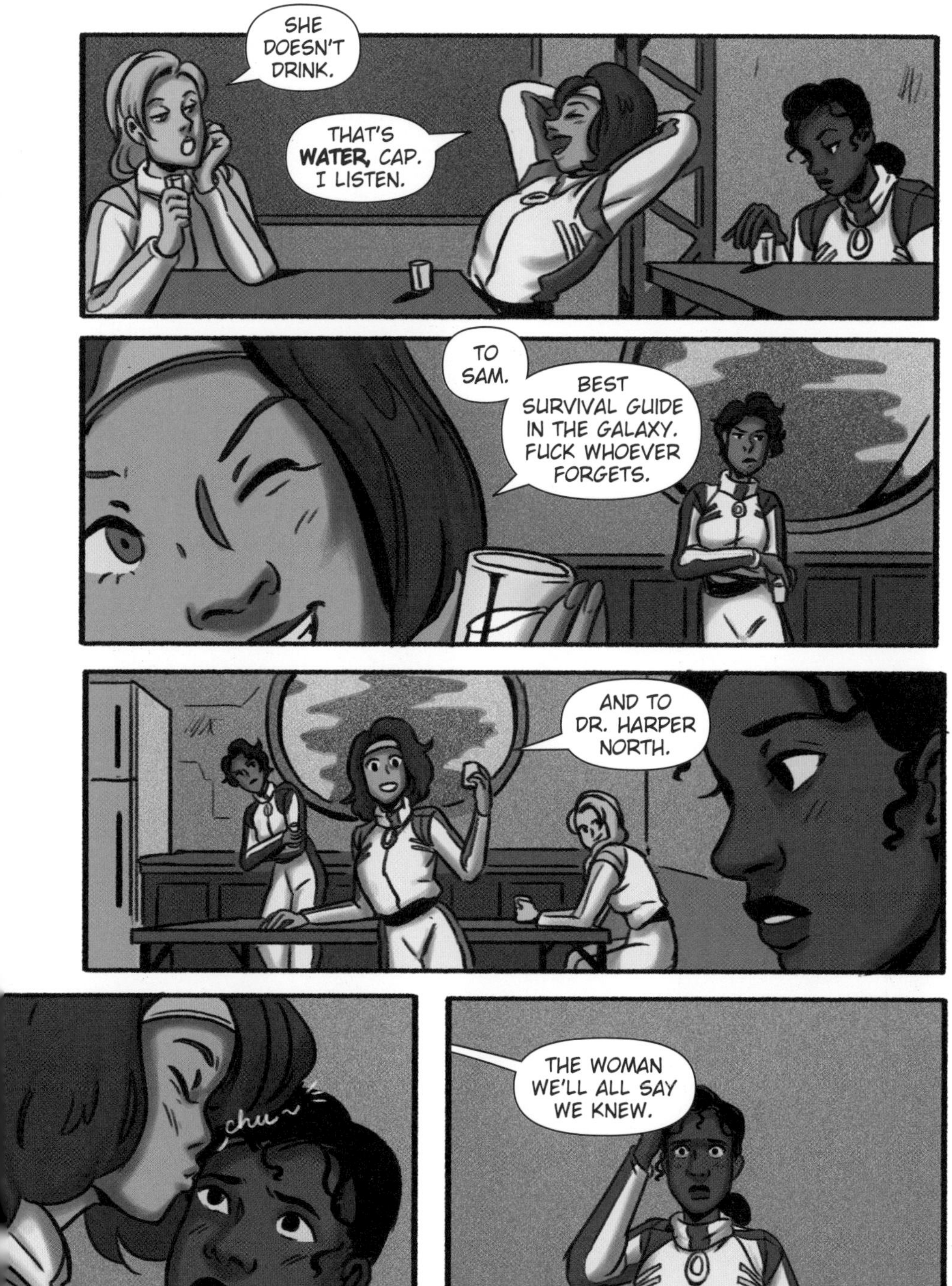
SHE DOESN'T DRINK.
THAT'S **WATER,** CAP. I LISTEN.
TO SAM.
BEST SURVIVAL GUIDE IN THE GALAXY. FUCK WHOEVER FORGETS.
AND TO DR. HARPER NORTH.
chu~
THE WOMAN WE'LL ALL SAY WE KNEW.

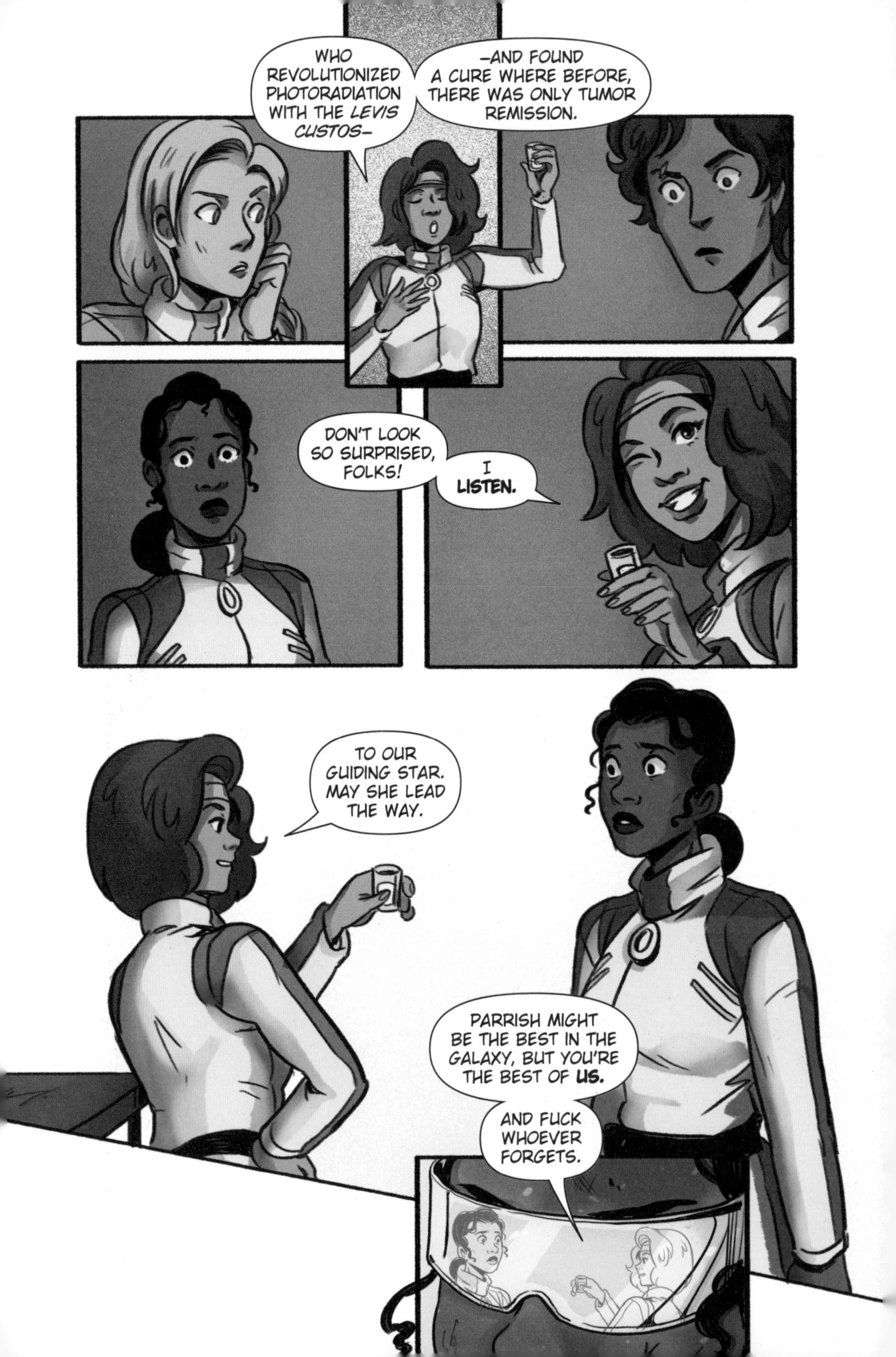
WHO REVOLUTIONIZED PHOTORADIATION WITH THE *LEVIS CUSTOS*–
–AND FOUND A CURE WHERE BEFORE, THERE WAS ONLY TUMOR REMISSION.
DON'T LOOK SO SURPRISED, FOLKS!
I **LISTEN.**
TO OUR GUIDING STAR. MAY SHE LEAD THE WAY.
PARRISH MIGHT BE THE BEST IN THE GALAXY, BUT YOU'RE THE BEST OF **US.**
AND FUCK WHOEVER FORGETS.

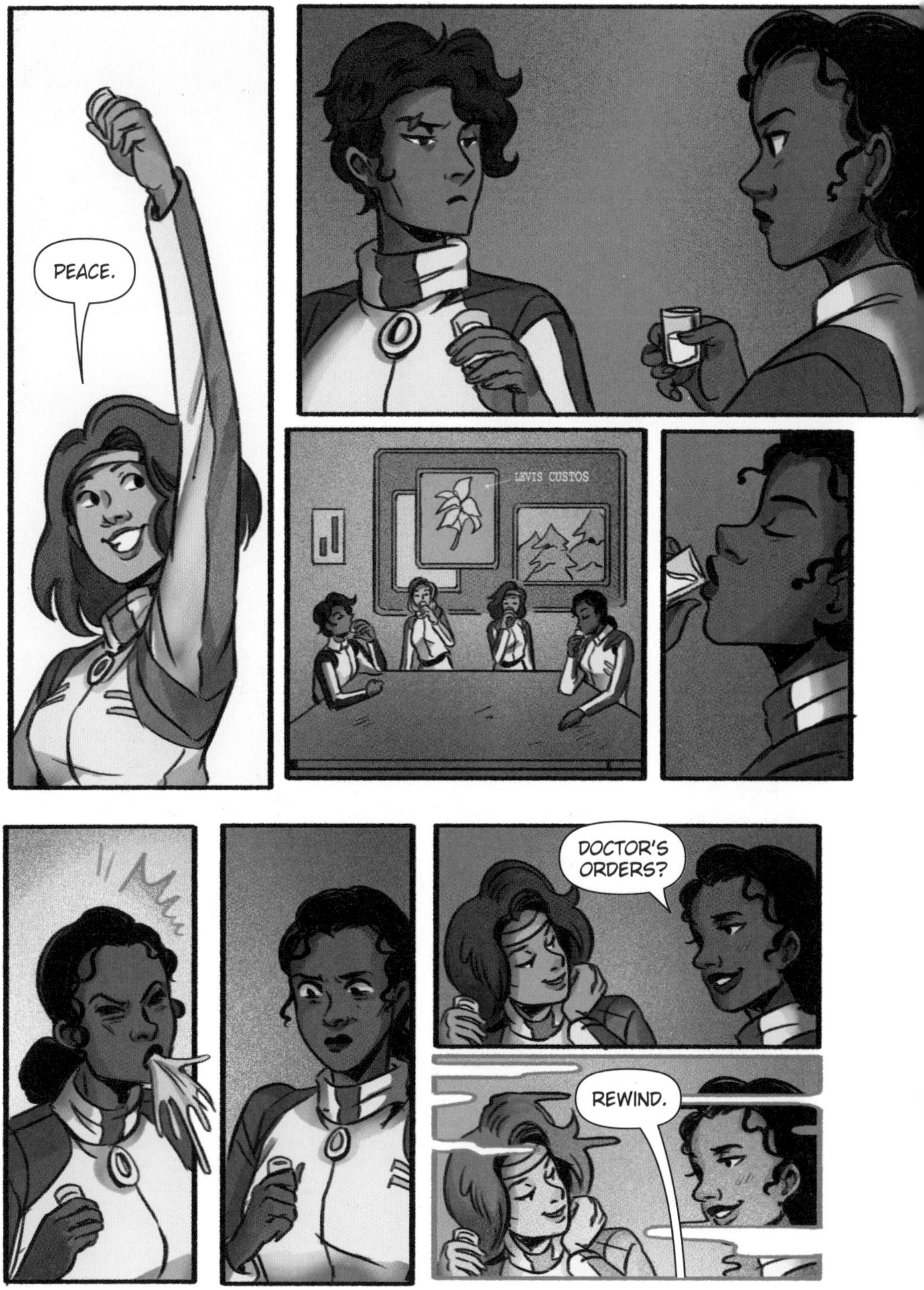
PEACE.
LEVIS CUSTOS
DOCTOR'S ORDERS?
REWIND.

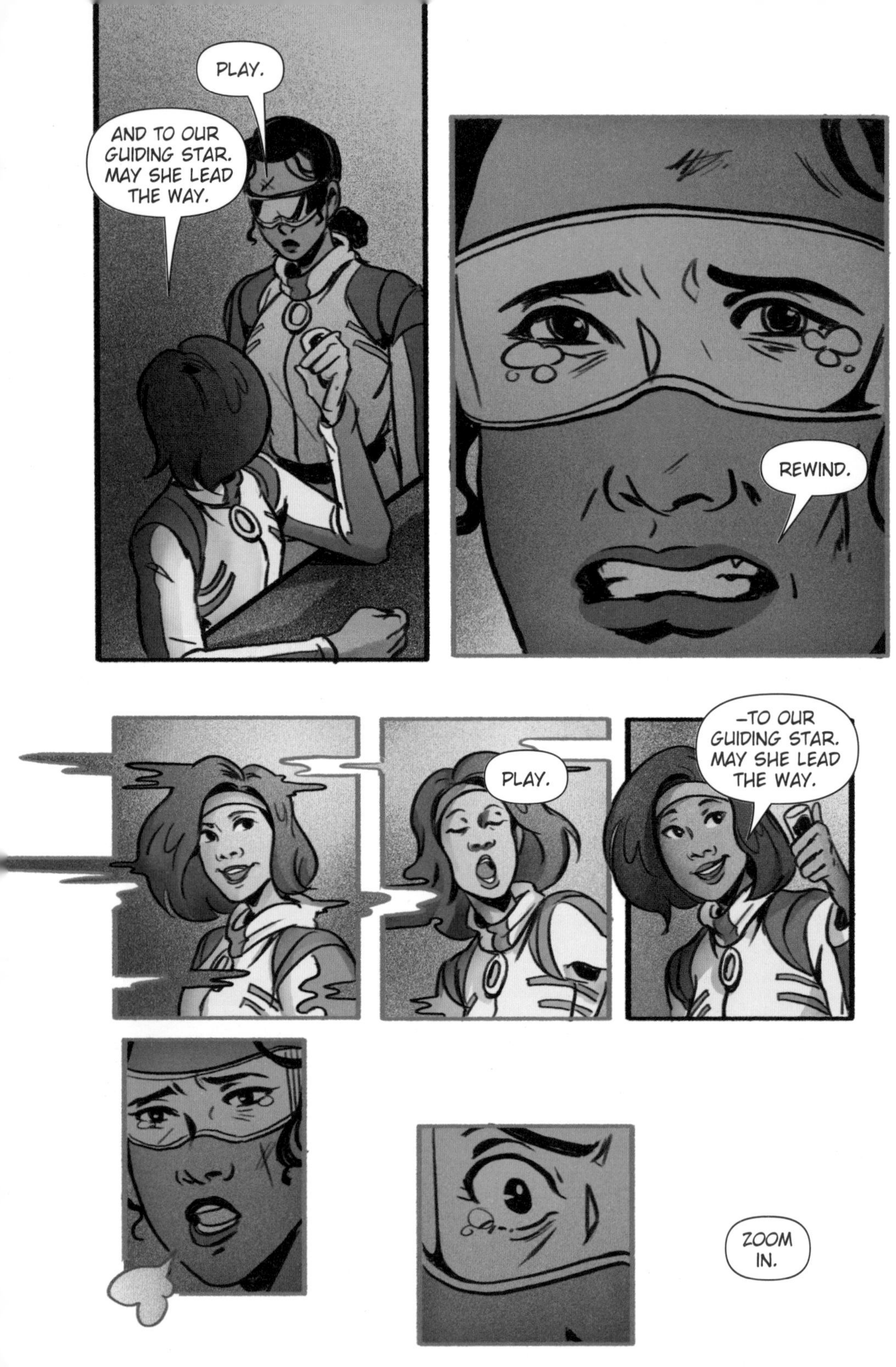
PLAY.
AND TO OUR GUIDING STAR. MAY SHE LEAD THE WAY.
REWIND.
PLAY.
–TO OUR GUIDING STAR. MAY SHE LEAD THE WAY.
ZOOM IN.

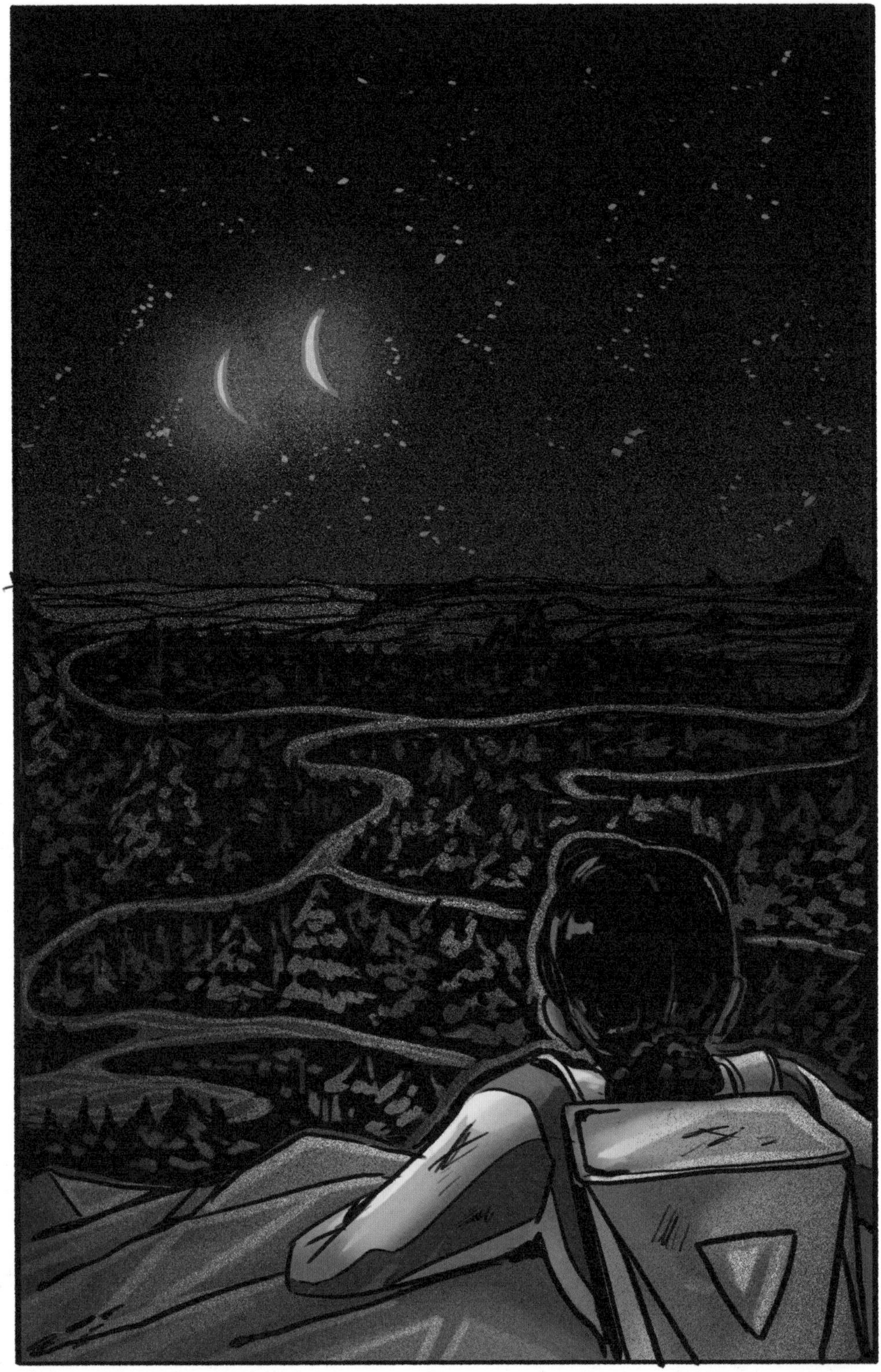

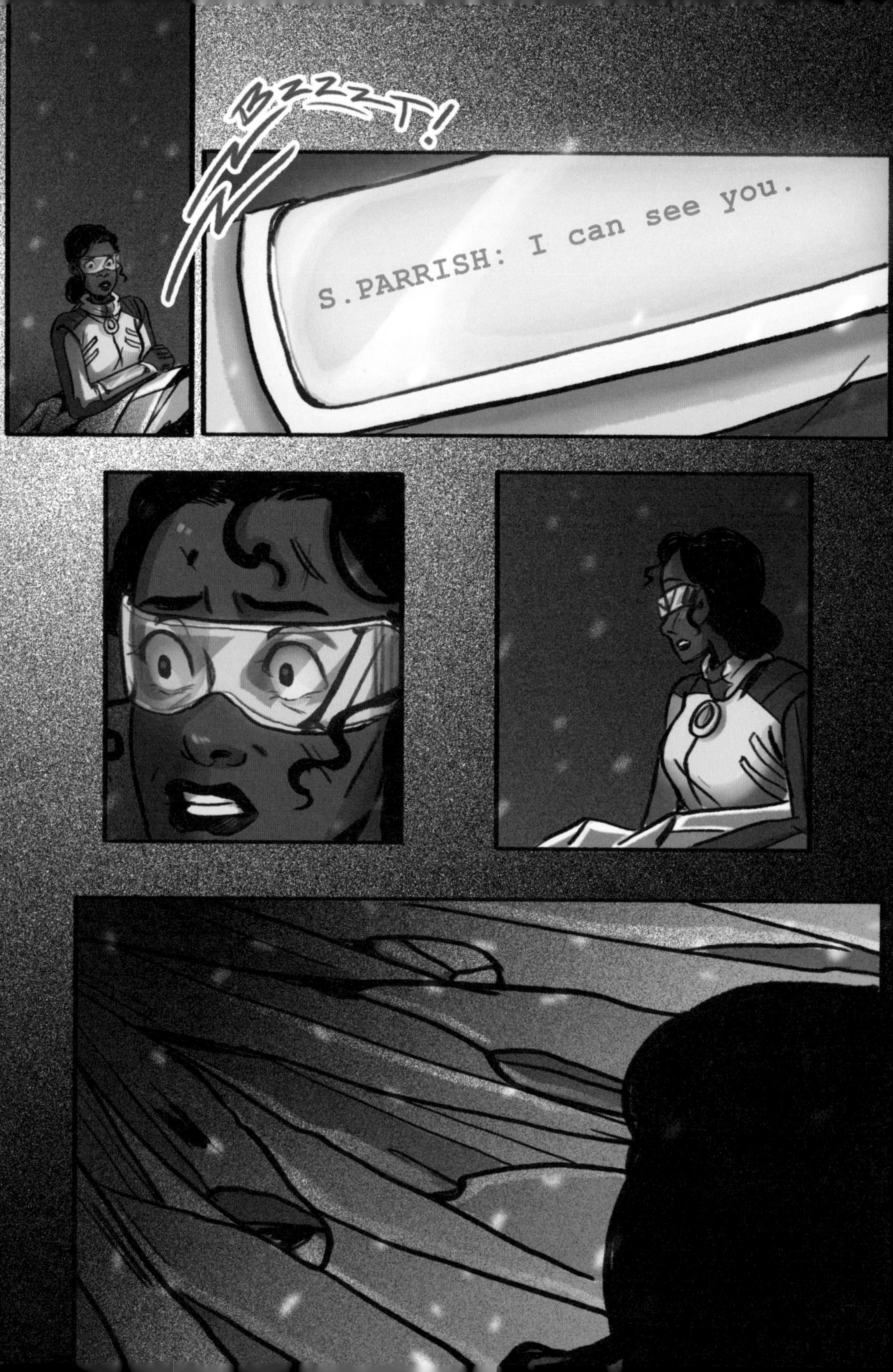
ZZ-BZZZZT!
S.PARRISH: I can see you.

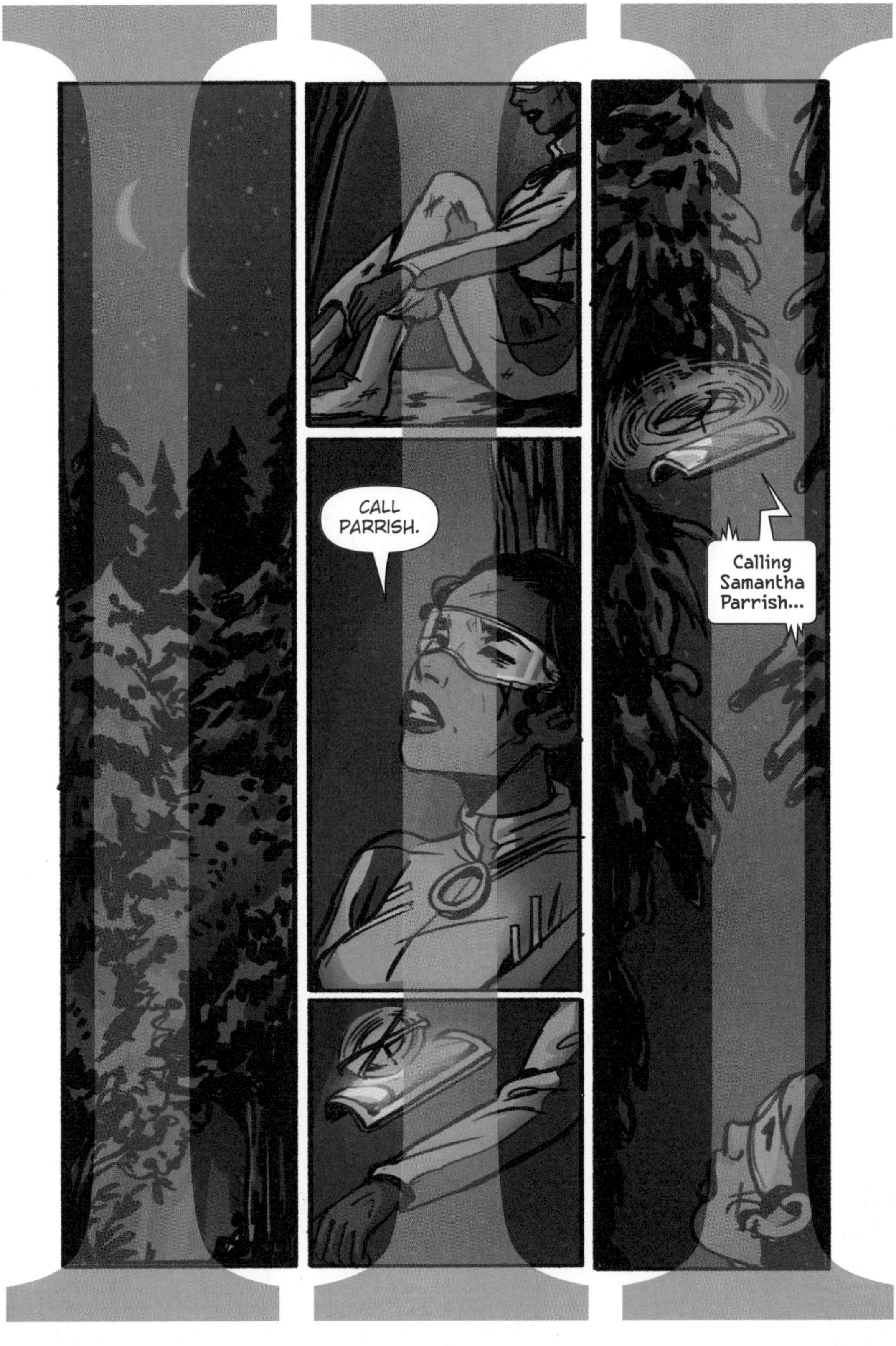
CALL PARRISH.
Calling Samantha Parrish...

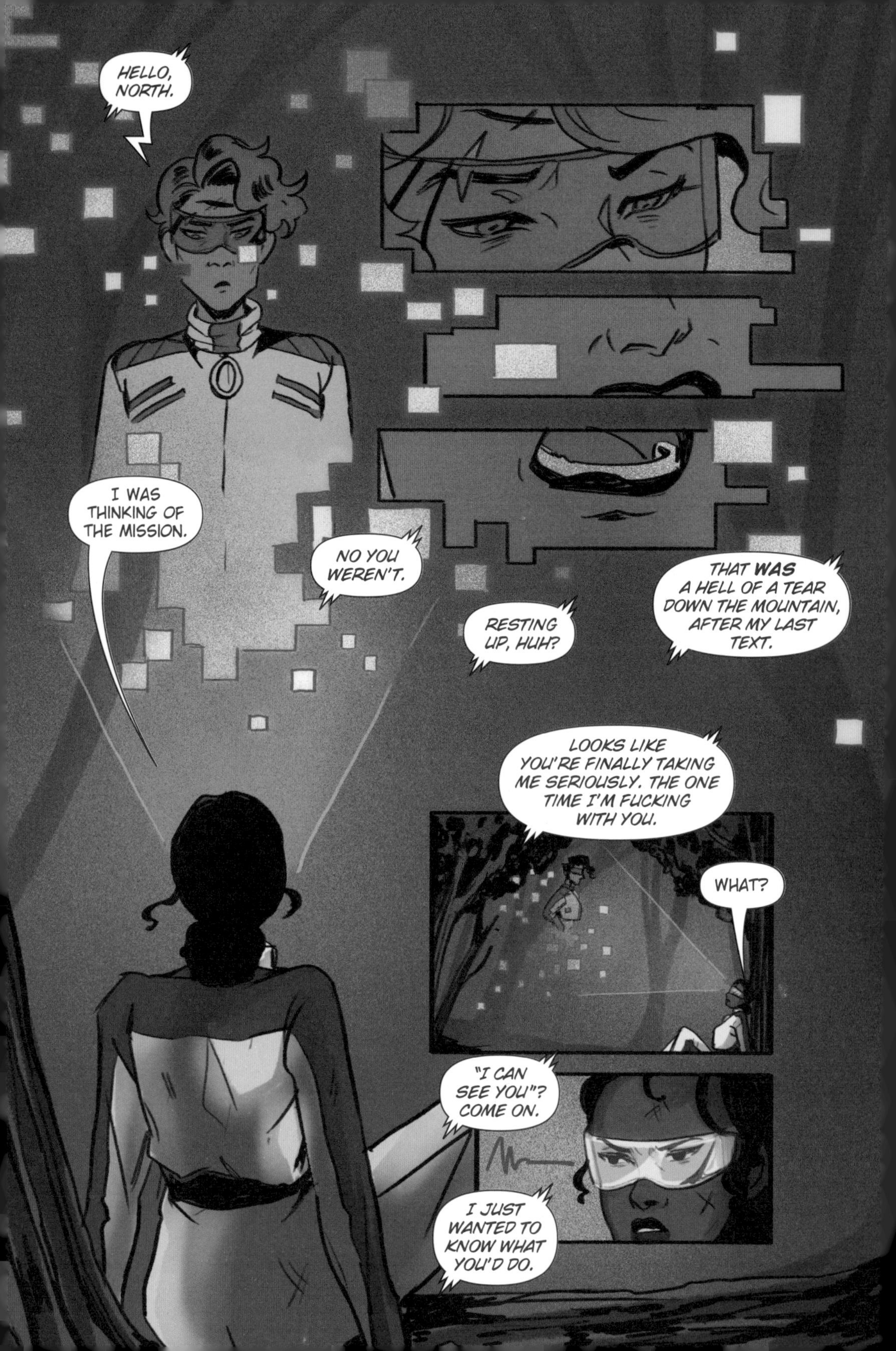
HELLO, NORTH.
I WAS THINKING OF THE MISSION.
NO YOU WEREN'T.
RESTING UP, HUH?
THAT **WAS** A HELL OF A TEAR DOWN THE MOUNTAIN, AFTER MY LAST TEXT.
LOOKS LIKE YOU'RE FINALLY TAKING ME SERIOUSLY. THE ONE TIME I'M FUCKING WITH YOU.
WHAT?
"I CAN SEE YOU"? COME ON.
I JUST WANTED TO KNOW WHAT YOU'D DO.

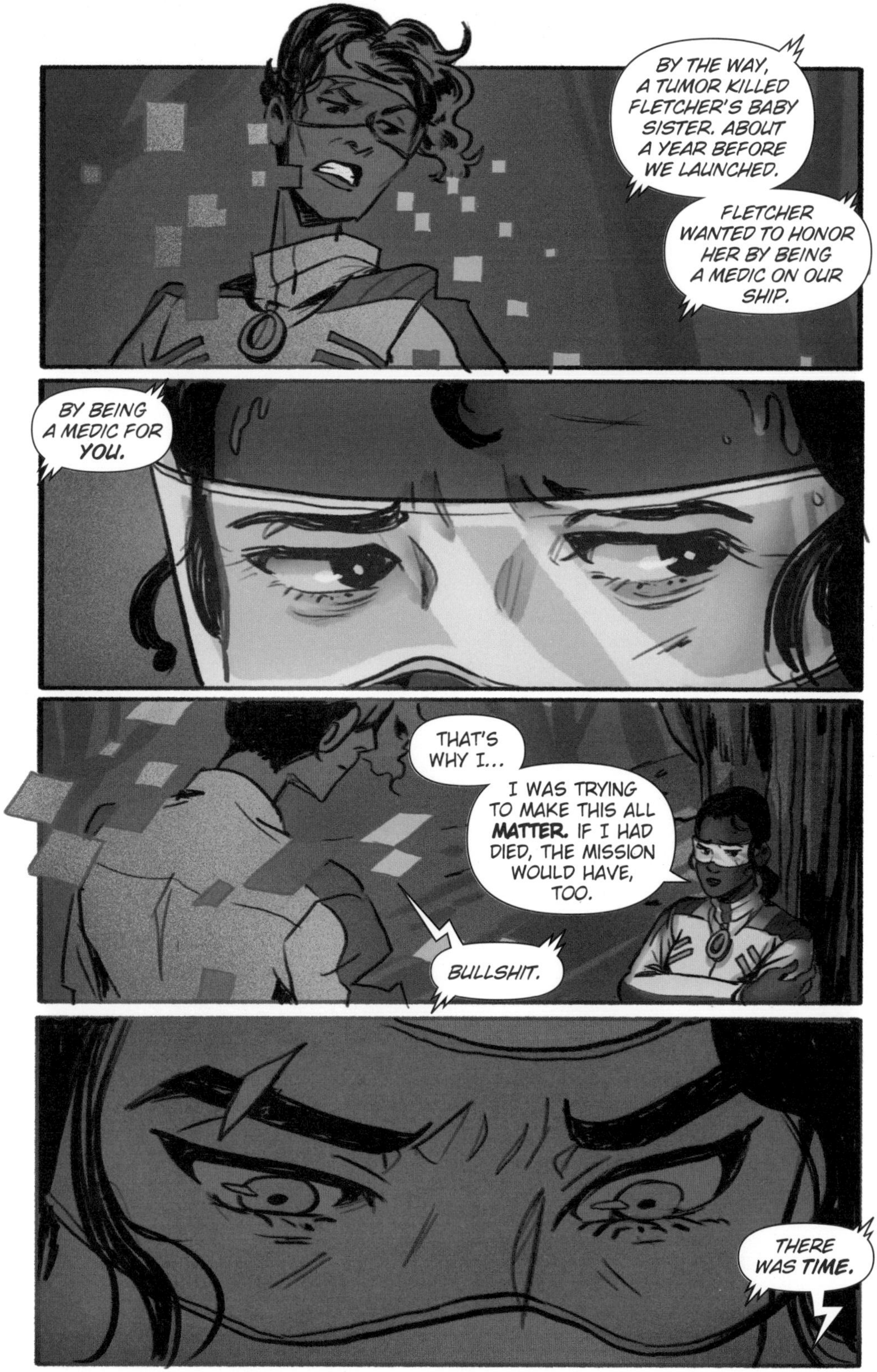
BY THE WAY, A TUMOR KILLED FLETCHER'S BABY SISTER. ABOUT A YEAR BEFORE WE LAUNCHED.
FLETCHER WANTED TO HONOR HER BY BEING A MEDIC ON OUR SHIP.
BY BEING A MEDIC FOR YOU.
THAT'S WHY I...
I WAS TRYING TO MAKE THIS ALL MATTER. IF I HAD DIED, THE MISSION WOULD HAVE, TOO.
BULLSHIT.
THERE WAS TIME.

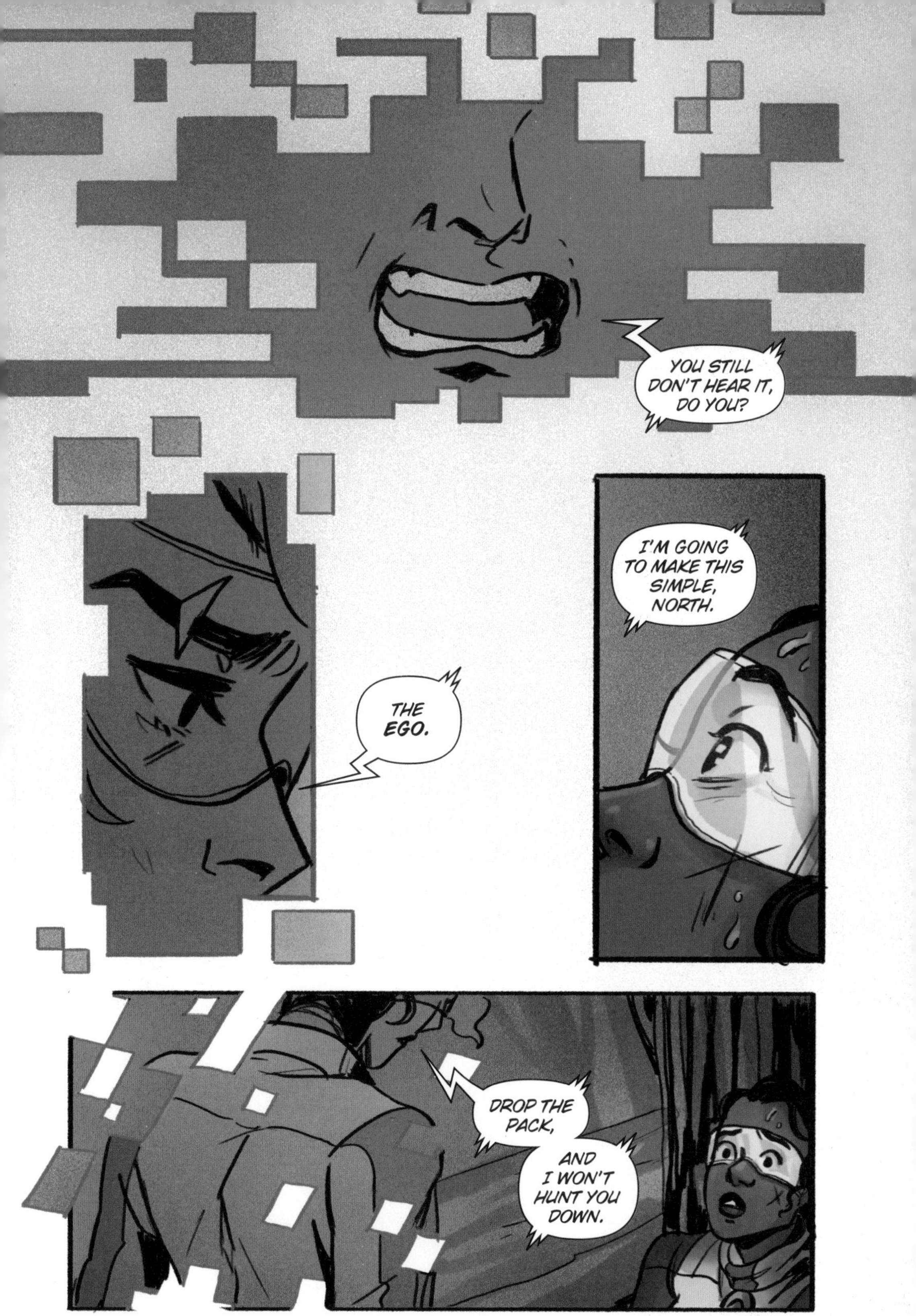
YOU STILL DON'T HEAR IT, DO YOU?
THE EGO.
I'M GOING TO MAKE THIS SIMPLE, NORTH.
DROP THE PACK,
AND I WON'T HUNT YOU DOWN.

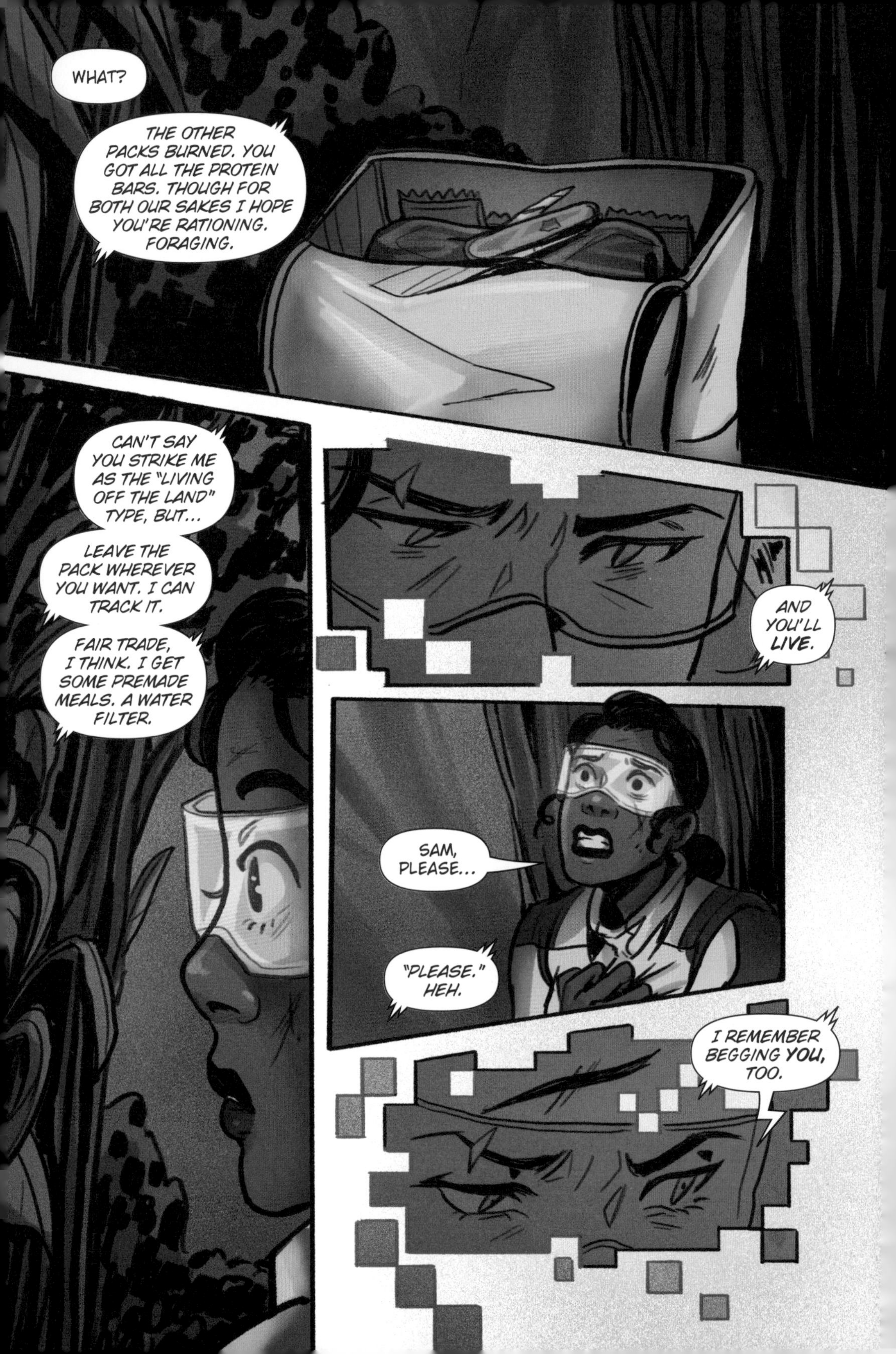
WHAT?
THE OTHER PACKS BURNED. YOU GOT ALL THE PROTEIN BARS. THOUGH FOR BOTH OUR SAKES I HOPE YOU'RE RATIONING. FORAGING.
CAN'T SAY YOU STRIKE ME AS THE "LIVING OFF THE LAND" TYPE, BUT...
LEAVE THE PACK WHEREVER YOU WANT. I CAN TRACK IT.
FAIR TRADE, I THINK. I GET SOME PREMADE MEALS. A WATER FILTER.
AND YOU'LL **LIVE.**
SAM, PLEASE...
"PLEASE." HEH.
I REMEMBER BEGGING **YOU,** TOO.

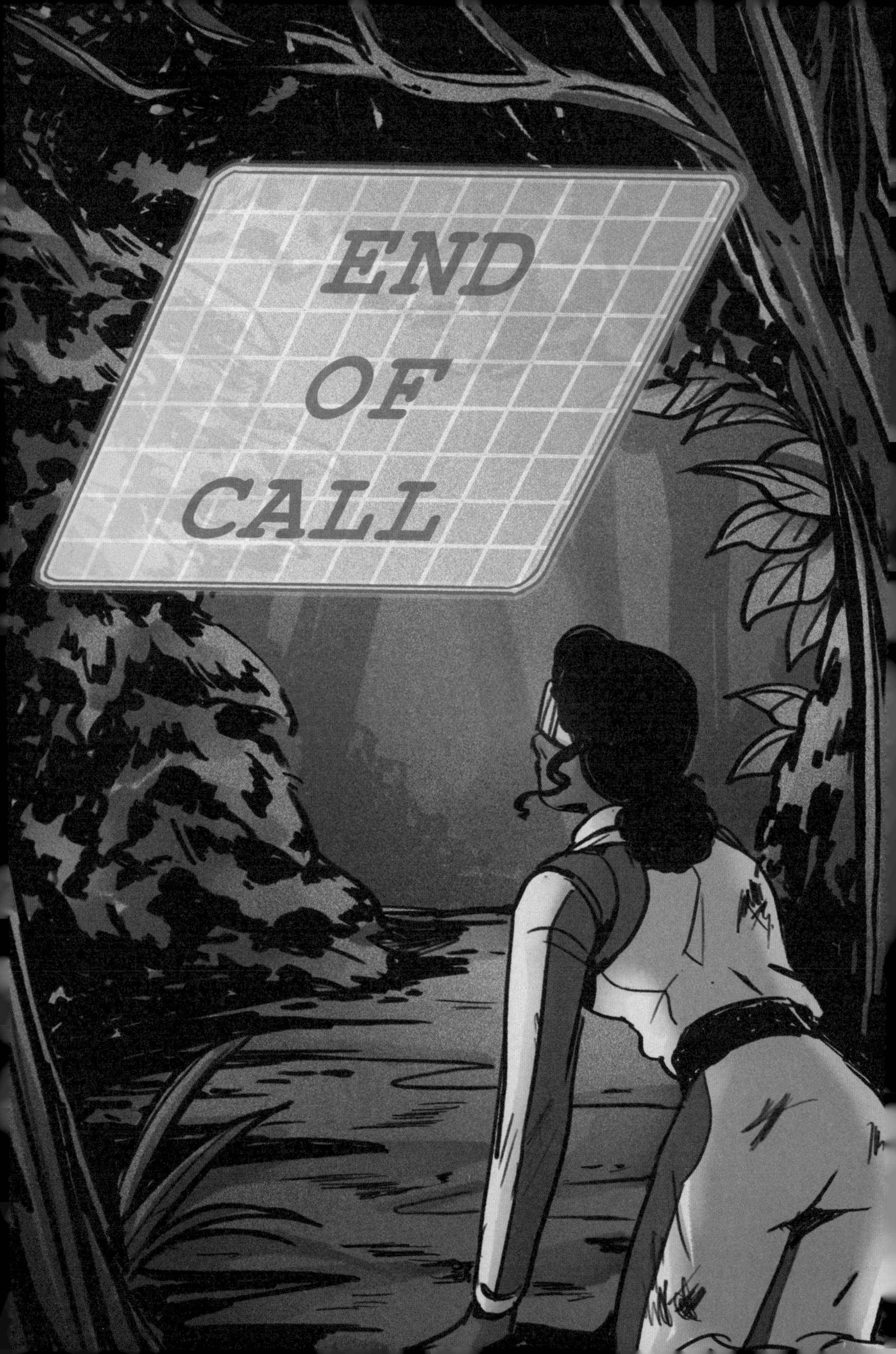
END
OF
CALL

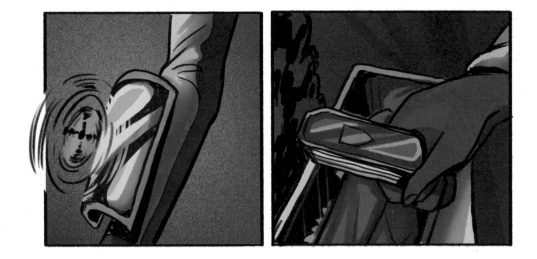

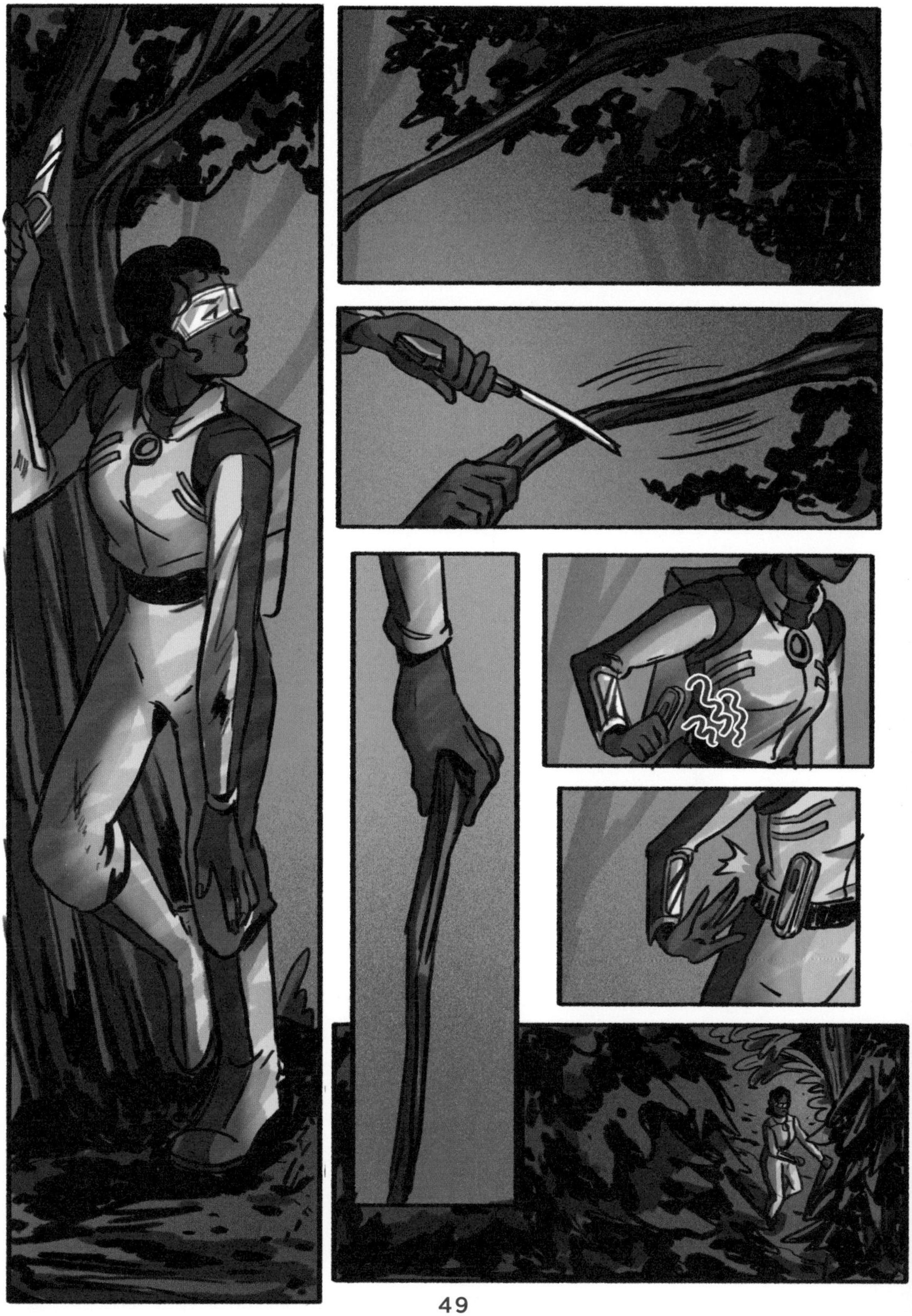

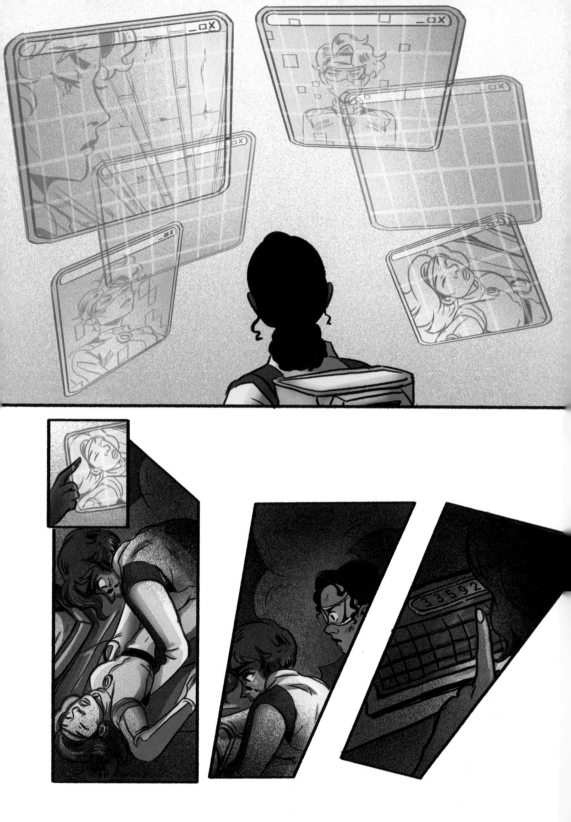

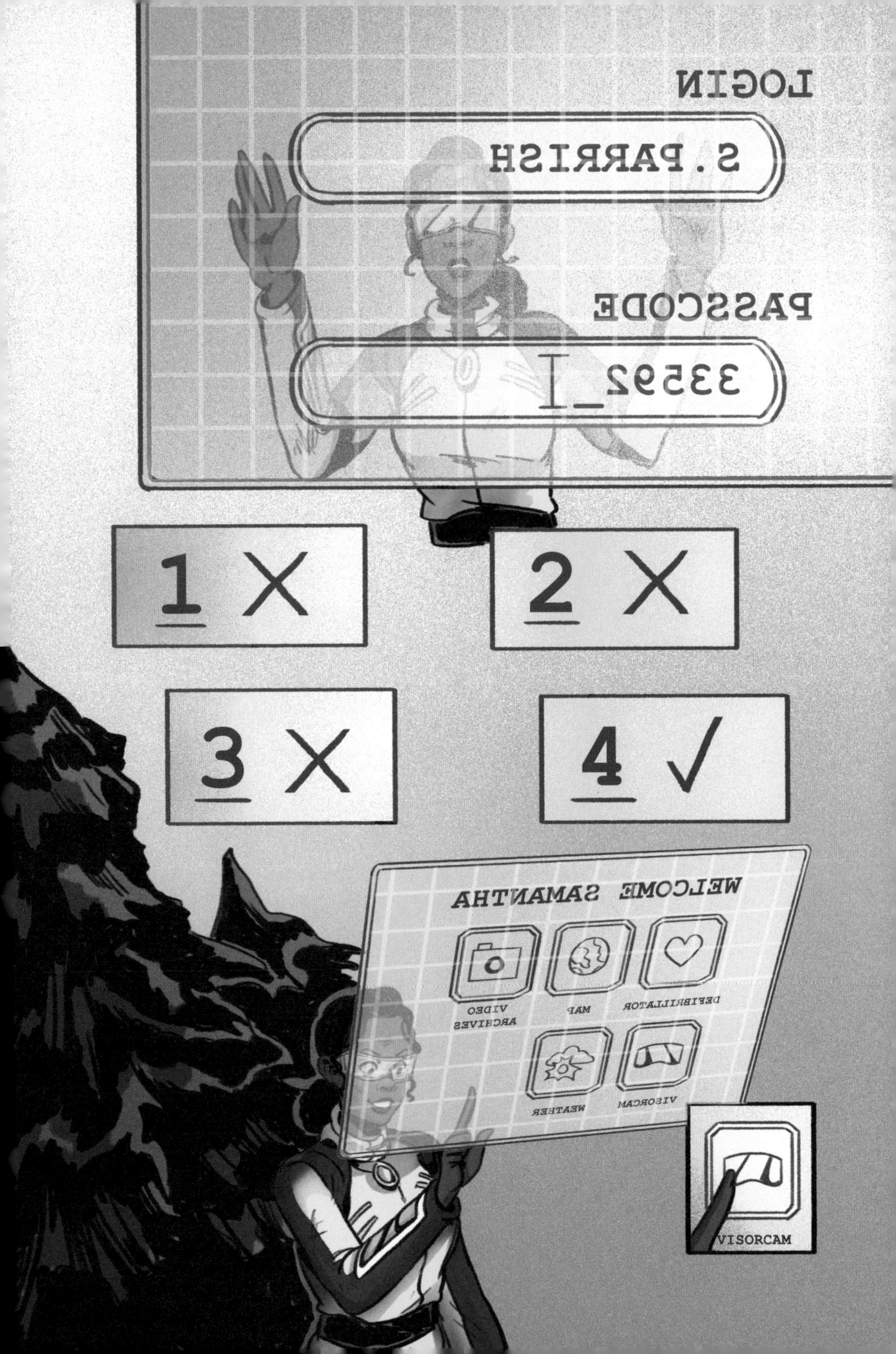
LOGIN
S.PARRISH
PASSCODE
33592_
1 X
2 X
3 X
4 ✓
WELCOME SAMANTHA
VIDEO ARCHIVES
MAP
DEFIBRILLATOR
WEATHER
VISORCAM
VISORCAM

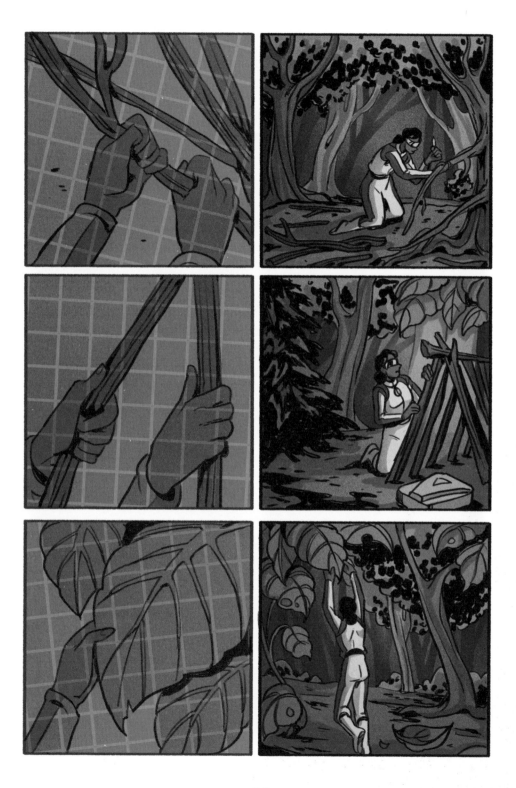

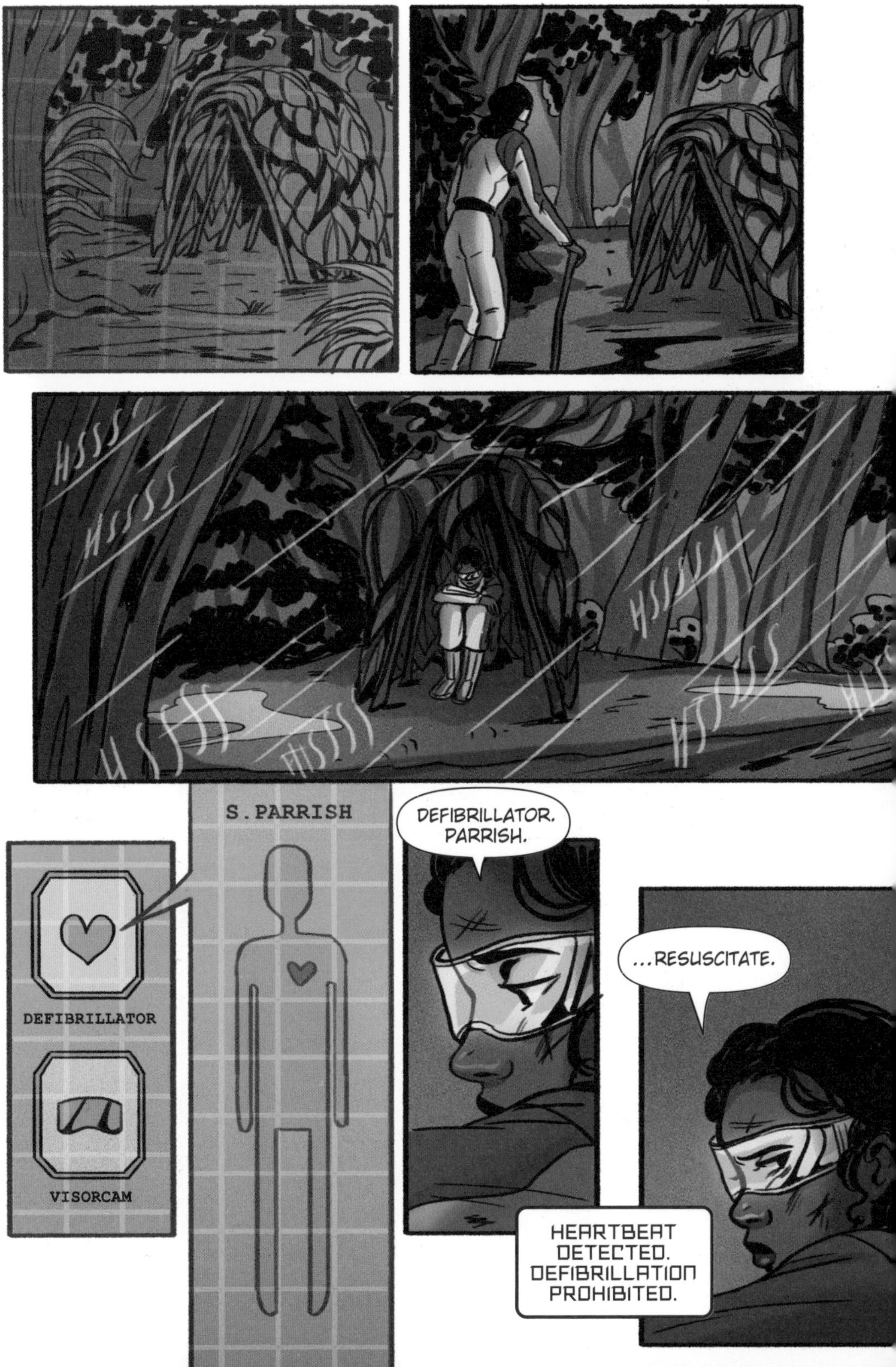
HSSSS
HSSSS
HSSSS
HSSSS
HSSSS
HSSSS
S.PARRISH
DEFIBRILLATOR
VISORCAM
DEFIBRILLATOR. PARRISH.
...RESUSCITATE.
HEARTBEAT DETECTED. DEFIBRILLATION PROHIBITED.

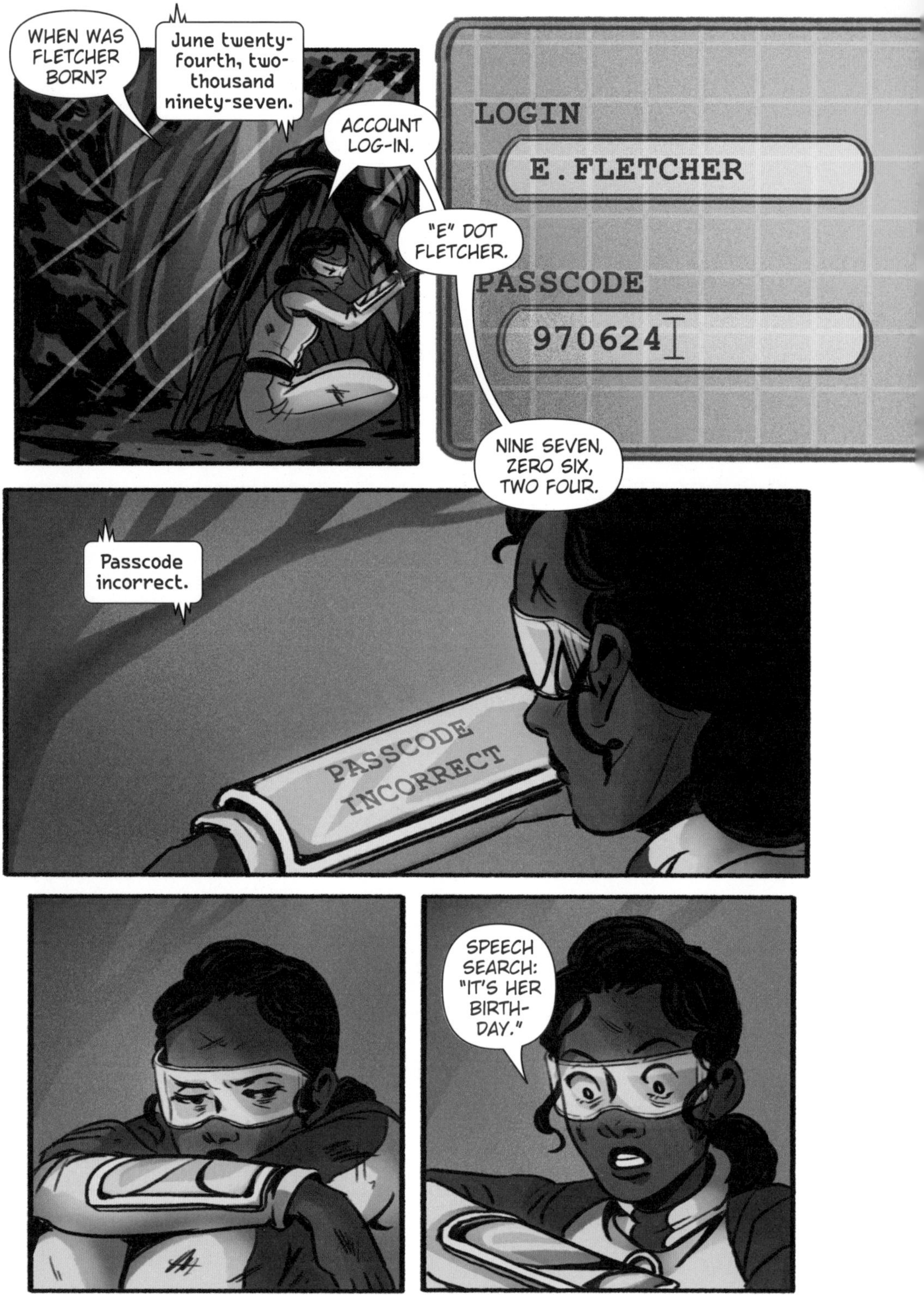
WHEN WAS FLETCHER BORN?
June twenty-fourth, two-thousand ninety-seven.
ACCOUNT LOG-IN.
LOGIN
E.FLETCHER
"E" DOT FLETCHER.
PASSCODE
970624
NINE SEVEN, ZERO SIX, TWO FOUR.
Passcode incorrect.
PASSCODE INCORRECT
SPEECH SEARCH: "IT'S HER BIRTH-DAY."

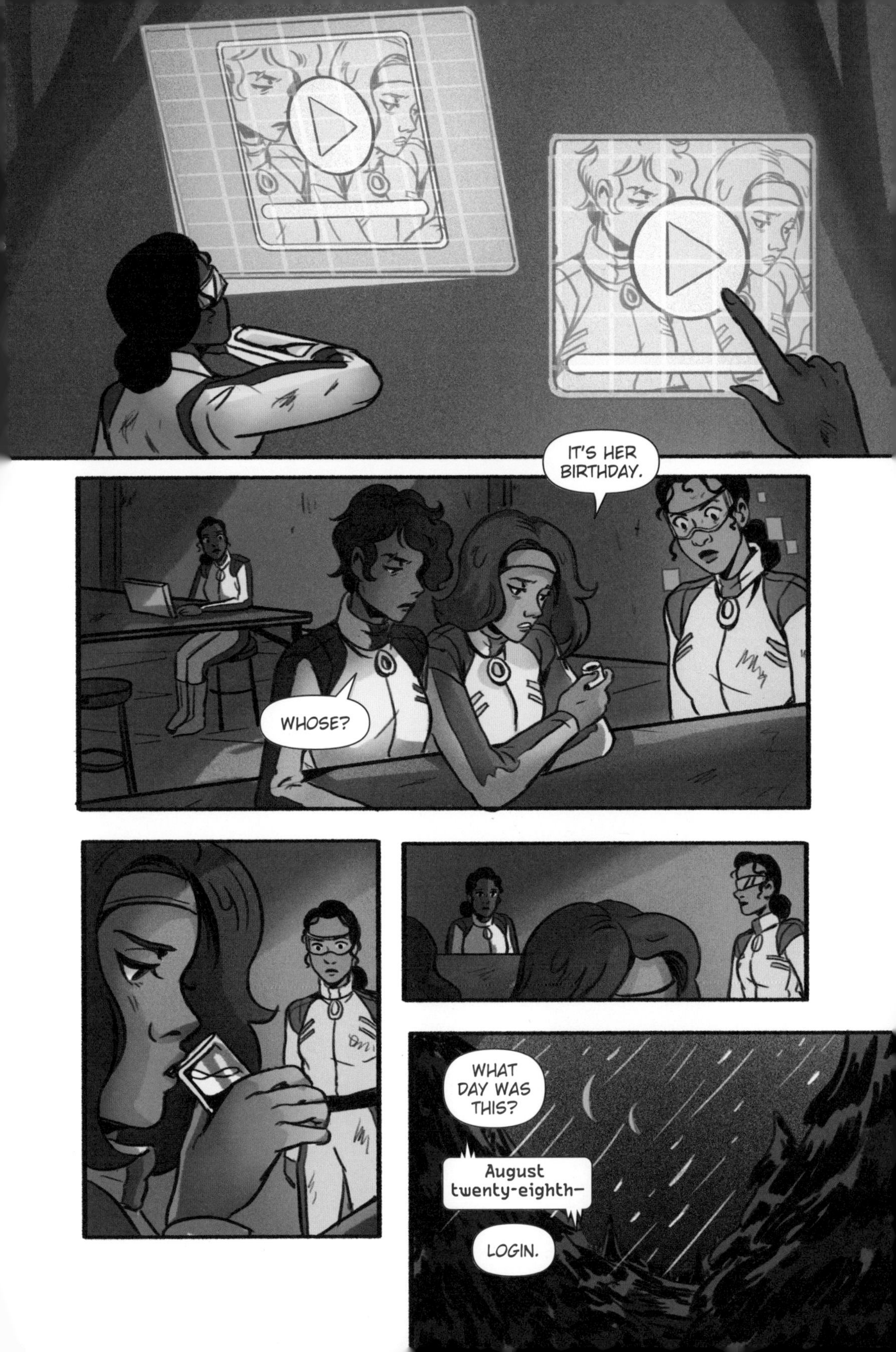

IT'S HER BIRTHDAY.
WHOSE?
WHAT DAY WAS THIS?
August twenty-eighth–
LOGIN.

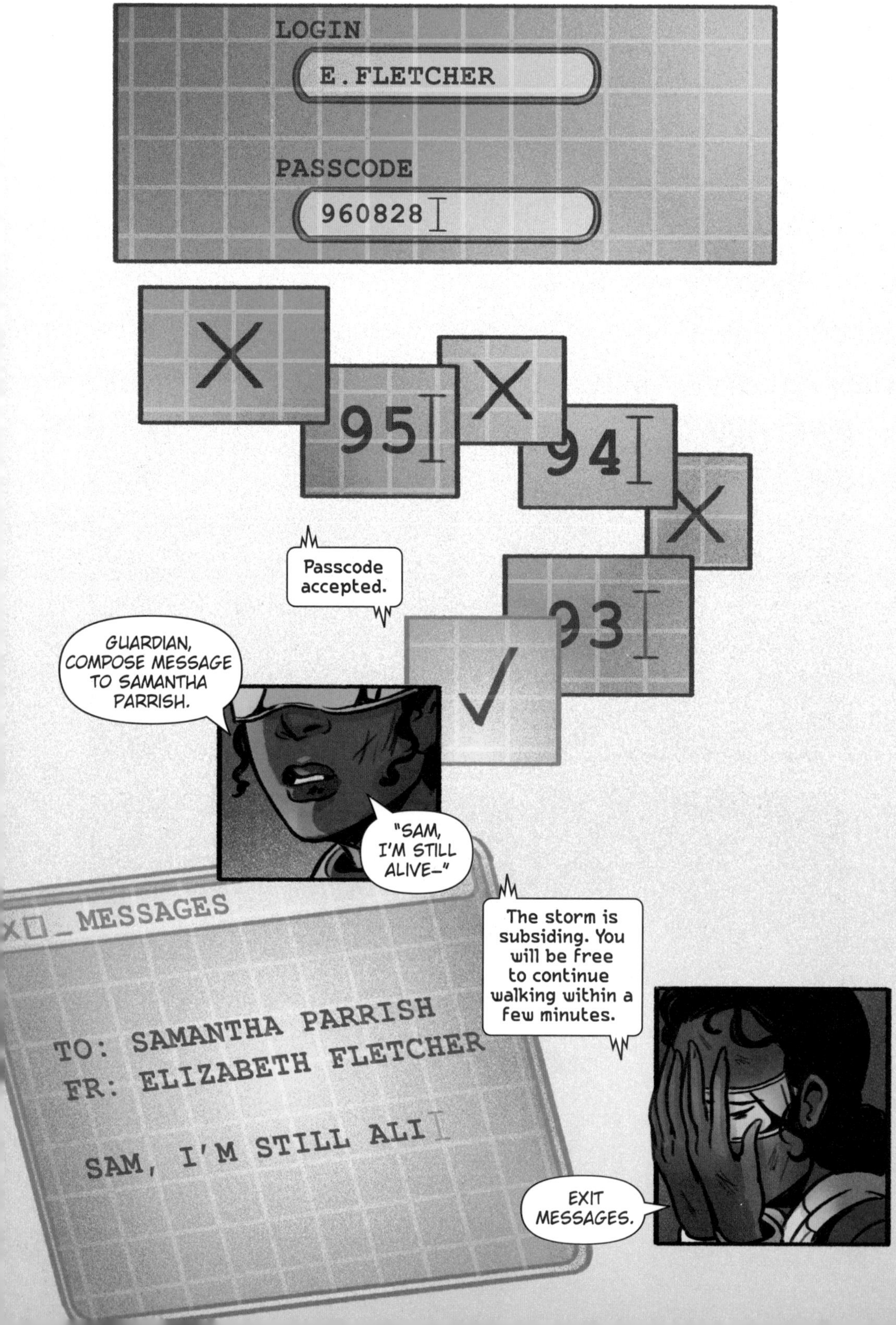
LOGIN
E.FLETCHER
PASSCODE
960828
95
94
93
Passcode accepted.
GUARDIAN, COMPOSE MESSAGE TO SAMANTHA PARRISH.
"SAM, I'M STILL ALIVE—"
MESSAGES
TO: SAMANTHA PARRISH
FR: ELIZABETH FLETCHER
SAM, I'M STILL ALI
The storm is subsiding. You will be free to continue walking within a few minutes.
EXIT MESSAGES.

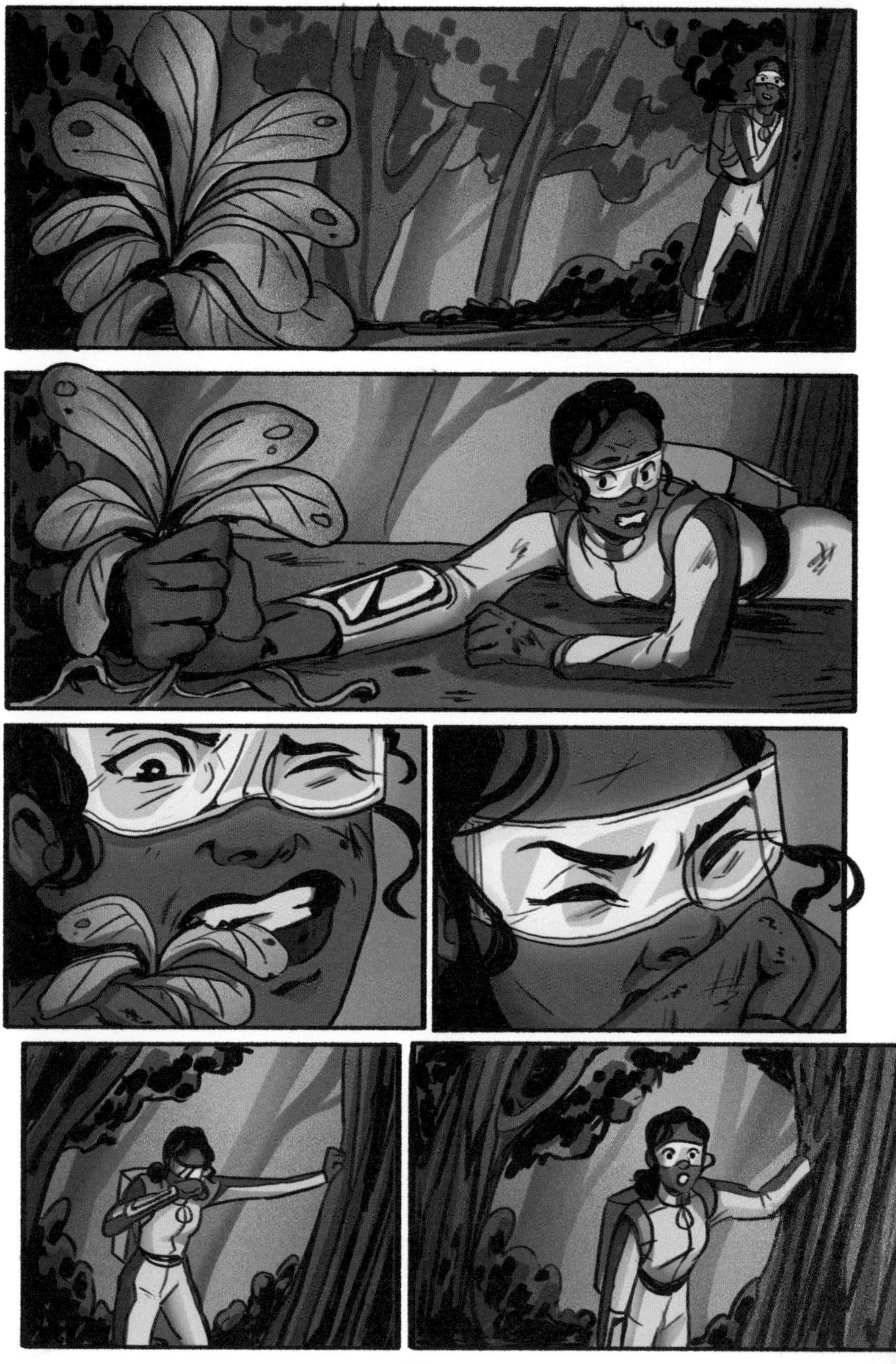

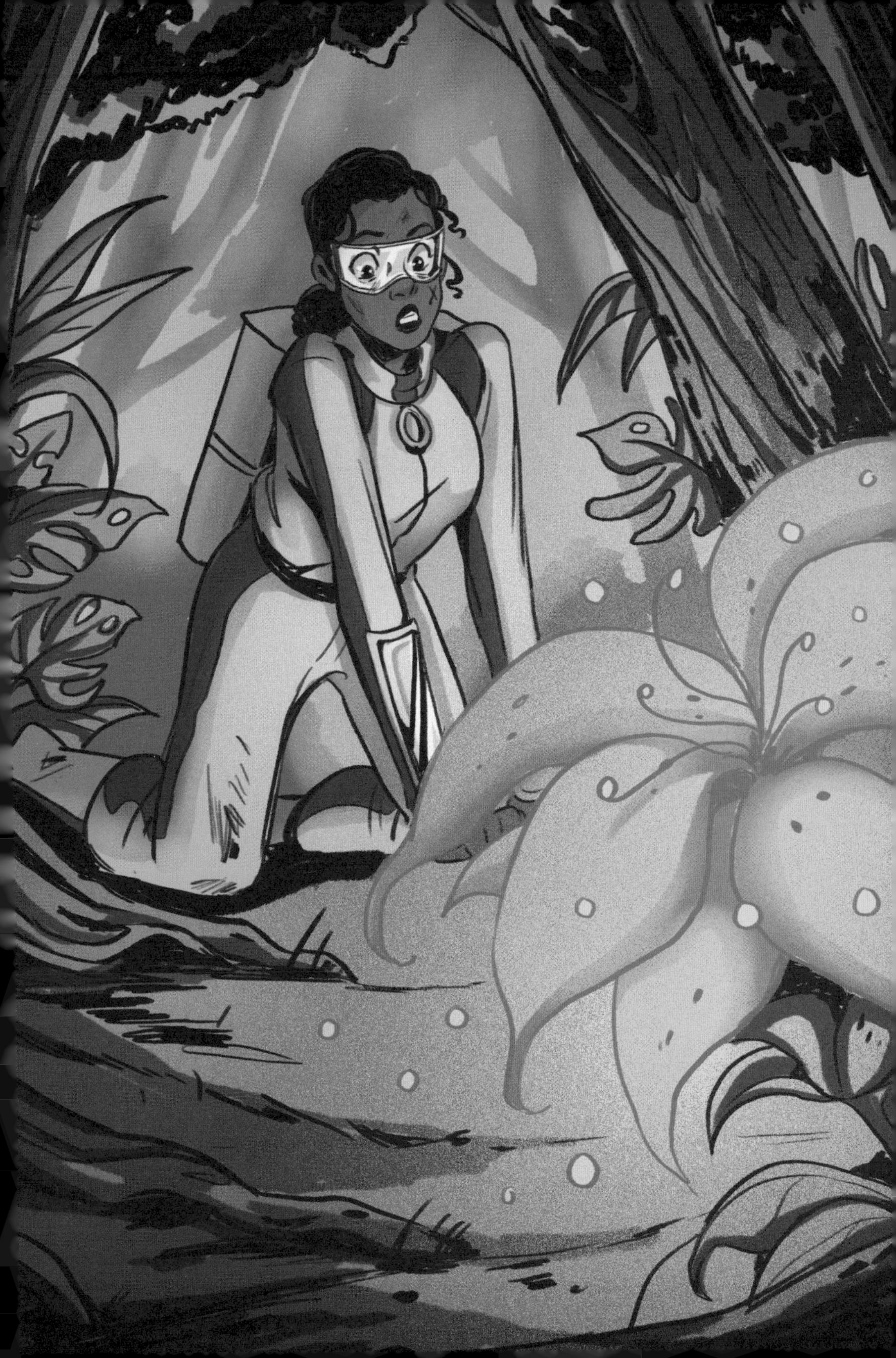

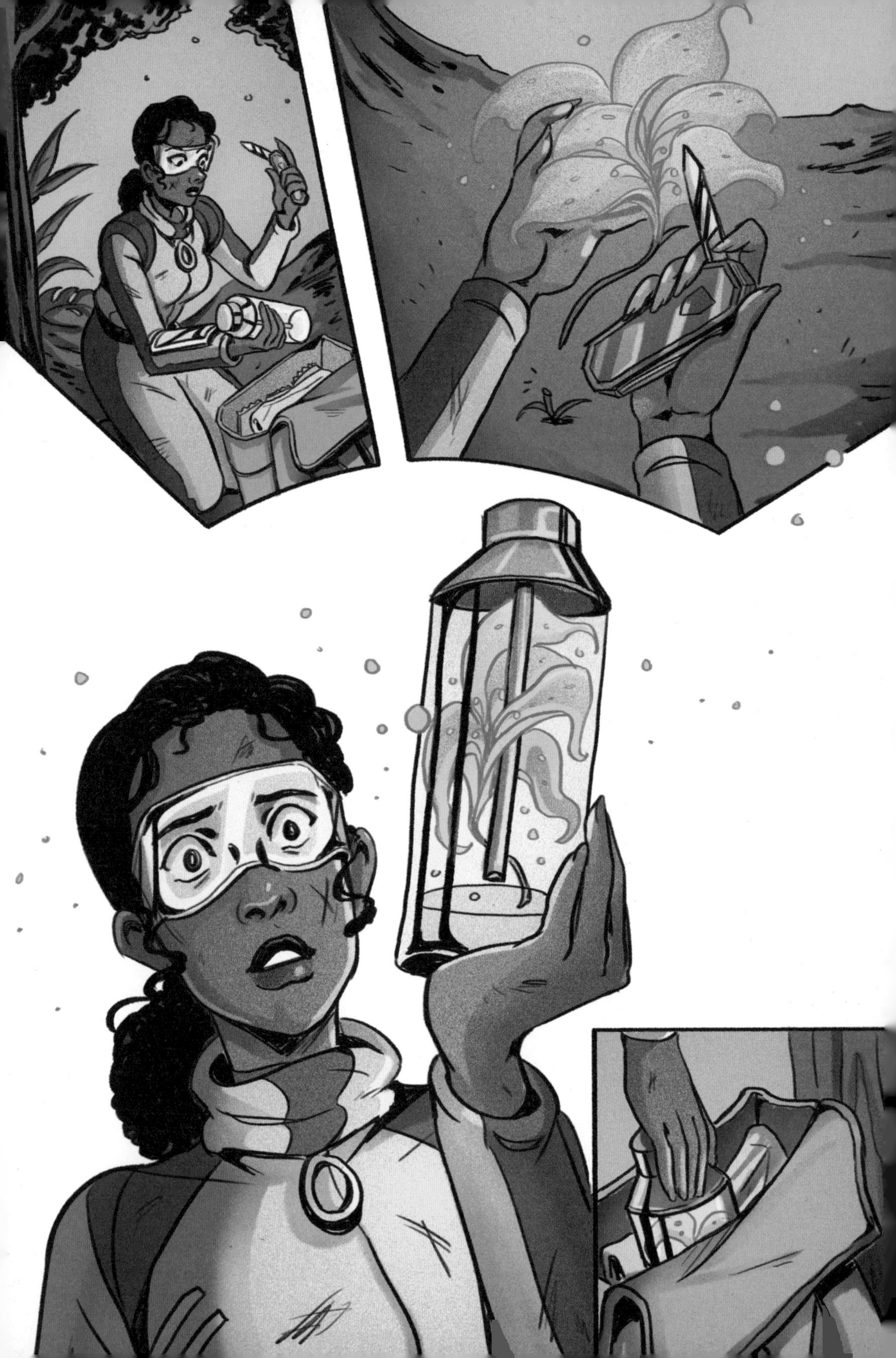

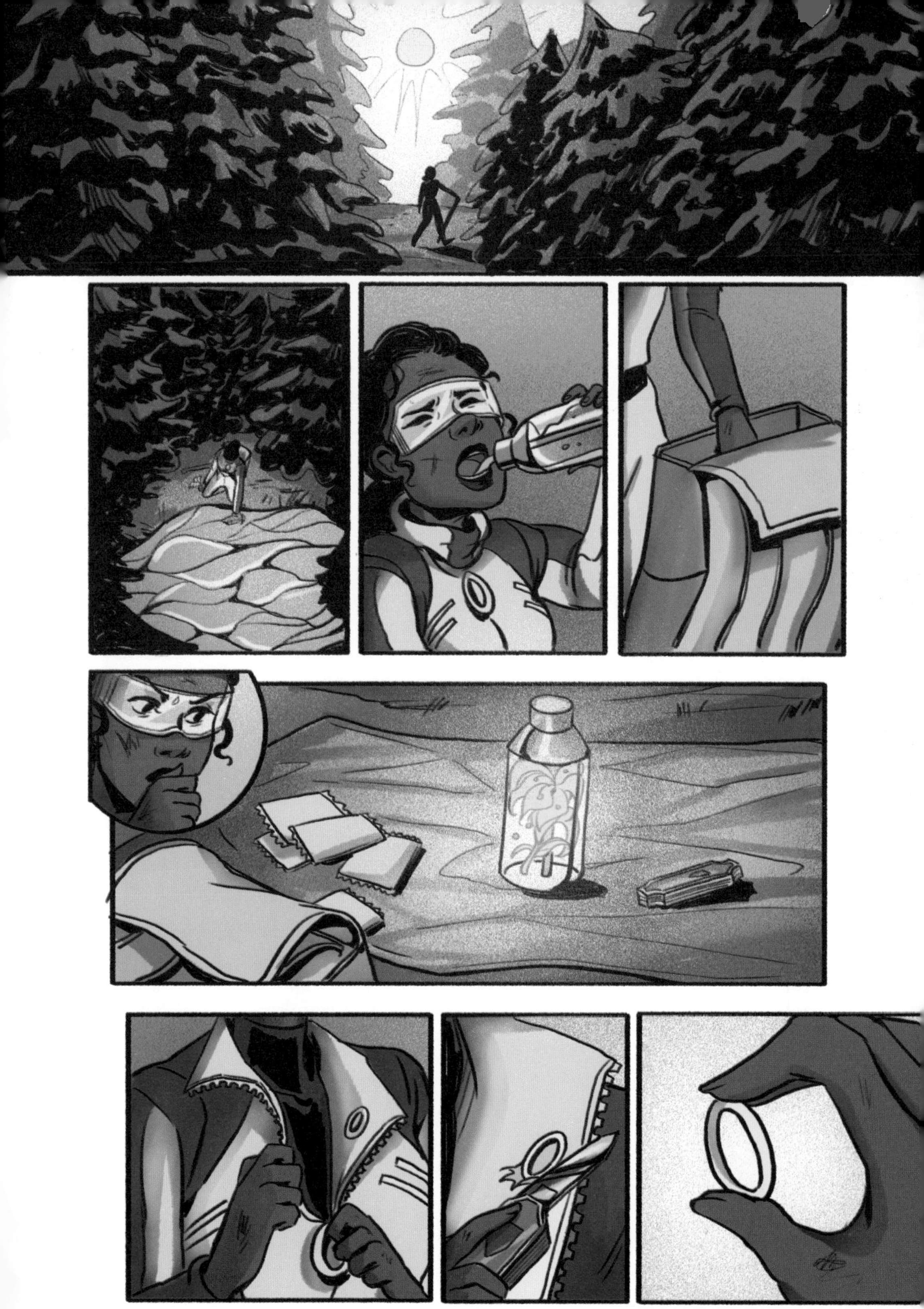

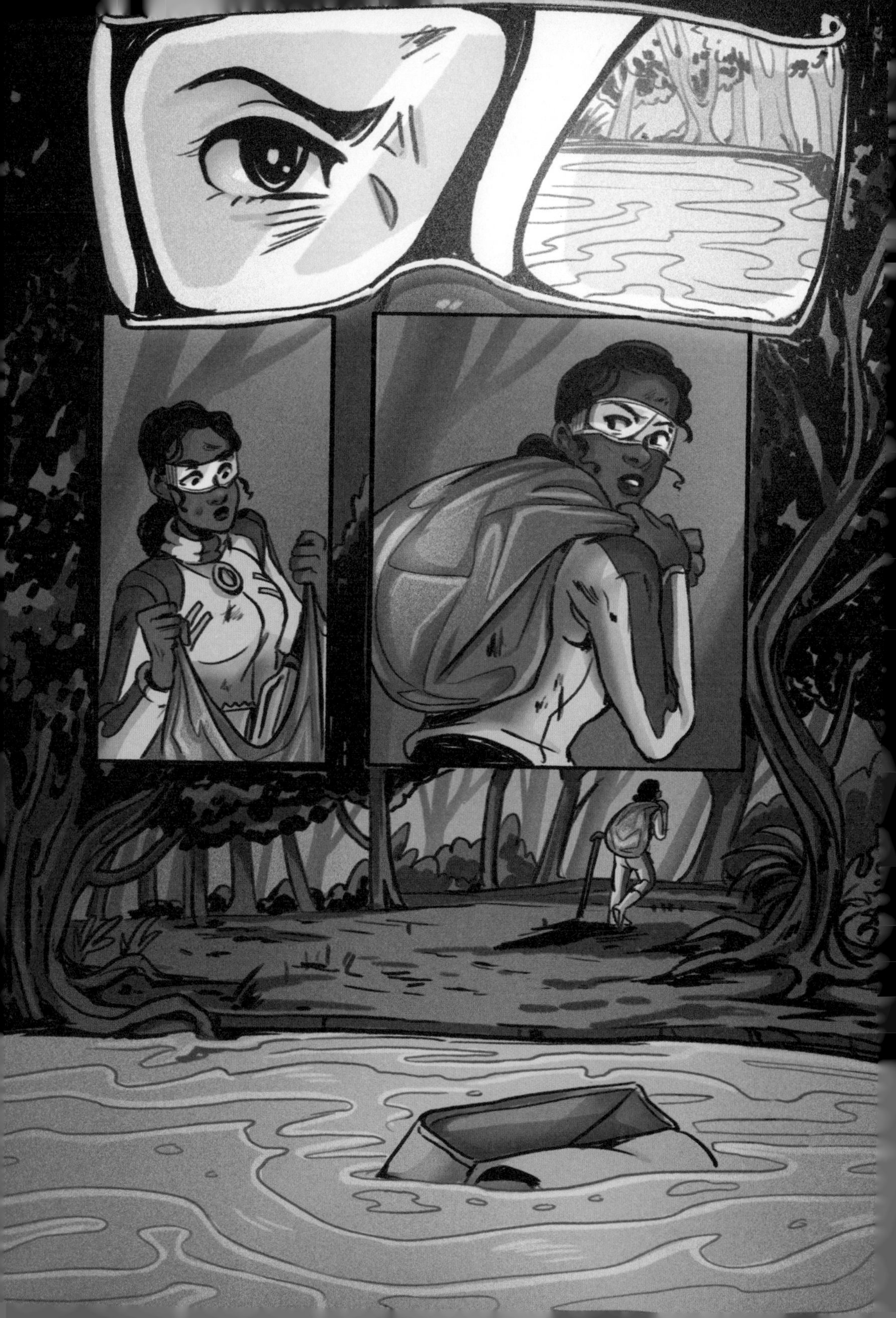

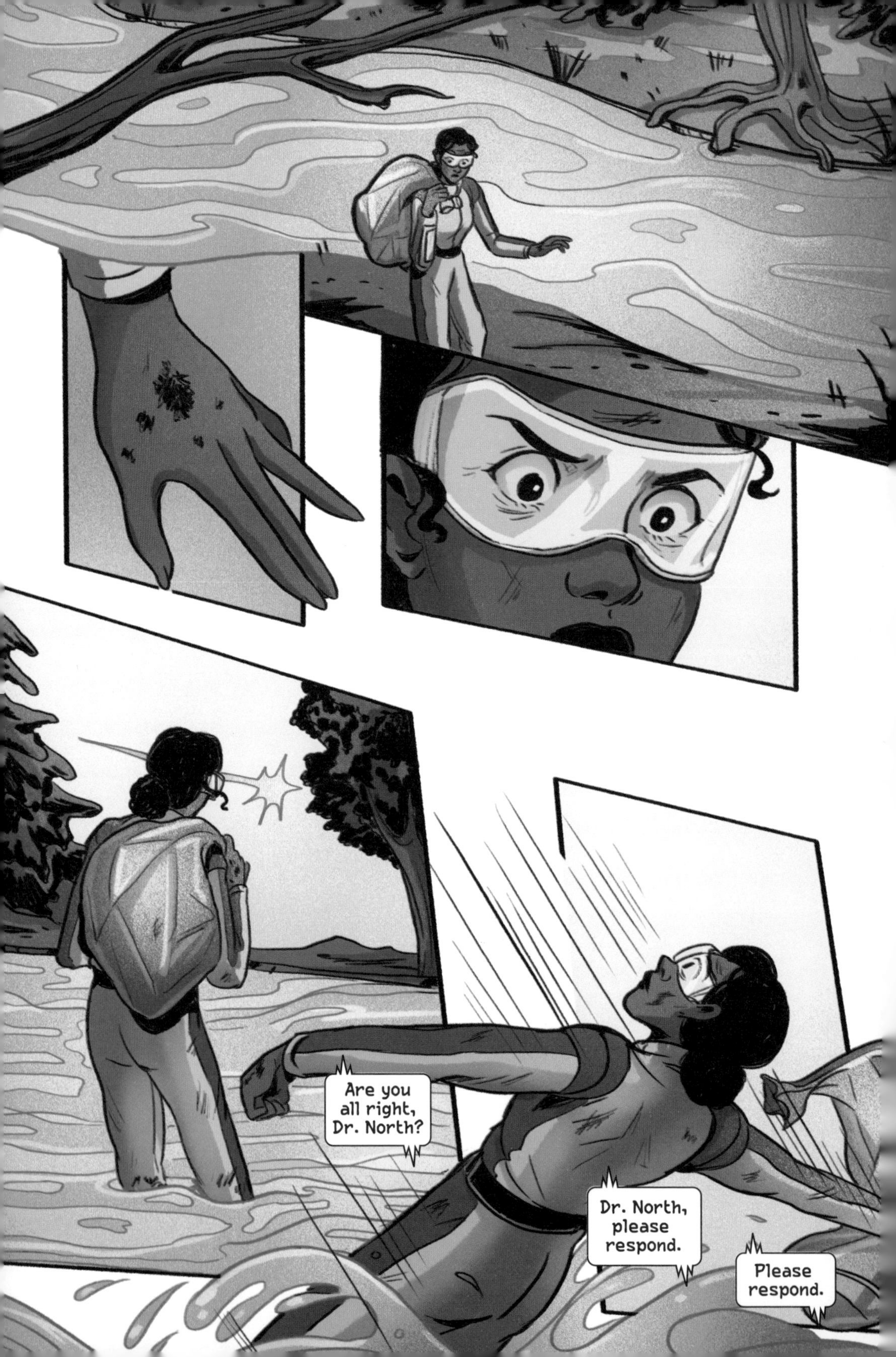
Are you all right, Dr. North?
Dr. North, please respond.
Please respond.

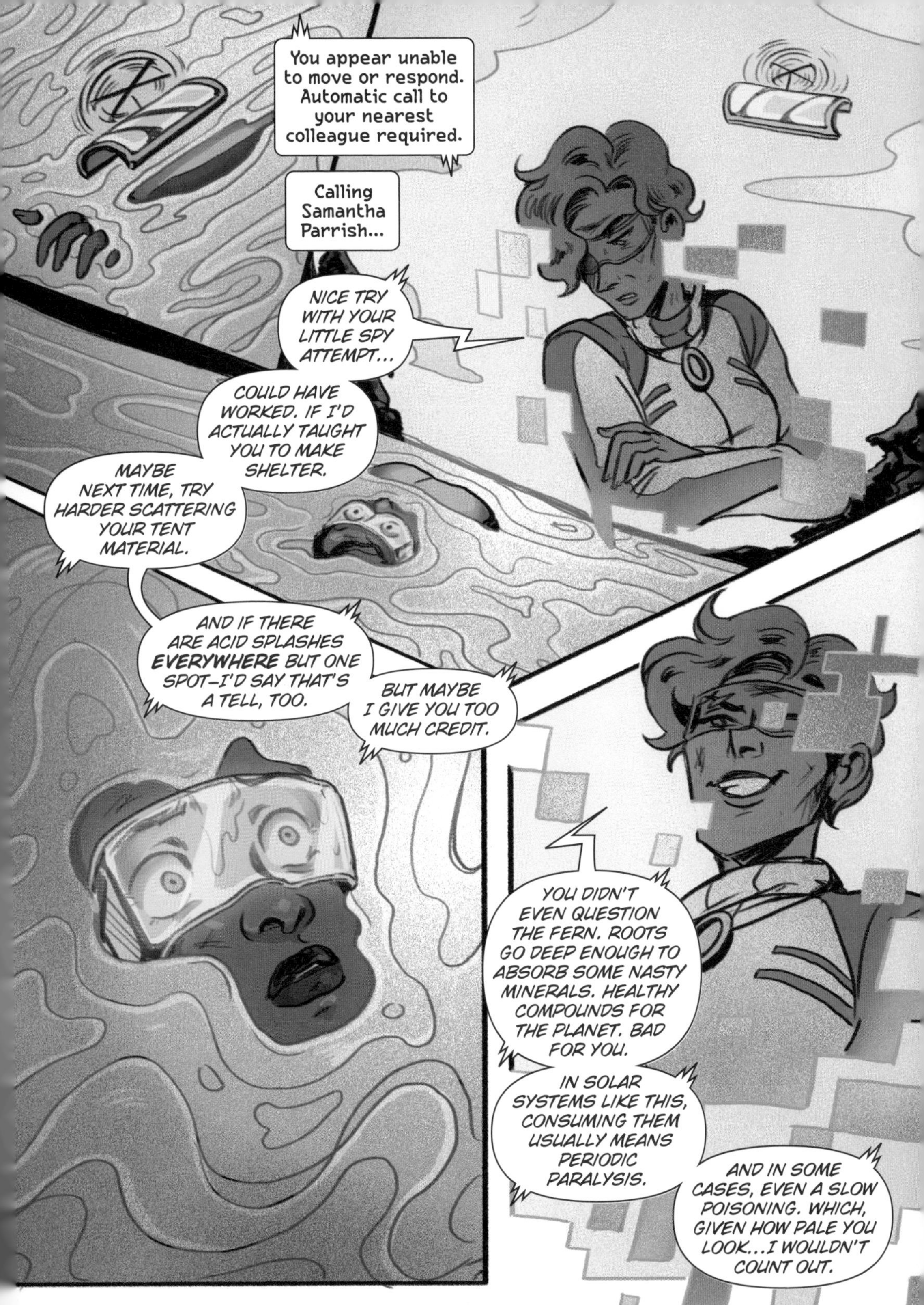
You appear unable to move or respond. Automatic call to your nearest colleague required.
Calling Samantha Parrish...
NICE TRY WITH YOUR LITTLE SPY ATTEMPT...
COULD HAVE WORKED. IF I'D ACTUALLY TAUGHT YOU TO MAKE SHELTER.
MAYBE NEXT TIME, TRY HARDER SCATTERING YOUR TENT MATERIAL.
AND IF THERE ARE ACID SPLASHES **EVERYWHERE** BUT ONE SPOT–I'D SAY THAT'S A TELL, TOO.
BUT MAYBE I GIVE YOU TOO MUCH CREDIT.
YOU DIDN'T EVEN QUESTION THE FERN. ROOTS GO DEEP ENOUGH TO ABSORB SOME NASTY MINERALS. HEALTHY COMPOUNDS FOR THE PLANET. BAD FOR YOU.
IN SOLAR SYSTEMS LIKE THIS, CONSUMING THEM USUALLY MEANS PERIODIC PARALYSIS.
AND IN SOME CASES, EVEN A SLOW POISONING. WHICH, GIVEN HOW PALE YOU LOOK...I WOULDN'T COUNT OUT.

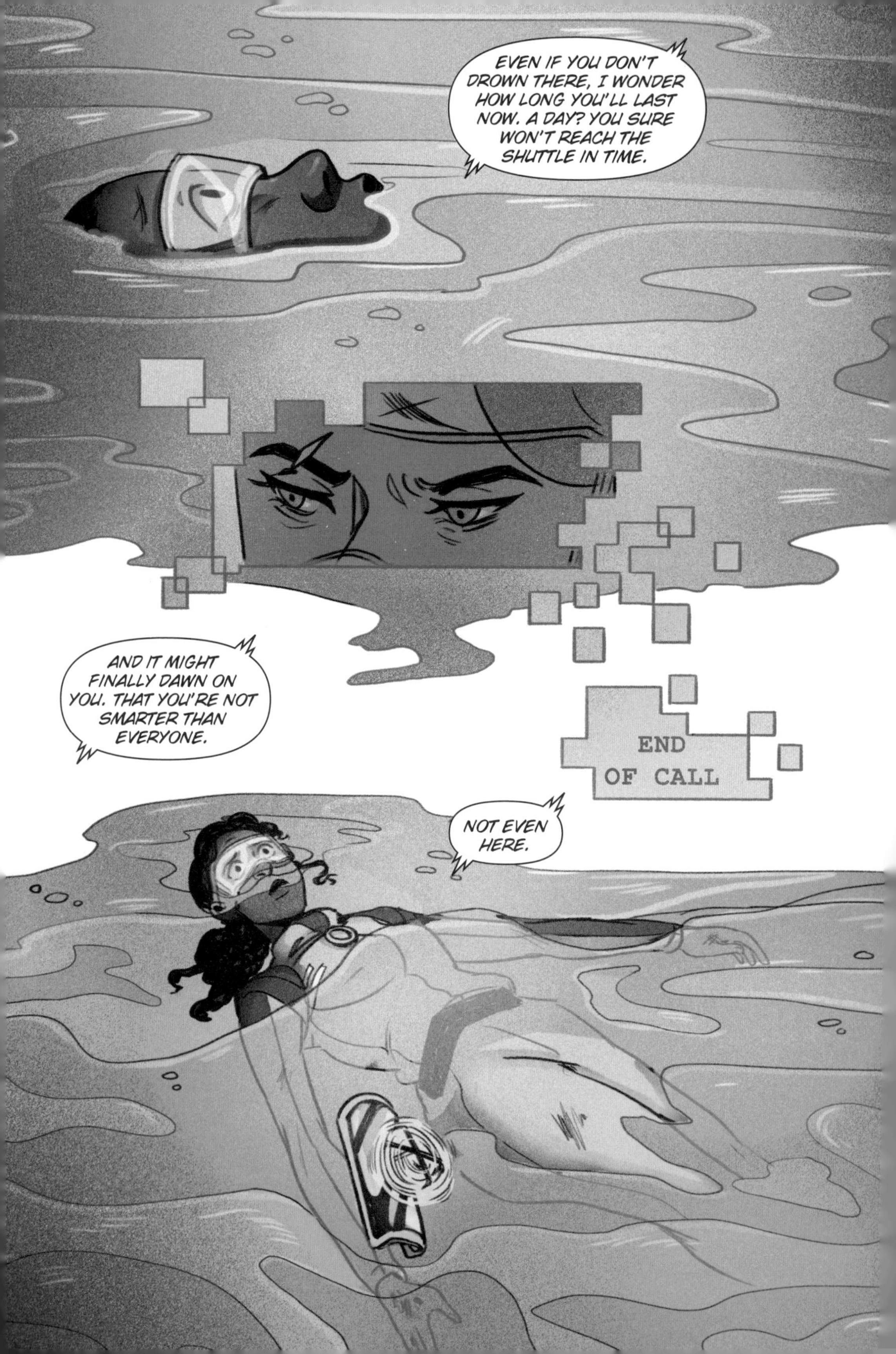
EVEN IF YOU DON'T DROWN THERE, I WONDER HOW LONG YOU'LL LAST NOW. A DAY? YOU SURE WON'T REACH THE SHUTTLE IN TIME.
AND IT MIGHT FINALLY DAWN ON YOU. THAT YOU'RE NOT SMARTER THAN EVERYONE.
END OF CALL
NOT EVEN HERE.

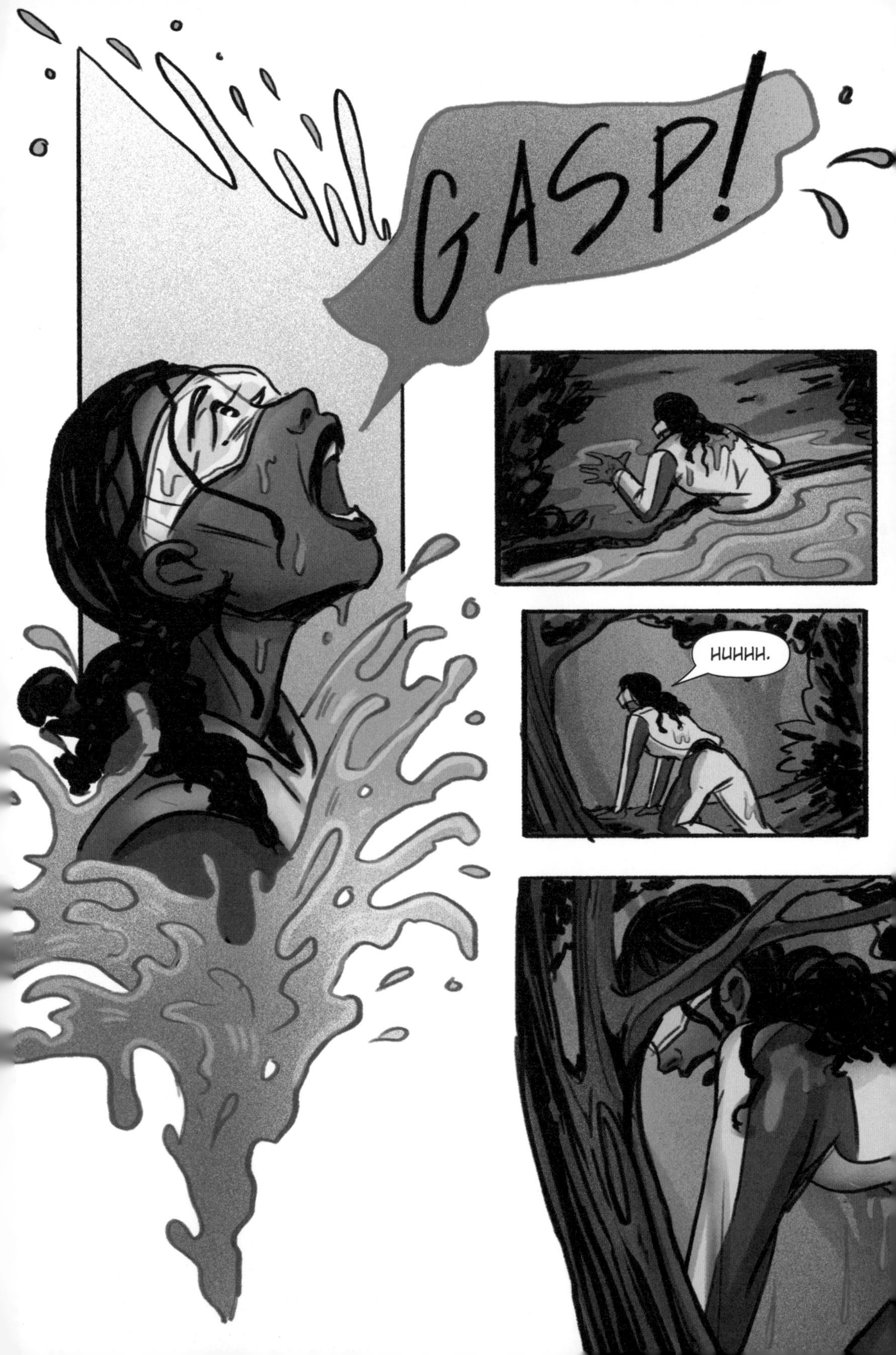
GASP!
HUHHH.

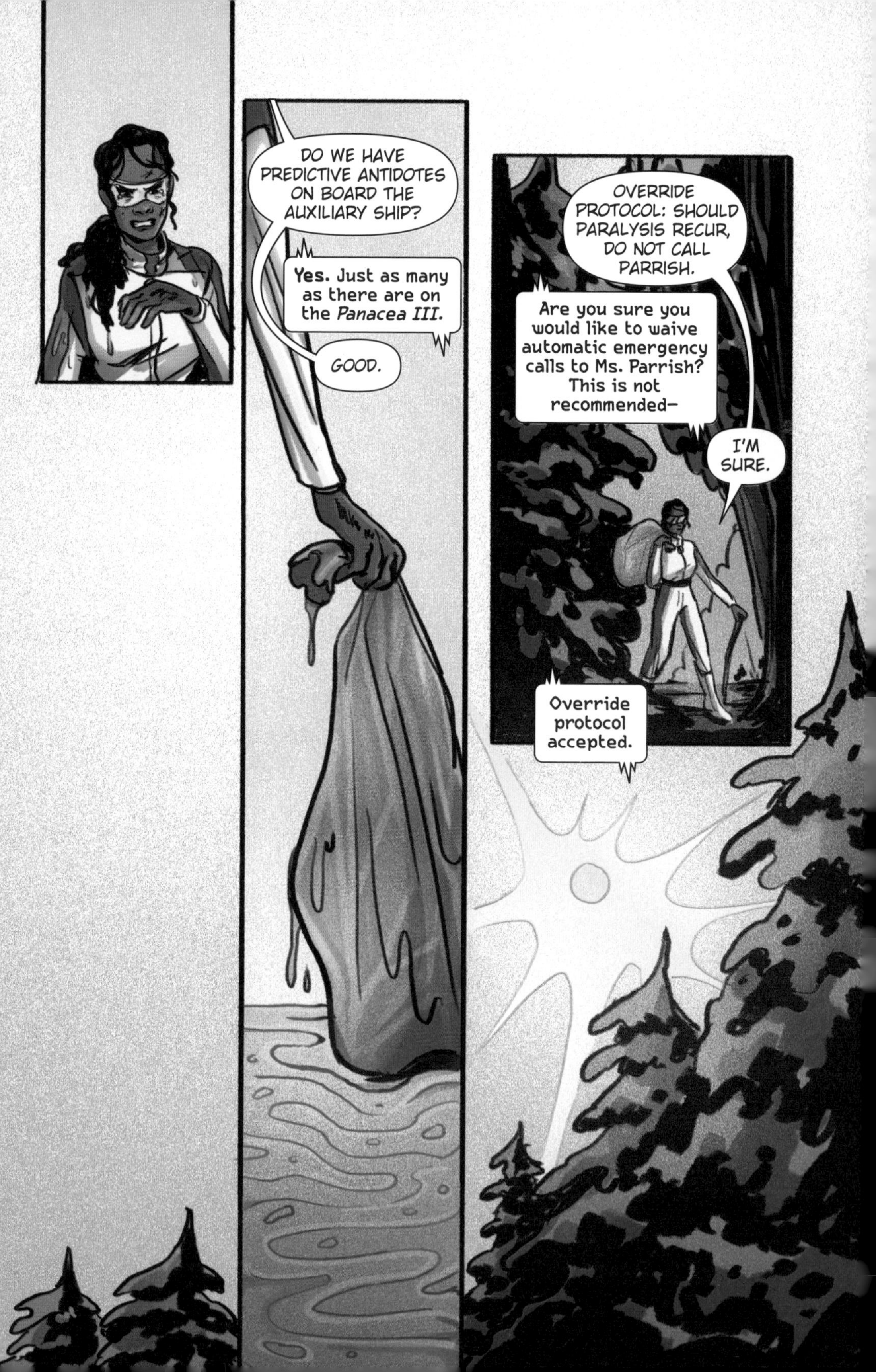

DO WE HAVE PREDICTIVE ANTIDOTES ON BOARD THE AUXILIARY SHIP?
Yes. Just as many as there are on the *Panacea III*.
GOOD.
OVERRIDE PROTOCOL: SHOULD PARALYSIS RECUR, DO NOT CALL PARRISH.
Are you sure you would like to waive automatic emergency calls to Ms. Parrish? This is not recommended—
I'M SURE.
Override protocol accepted.

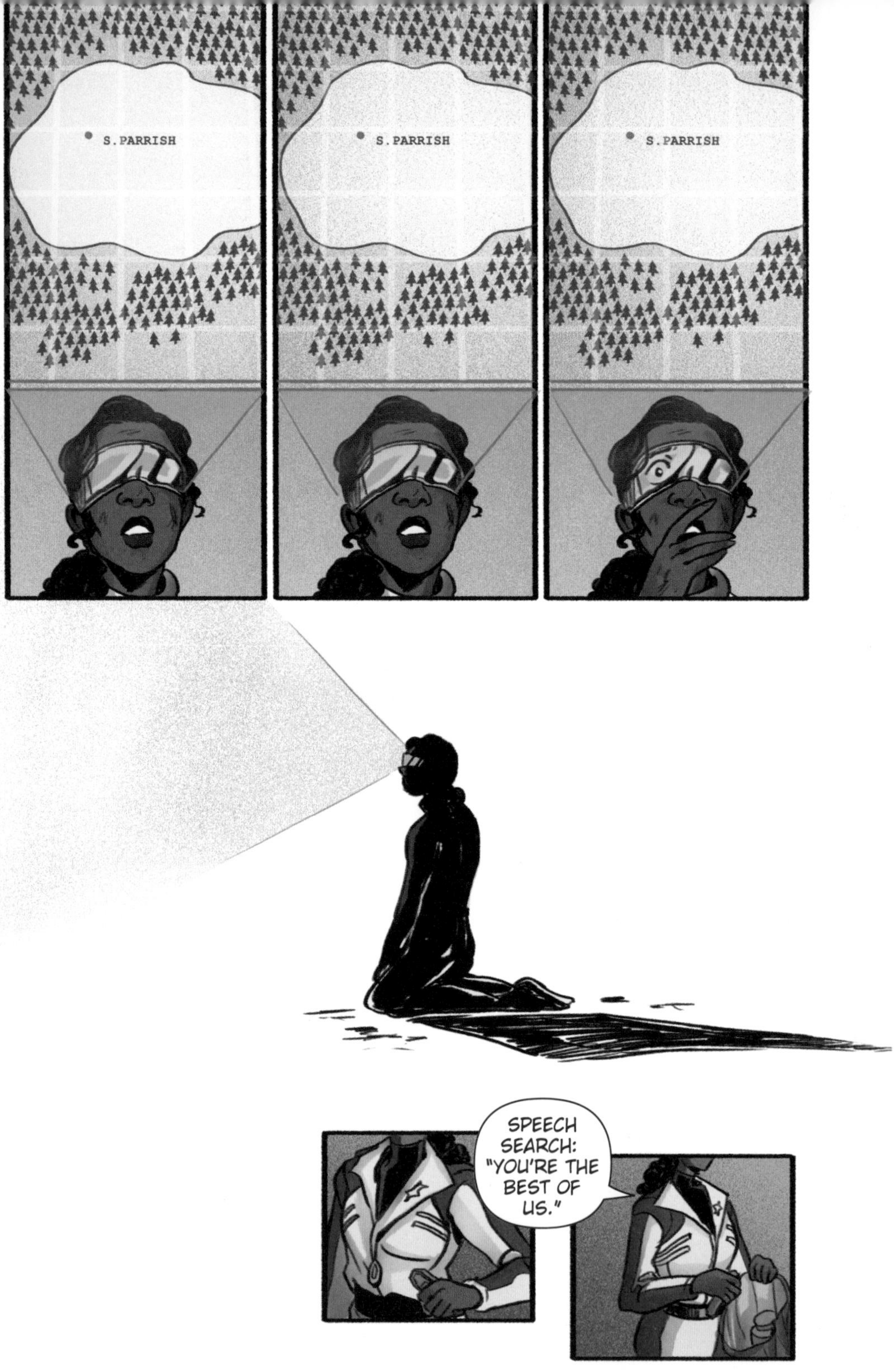
S.PARRISH
S.PARRISH
S.PARRISH
SPEECH SEARCH: "YOU'RE THE BEST OF US."

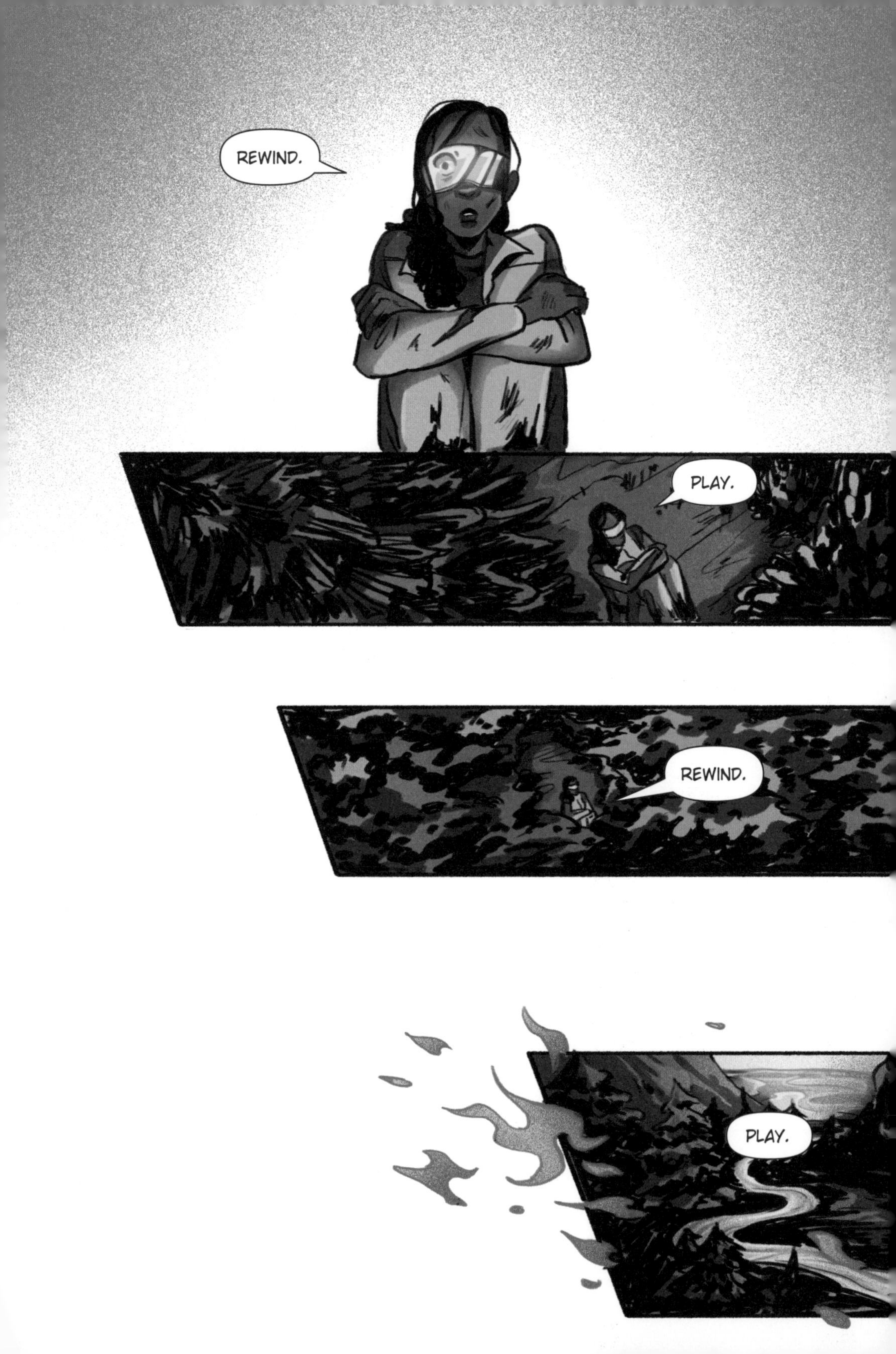
REWIND.
PLAY.
REWIND.
PLAY.

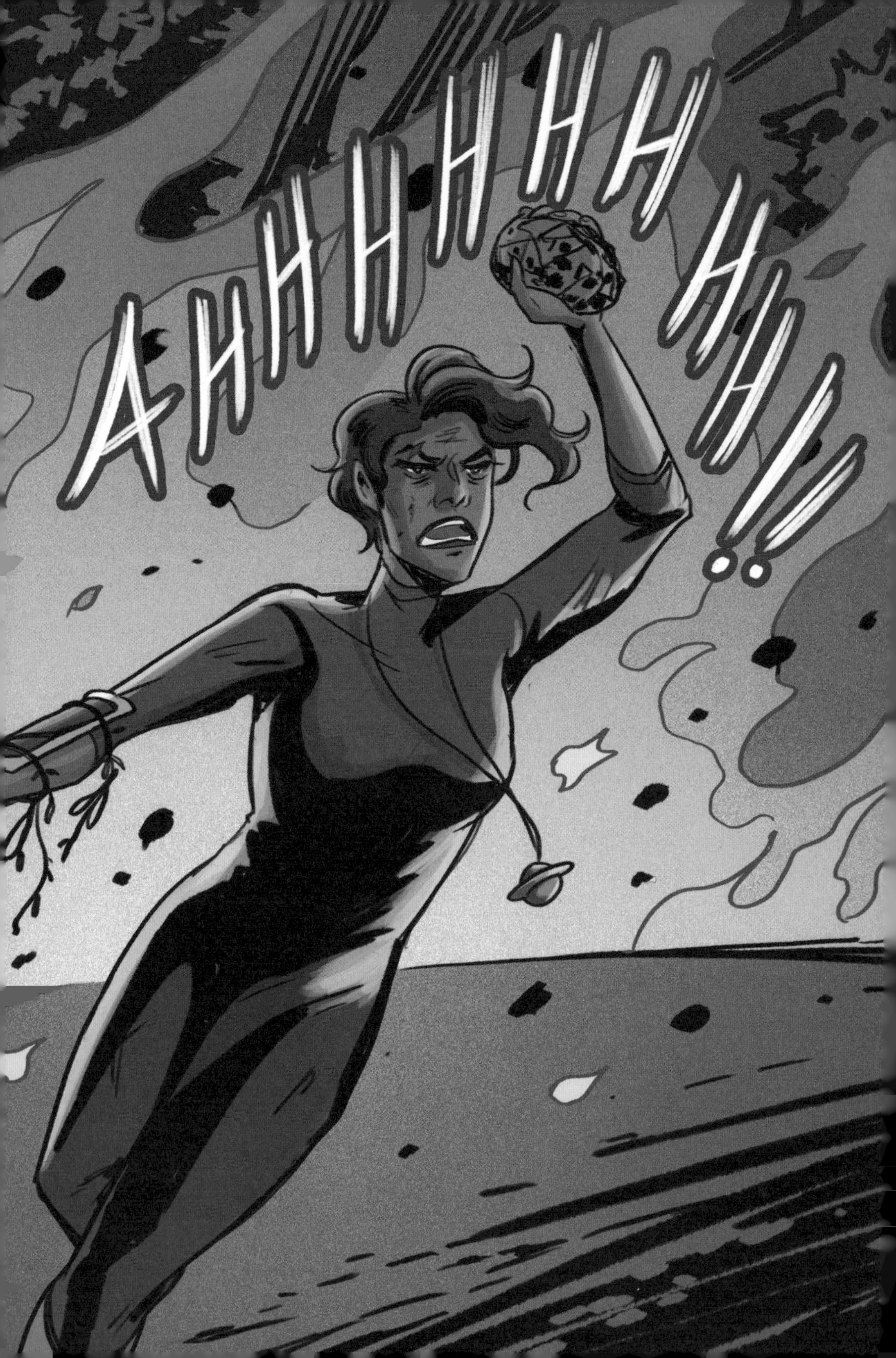
AHHHHHHHHH!!

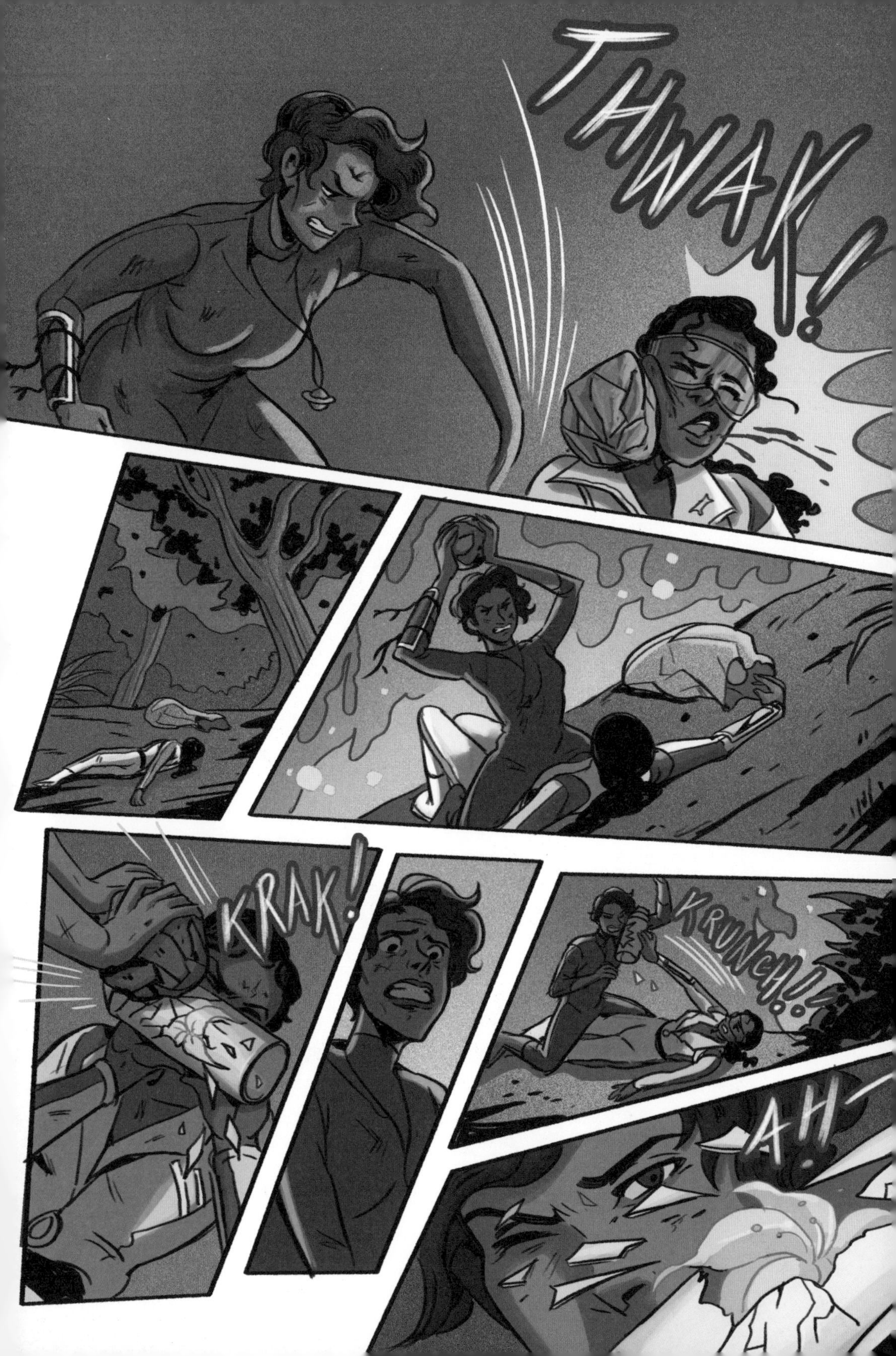
THWAK!
KRAK!
KRUNCH!!
AH-

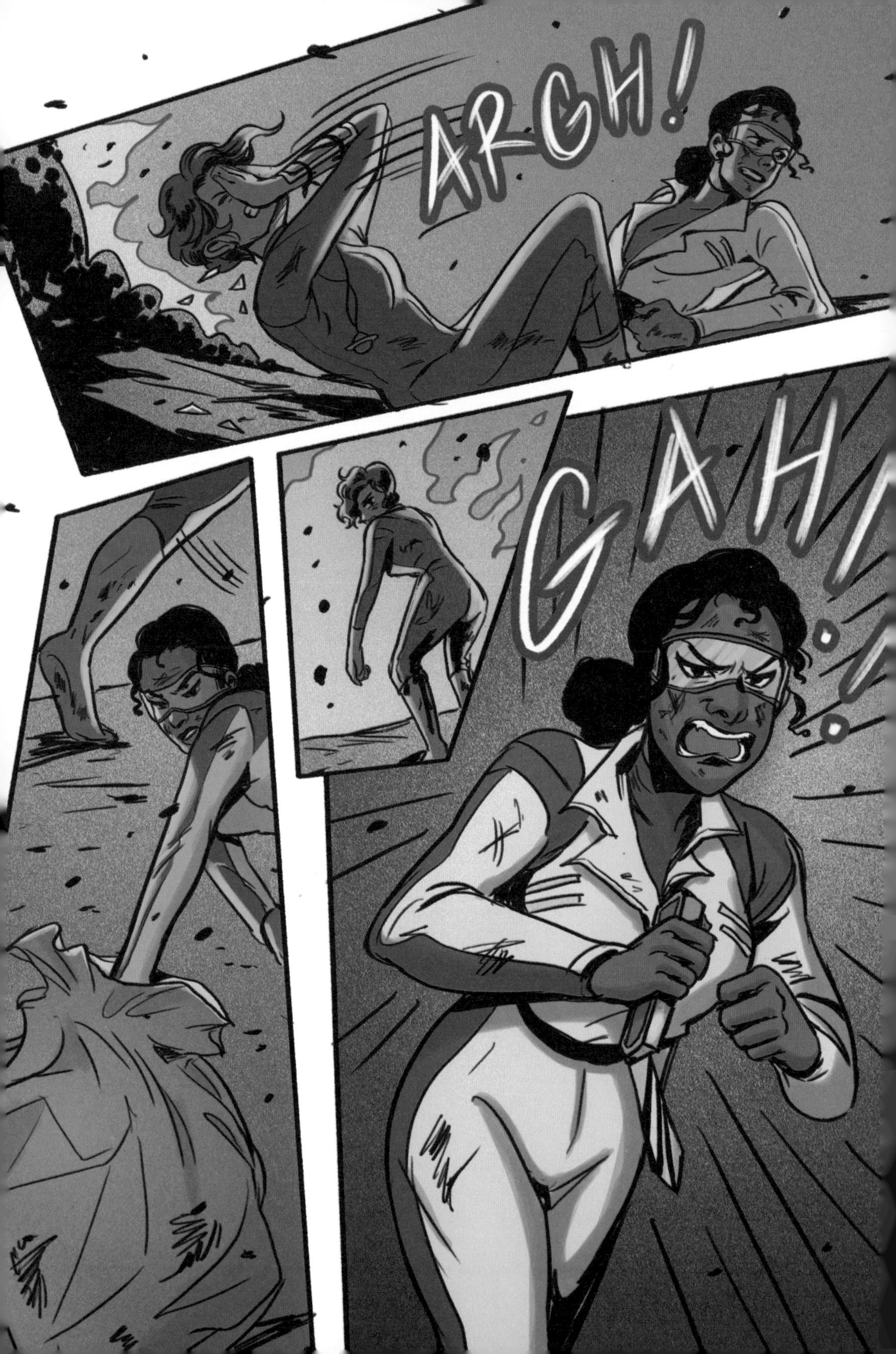
ARGH!
GAH!!

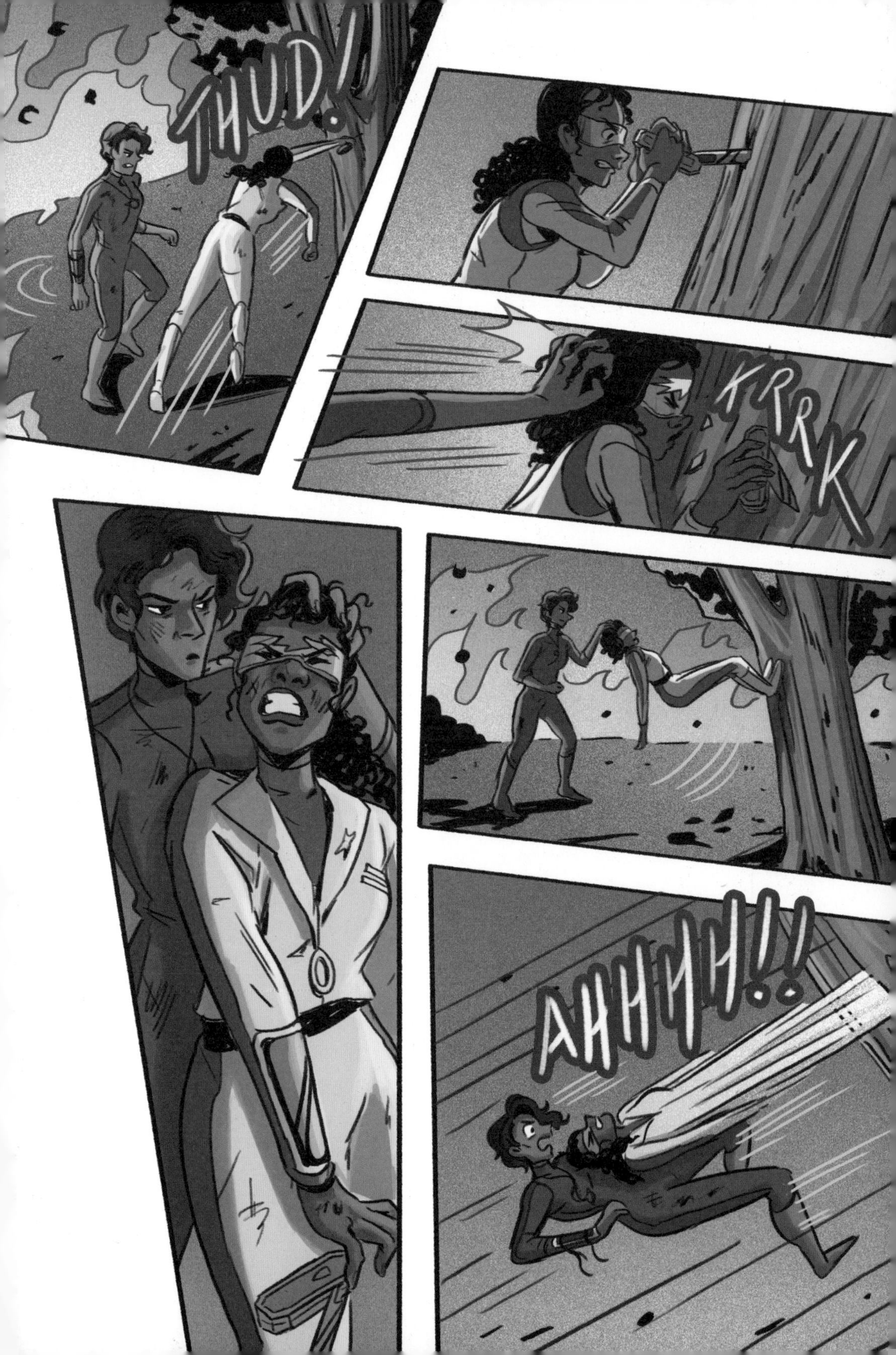
THUD!
KRRK
AHHHH!!

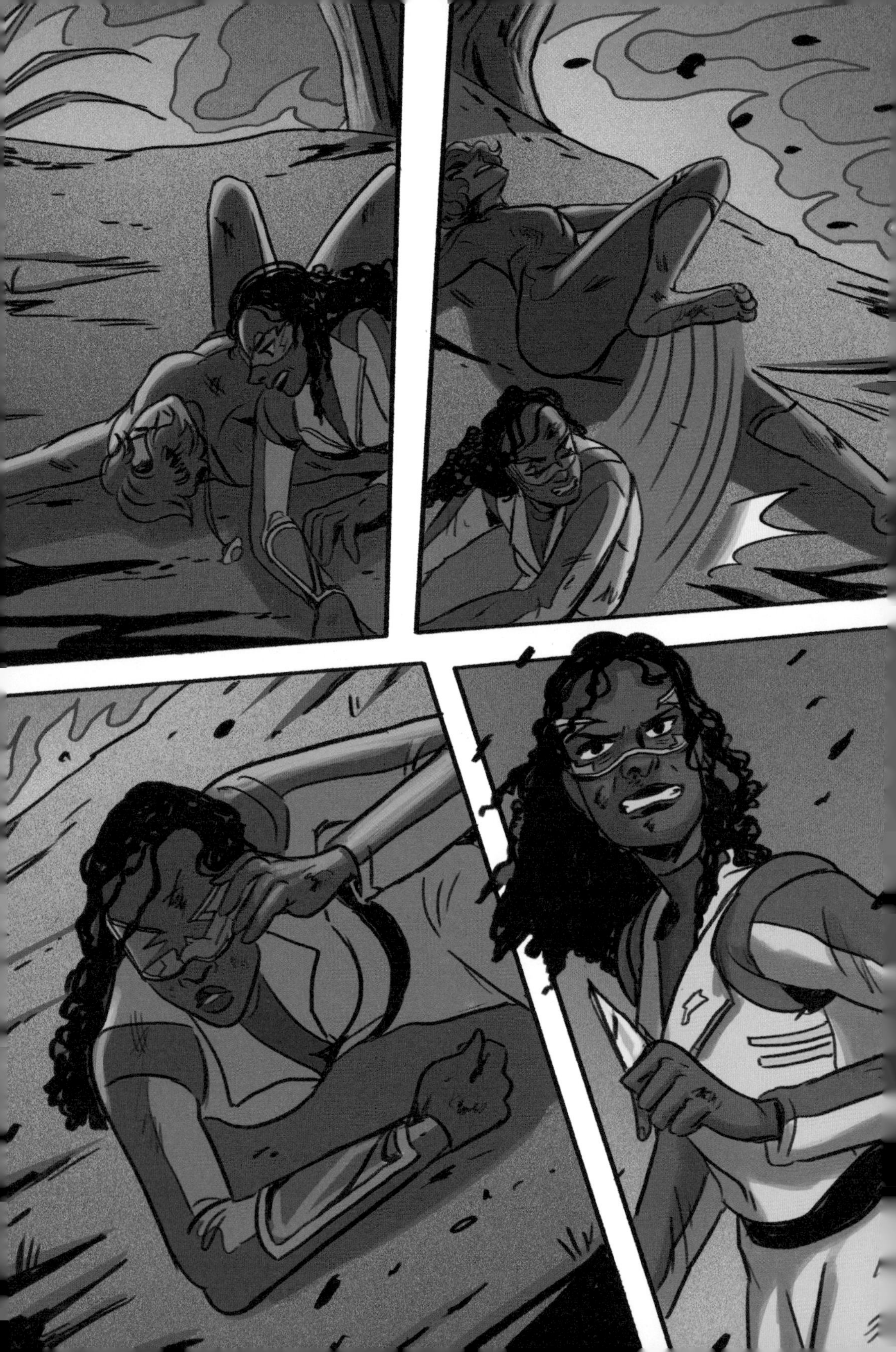

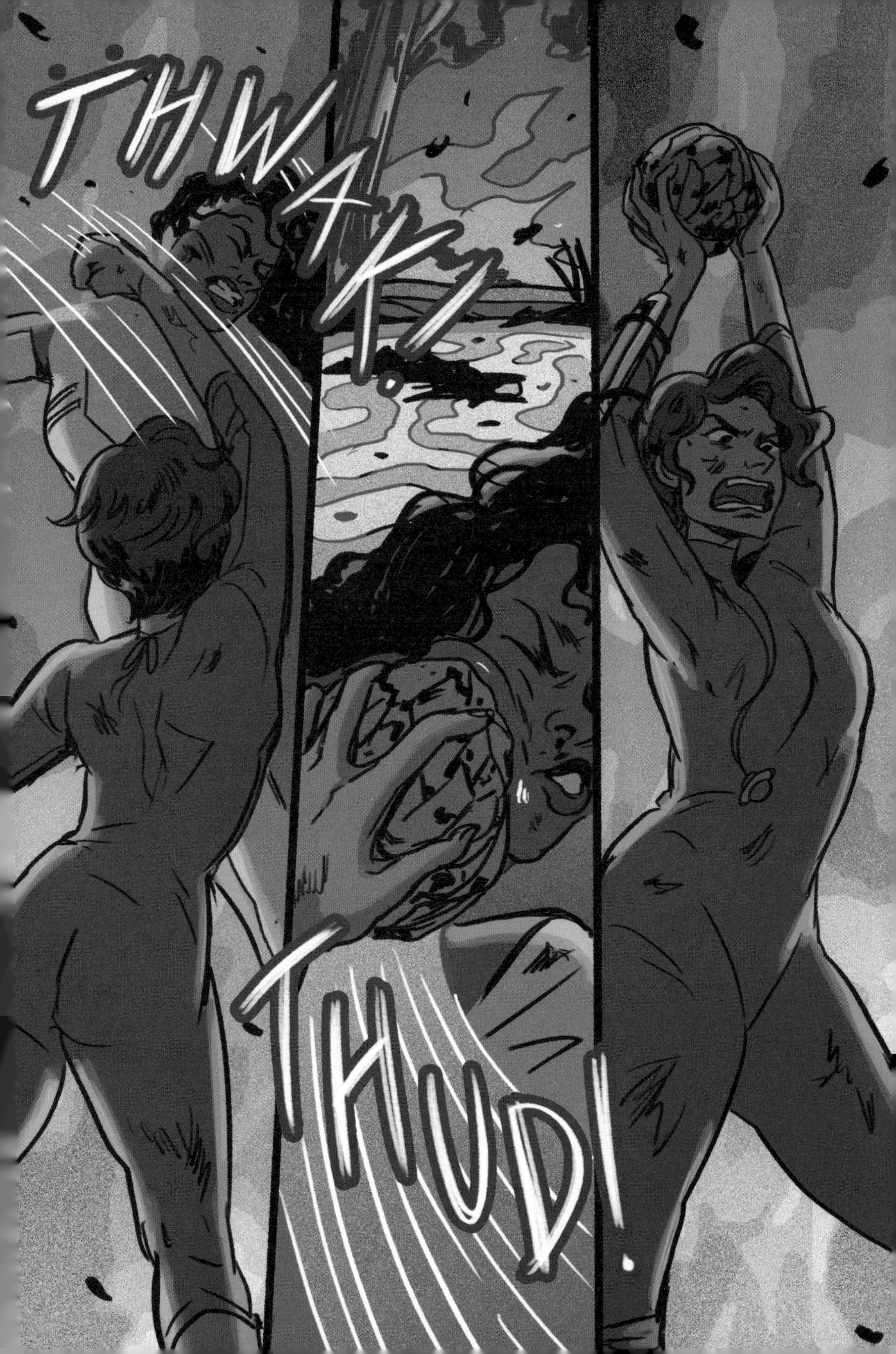
THWAK!
THUD!

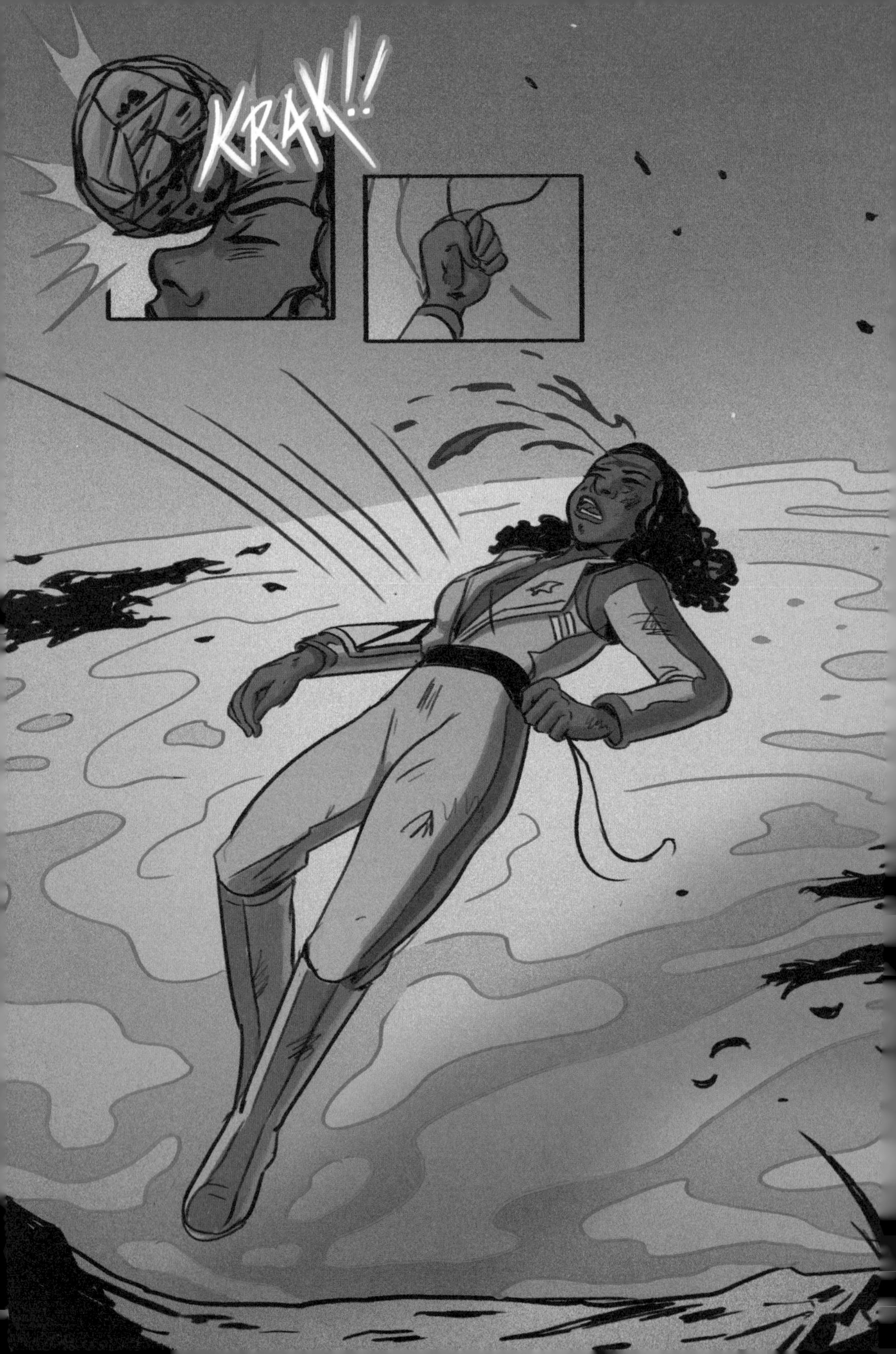
KRAK!!

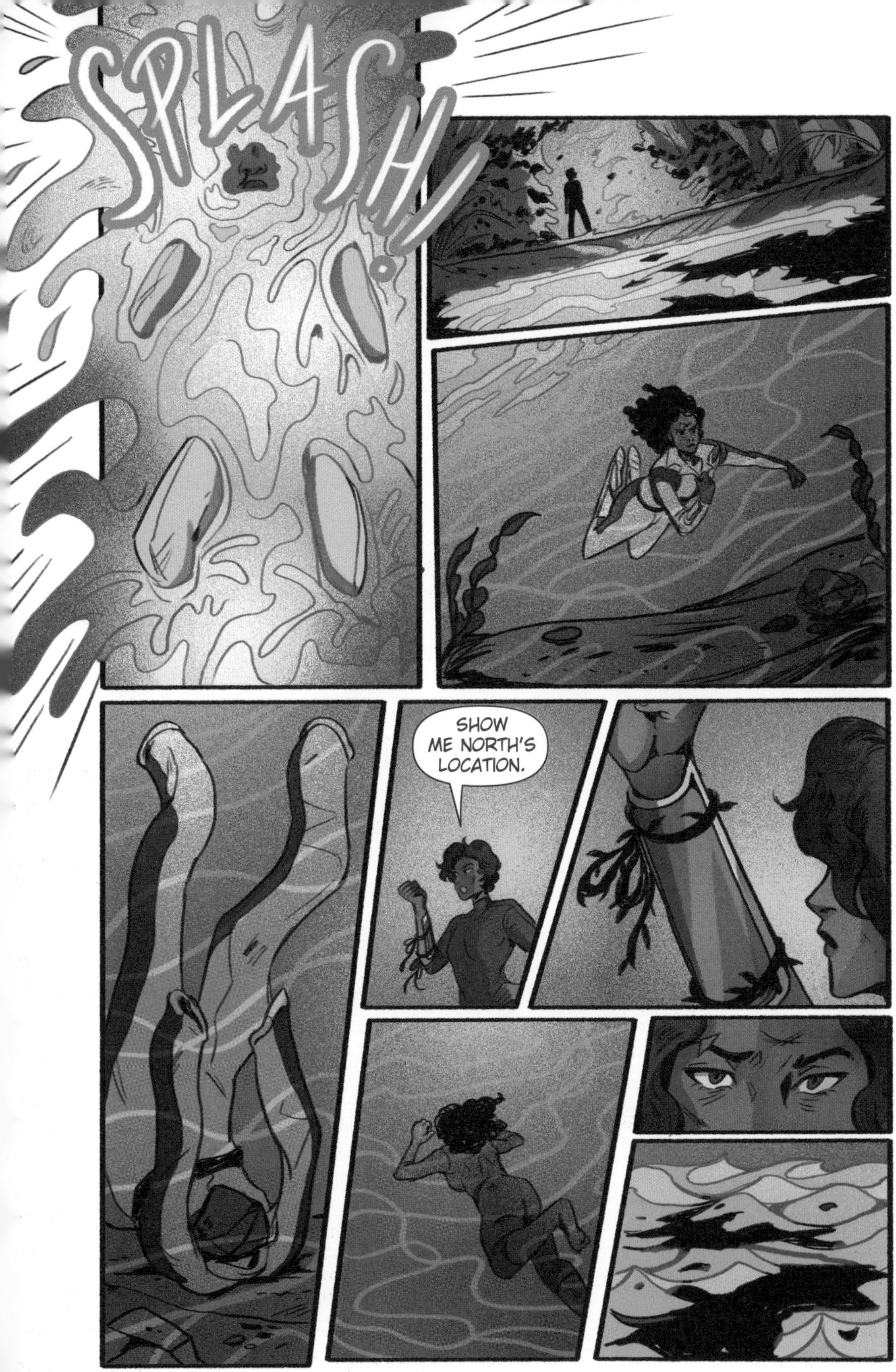
SPLASH!
SHOW ME NORTH'S LOCATION.

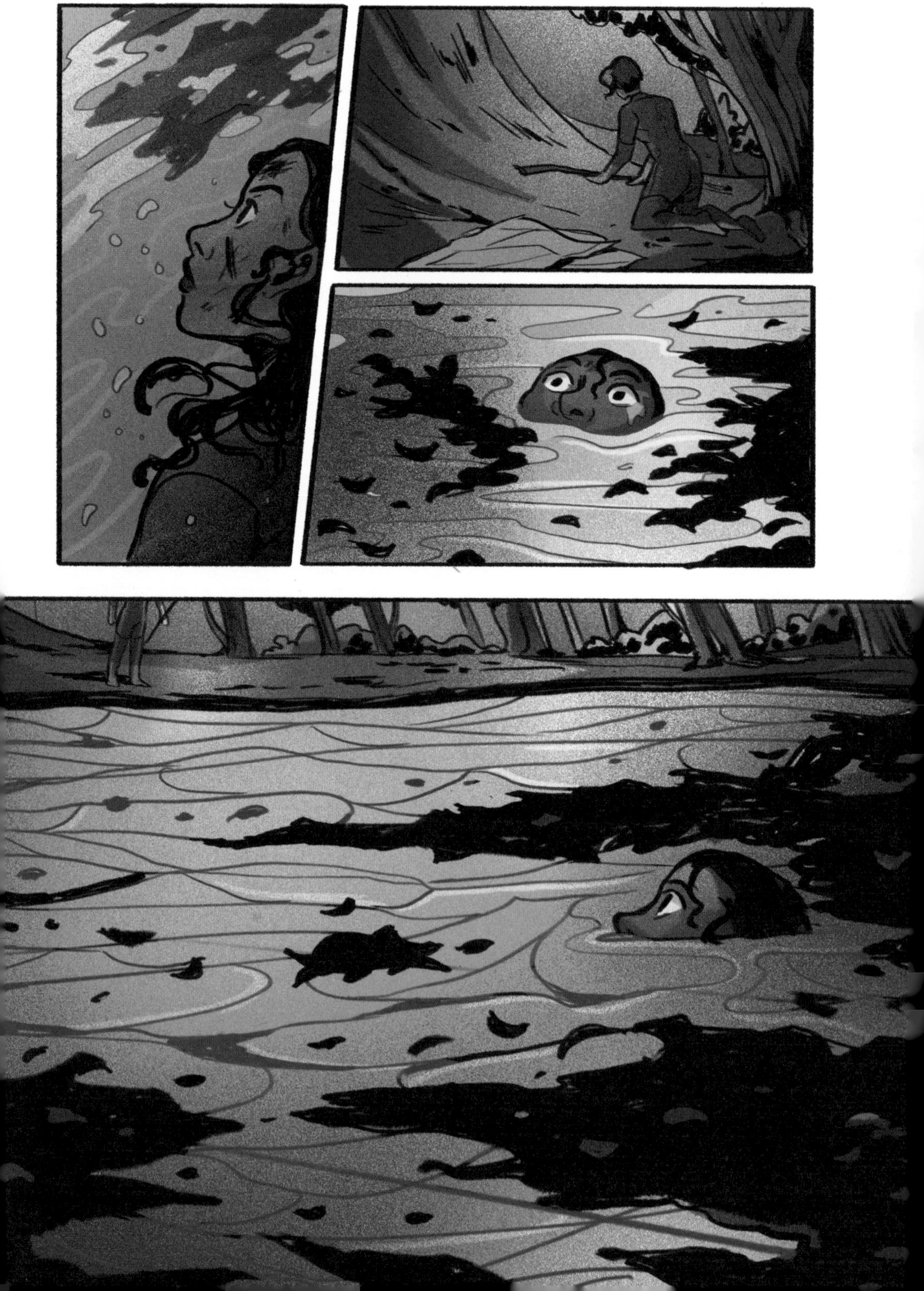

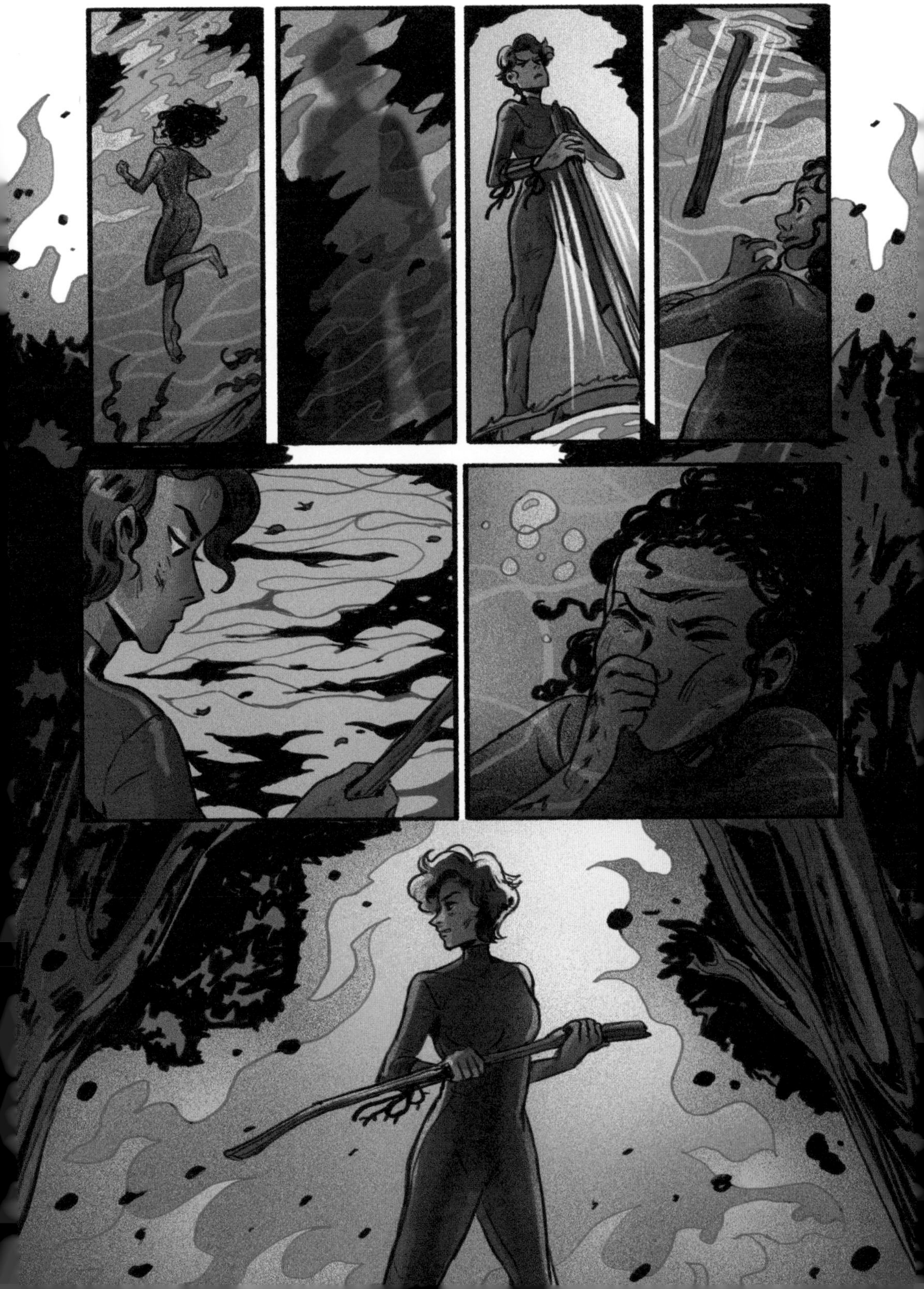

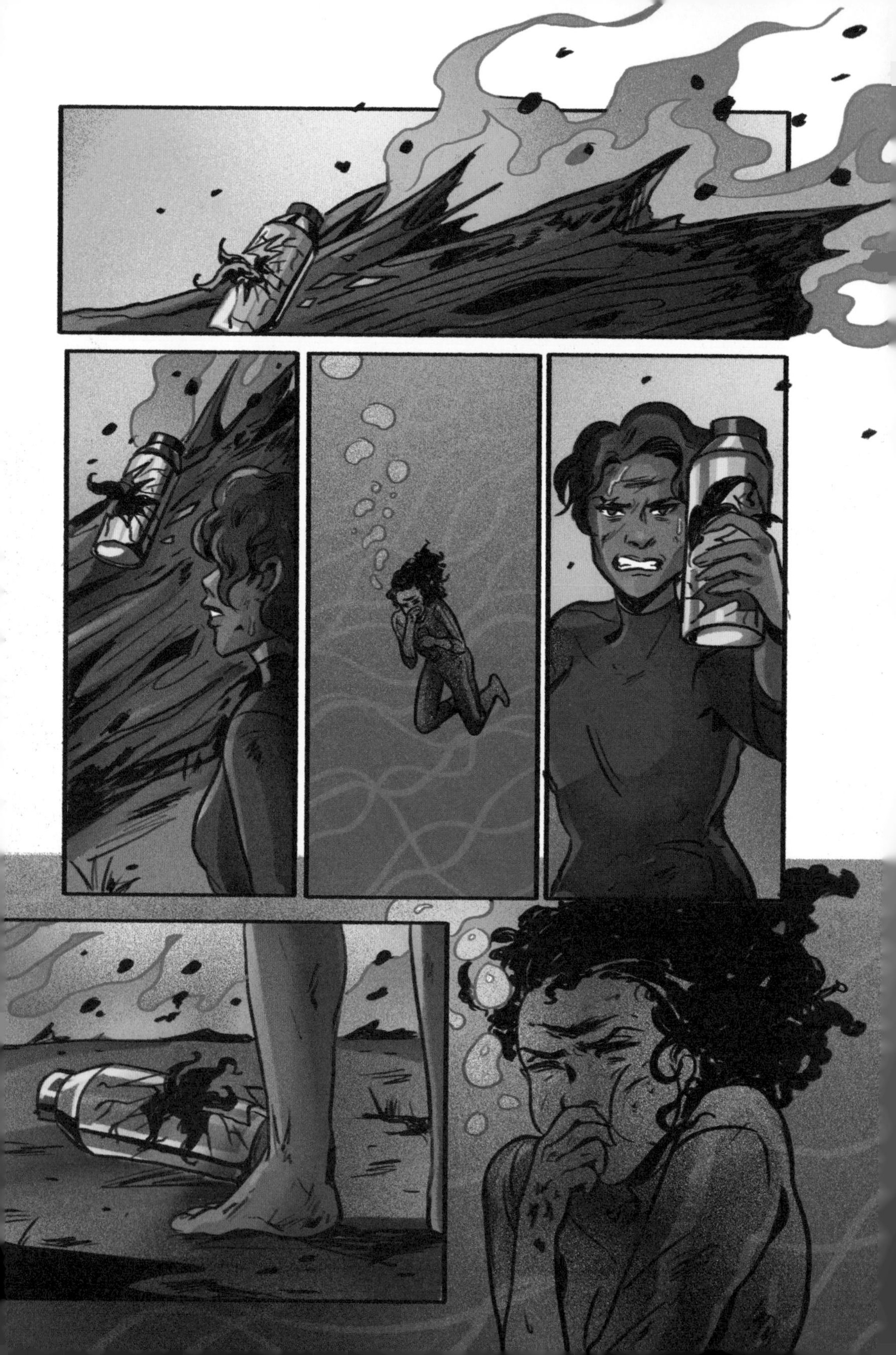

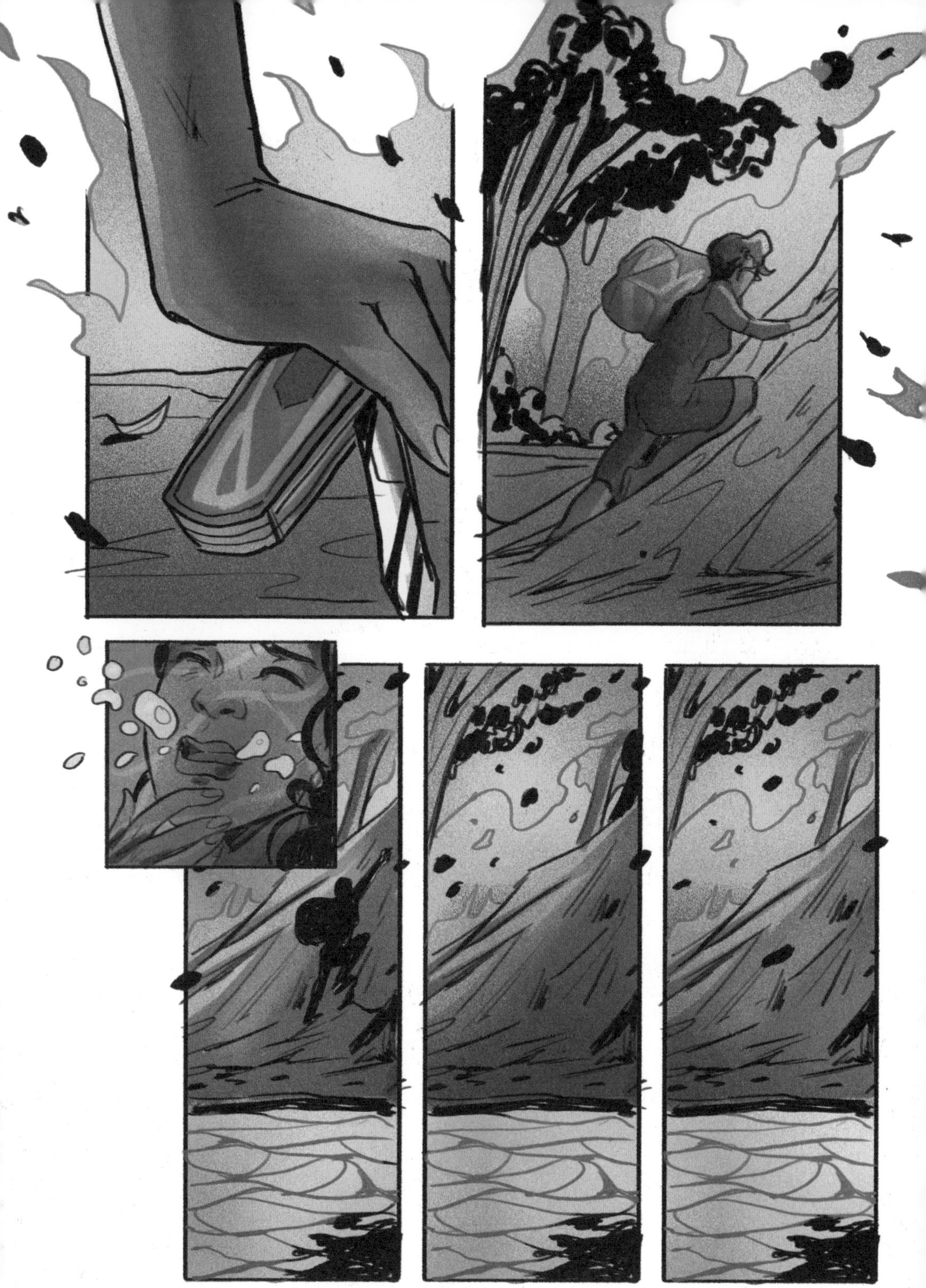

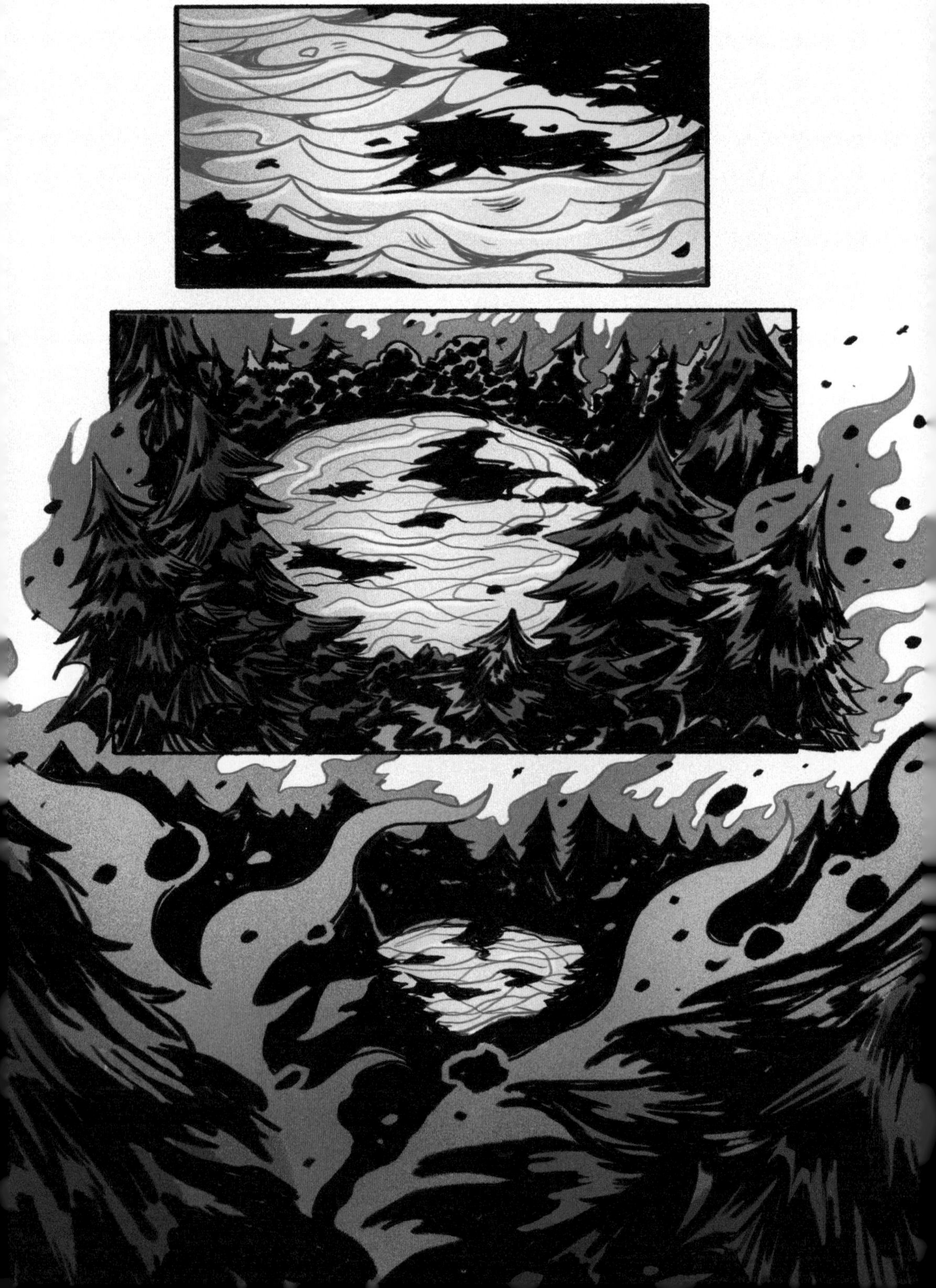

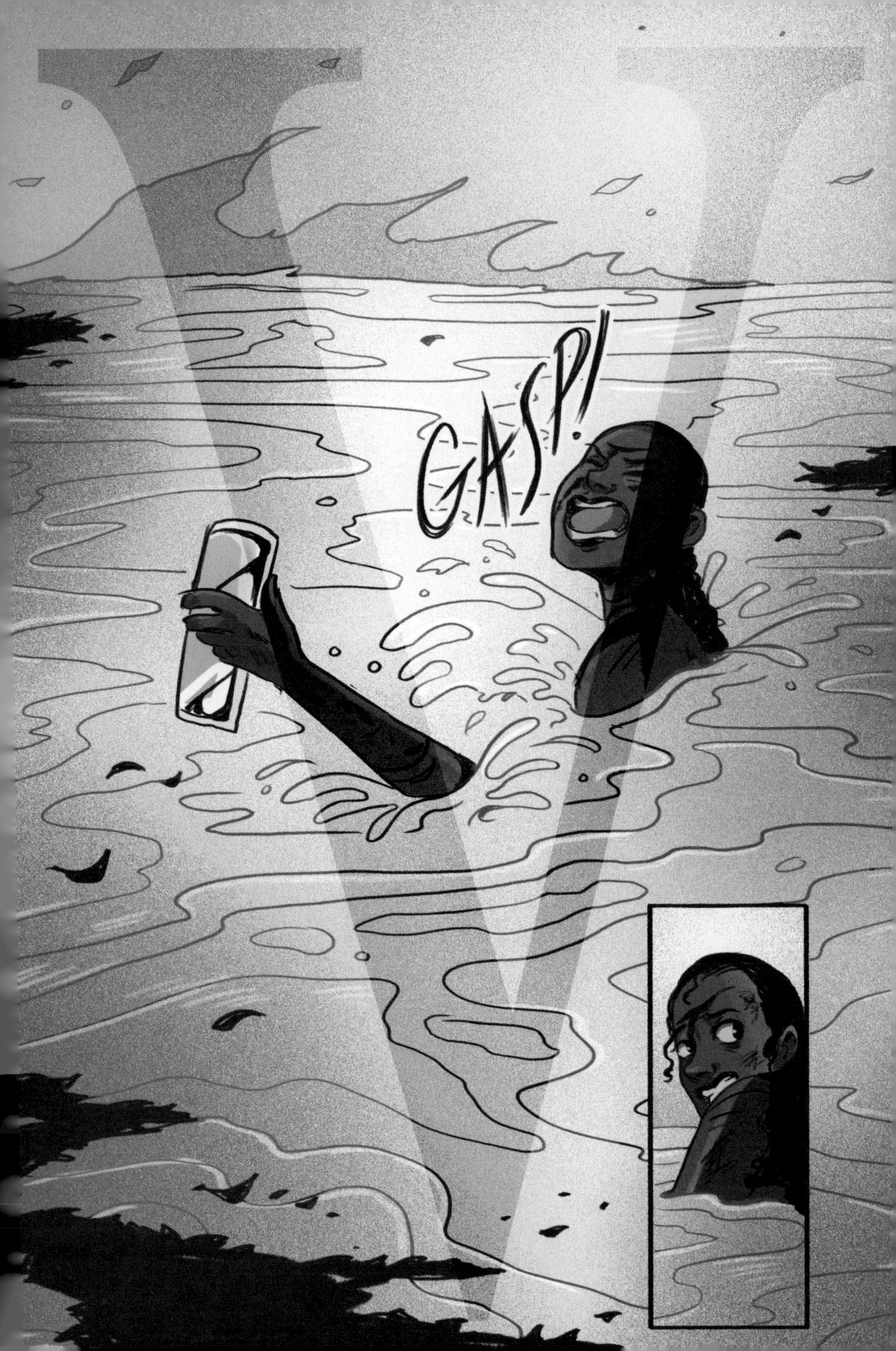
GASP!

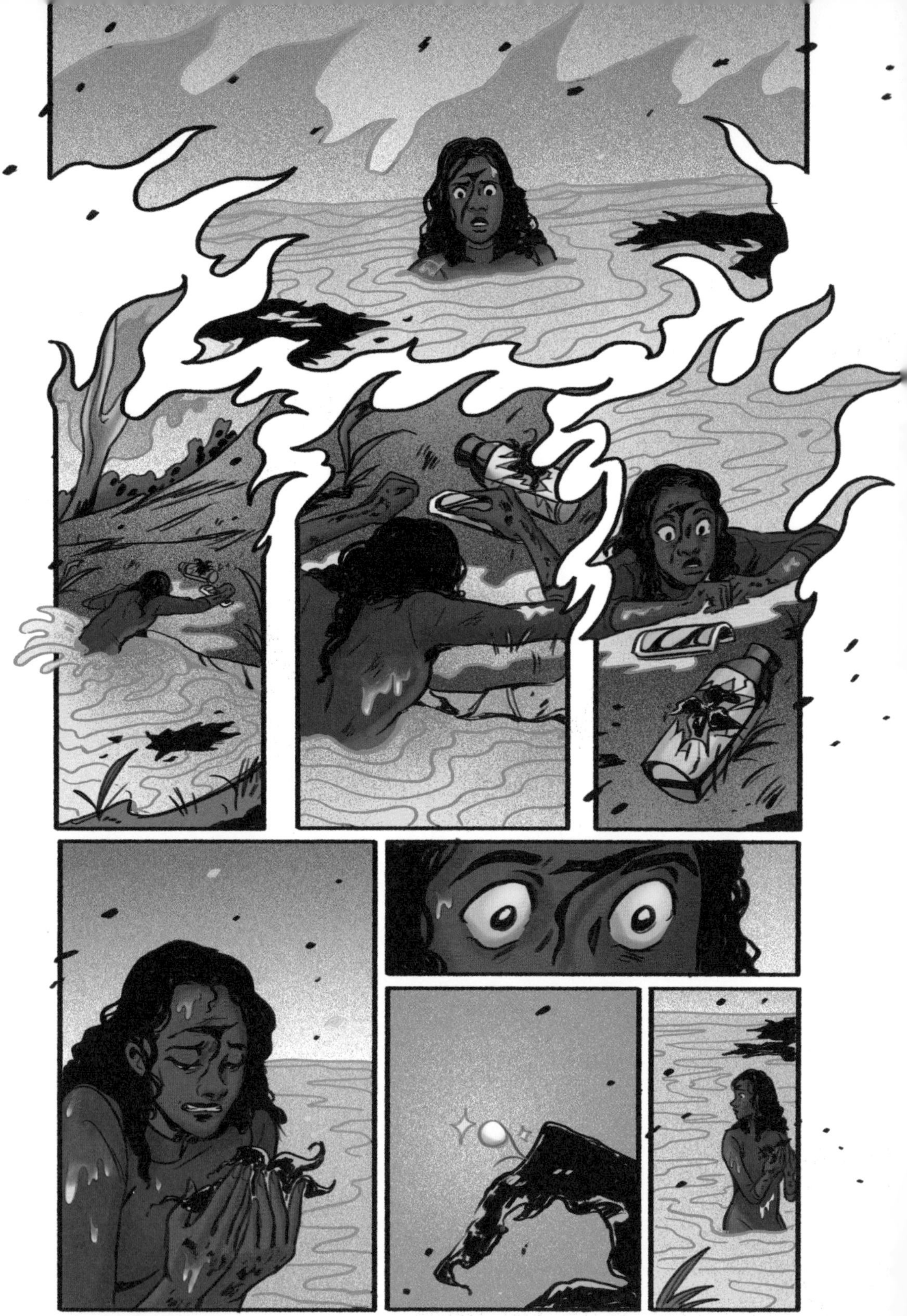

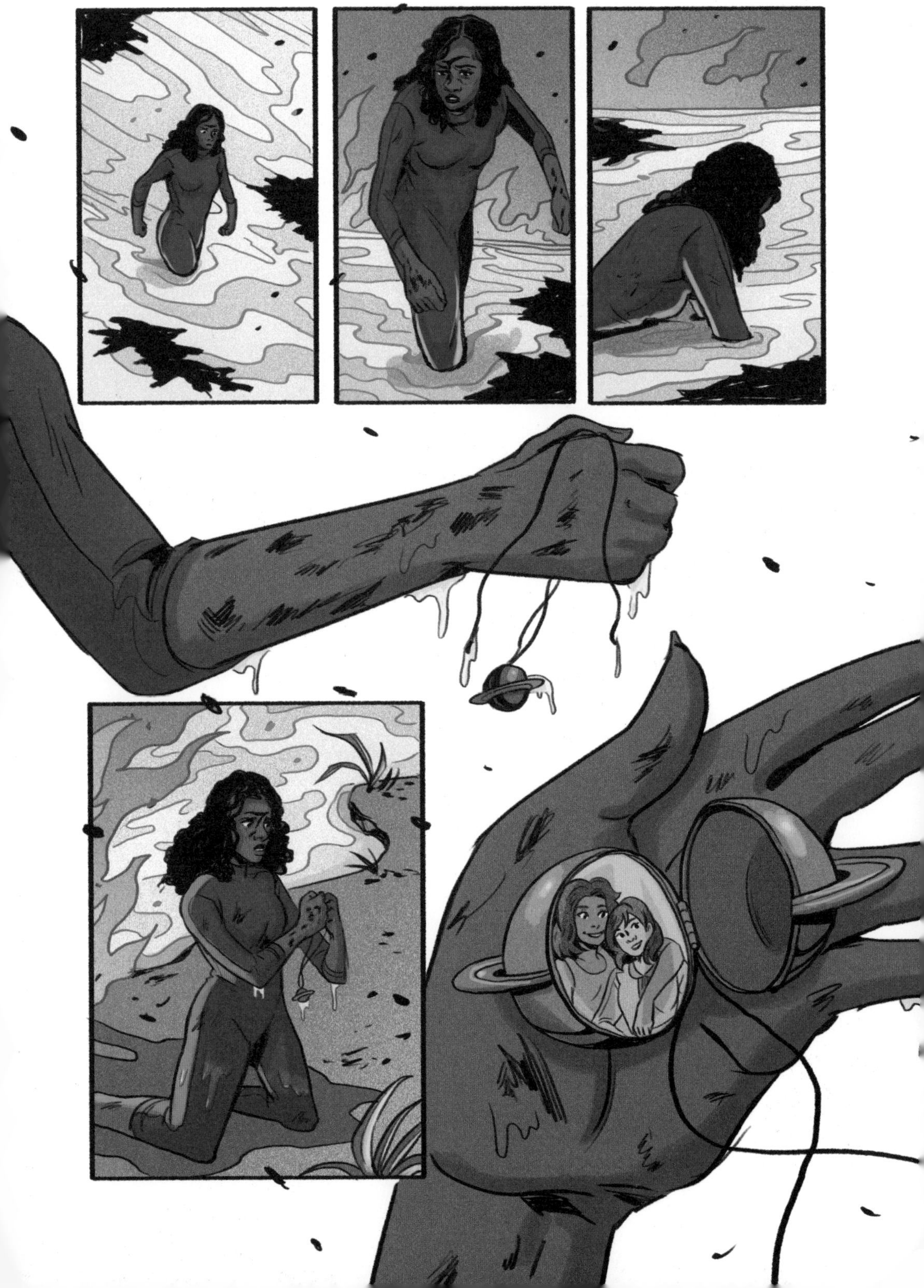

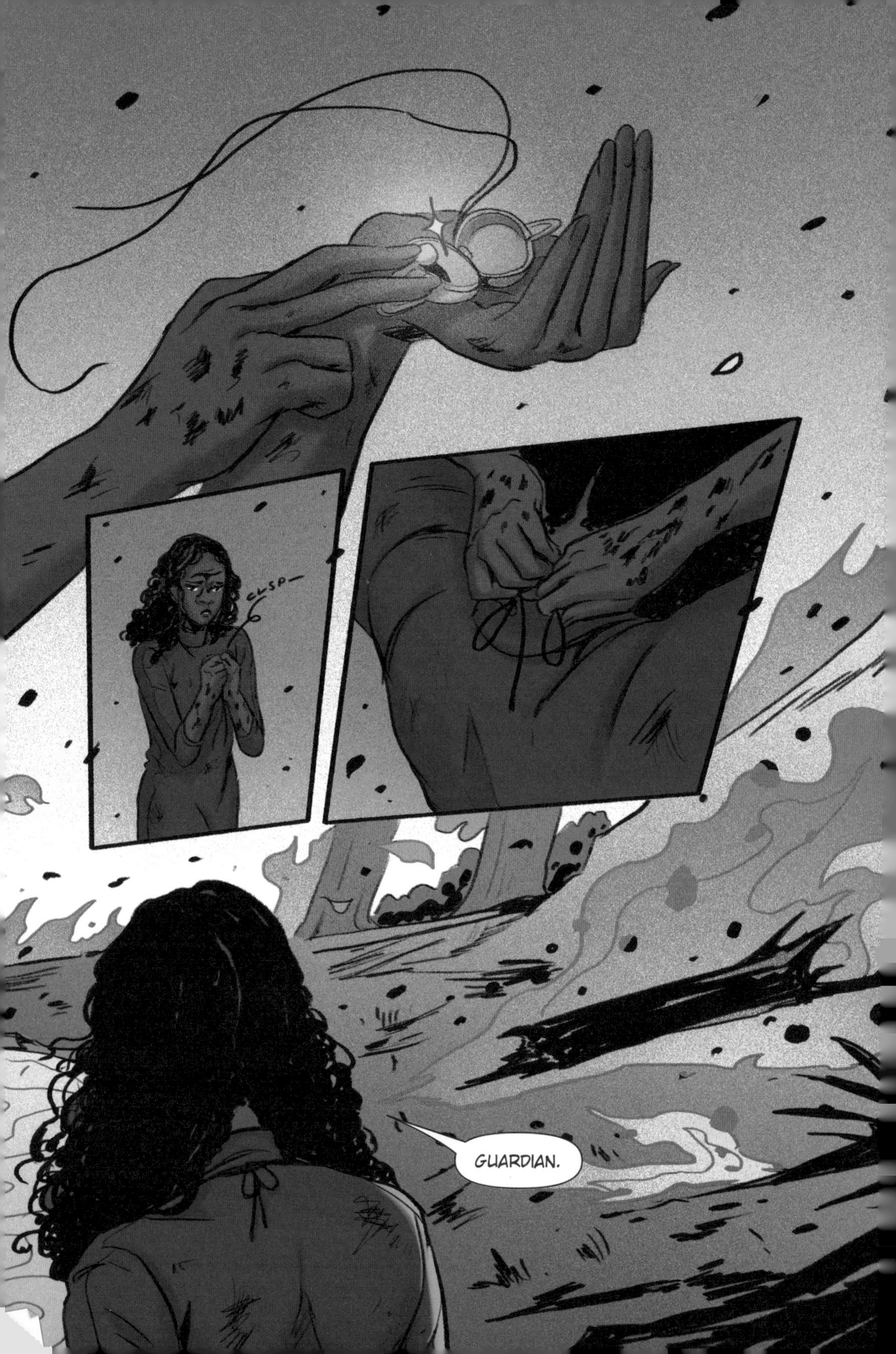
CLSP—
GUARDIAN.

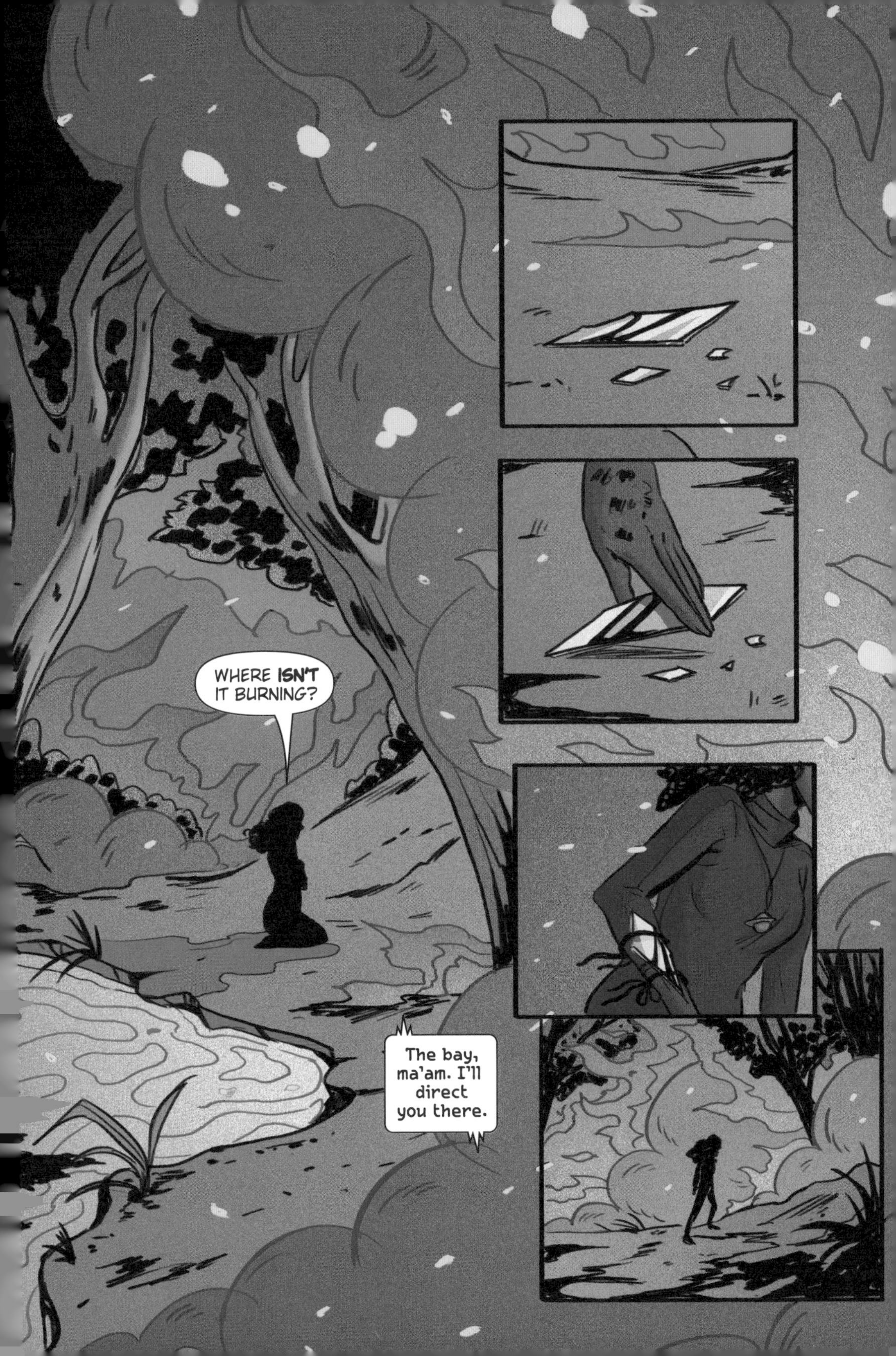
WHERE ISN'T IT BURNING?
The bay, ma'am. I'll direct you there.

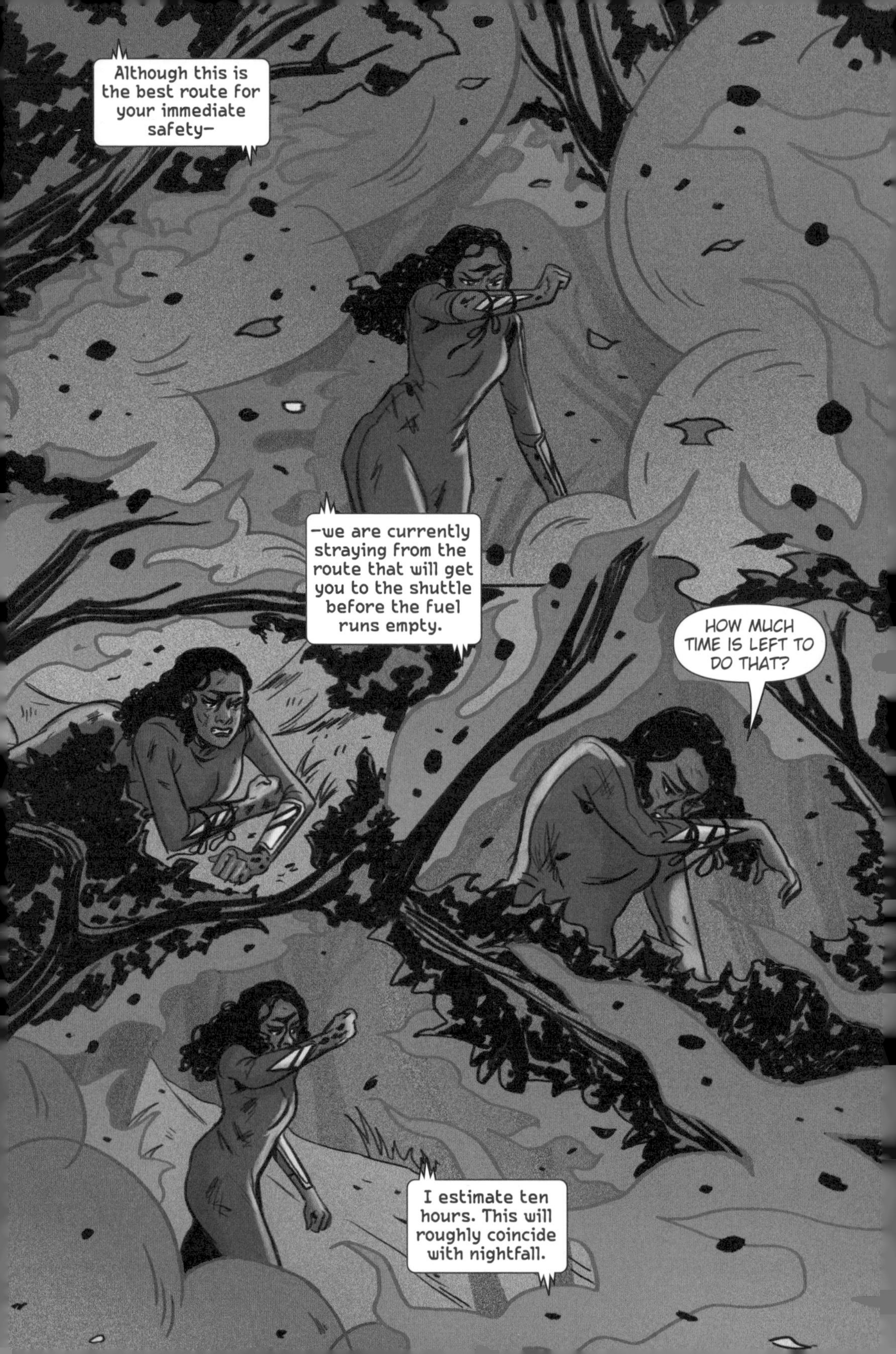
Although this is the best route for your immediate safety—
—we are currently straying from the route that will get you to the shuttle before the fuel runs empty.
HOW MUCH TIME IS LEFT TO DO THAT?
I estimate ten hours. This will roughly coincide with nightfall.

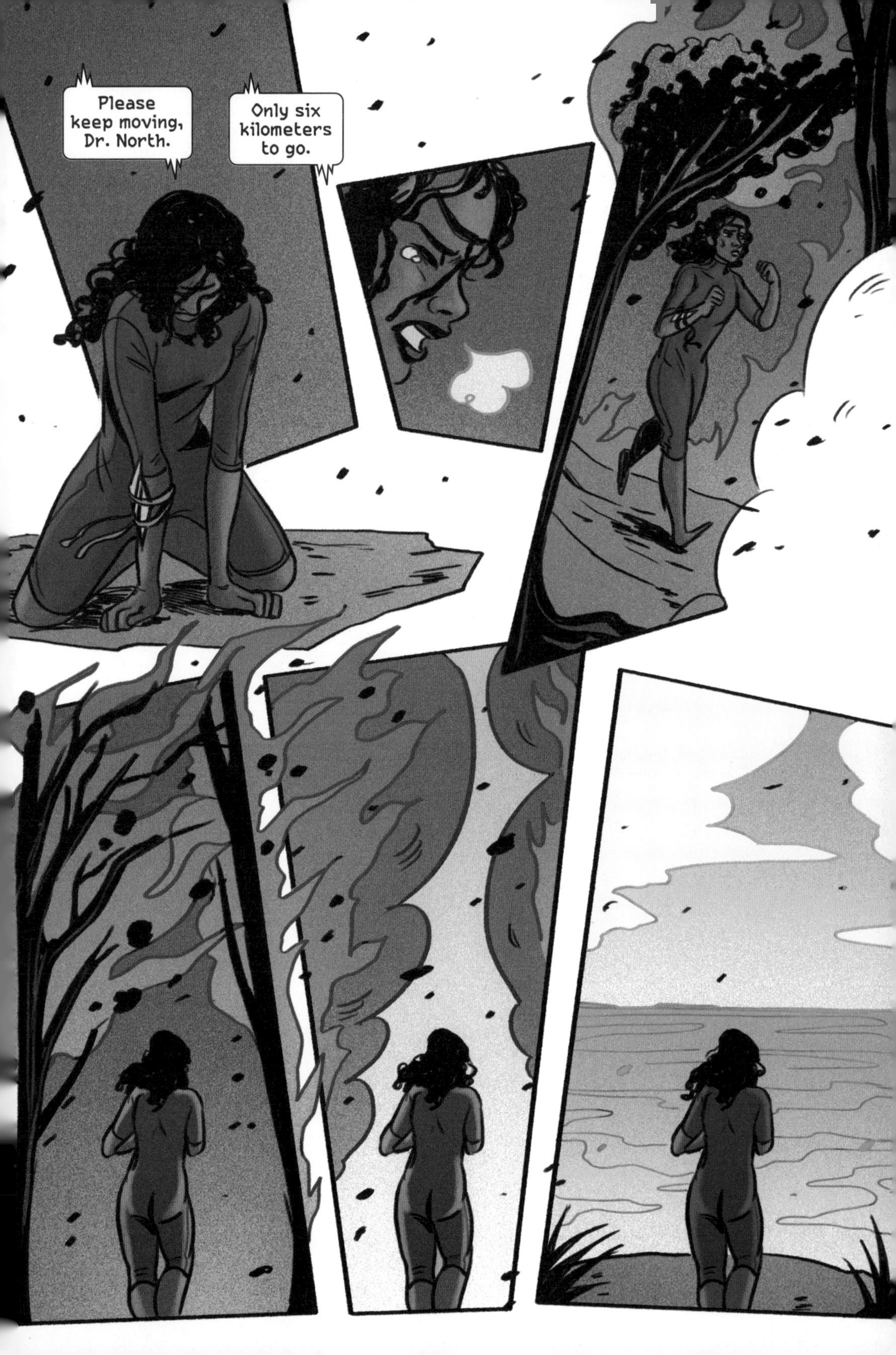
Please keep moving, Dr. North.
Only six kilometers to go.

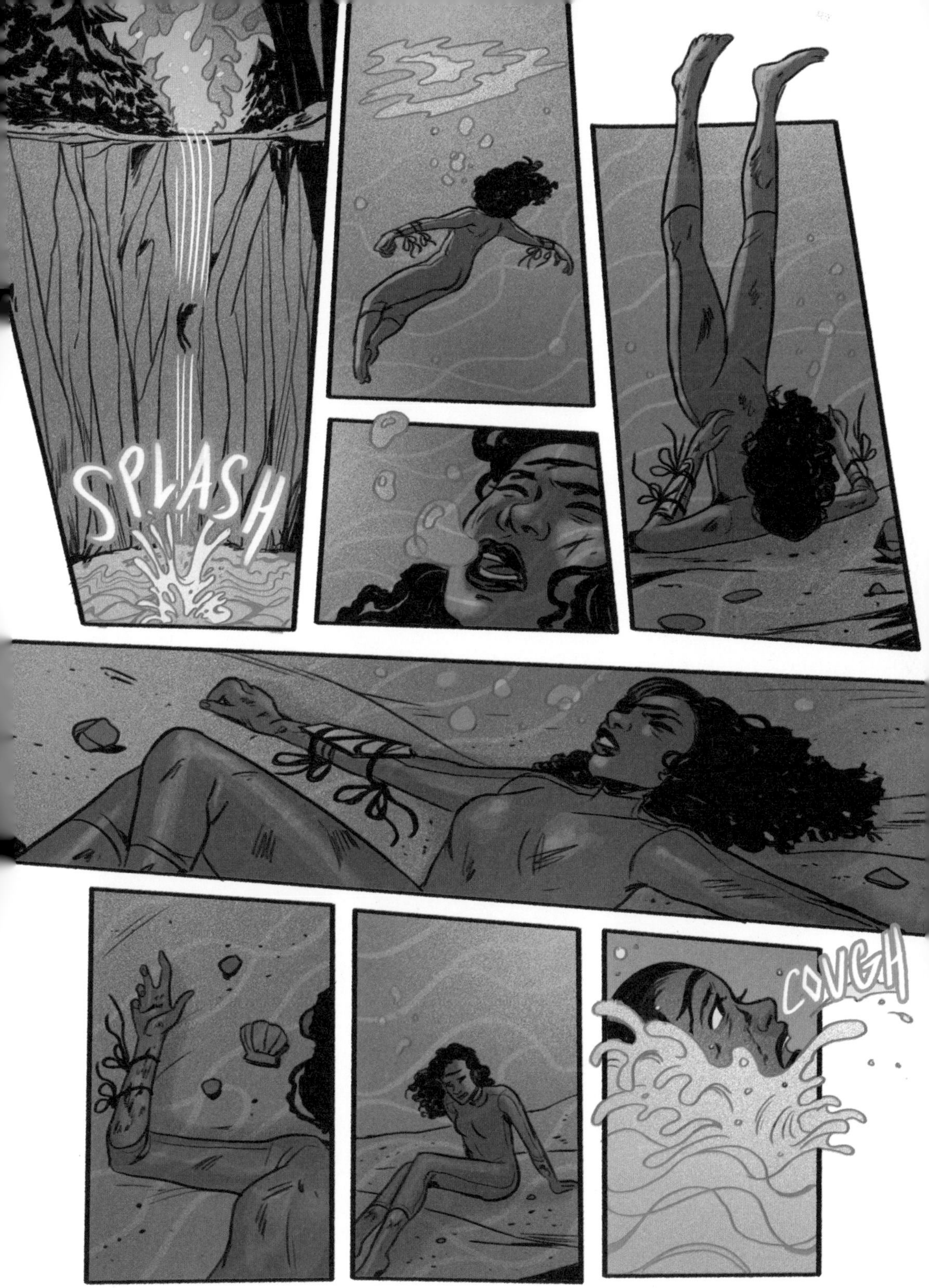
SPLASH
COUGH

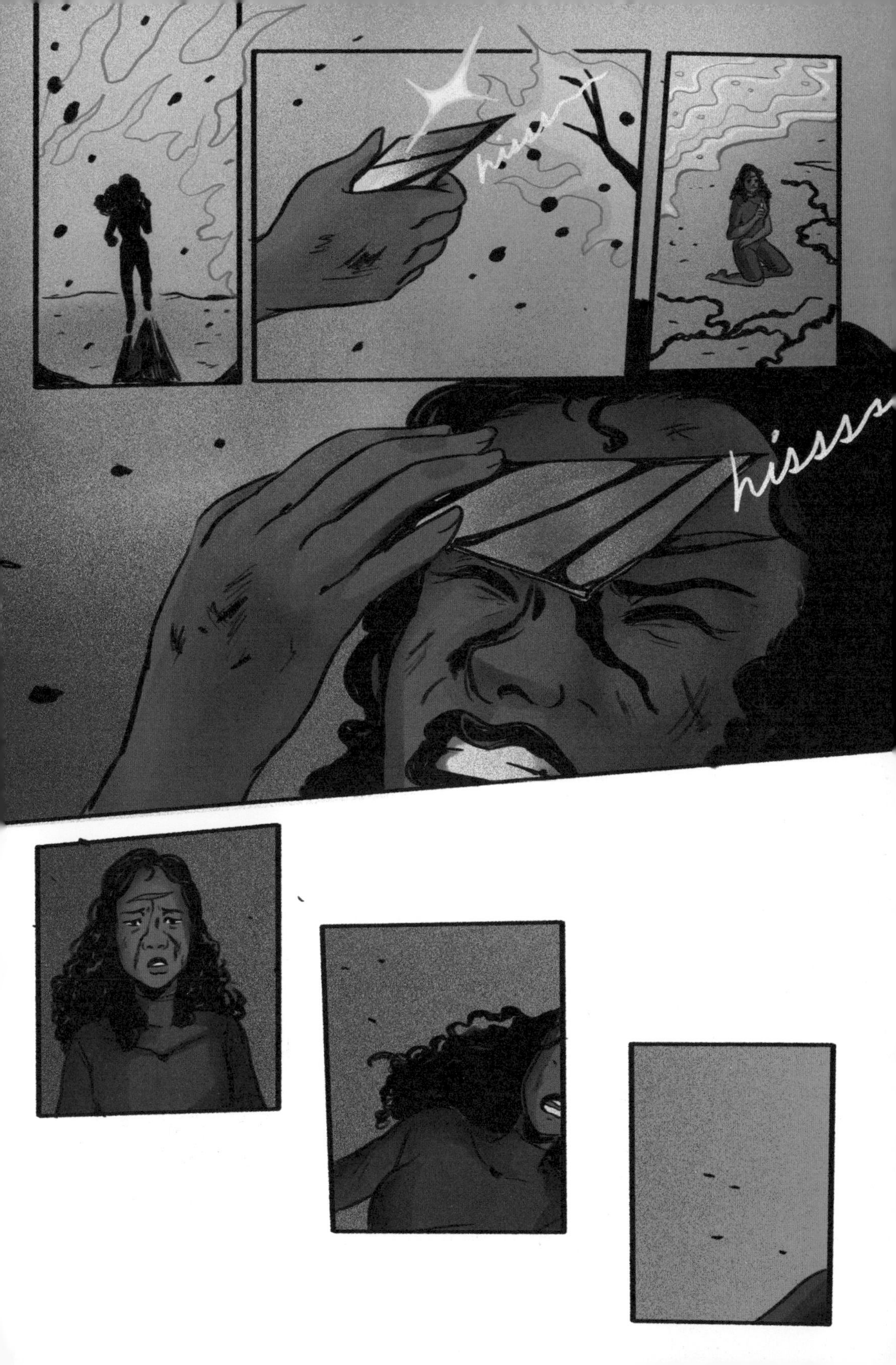
hiss
hissss

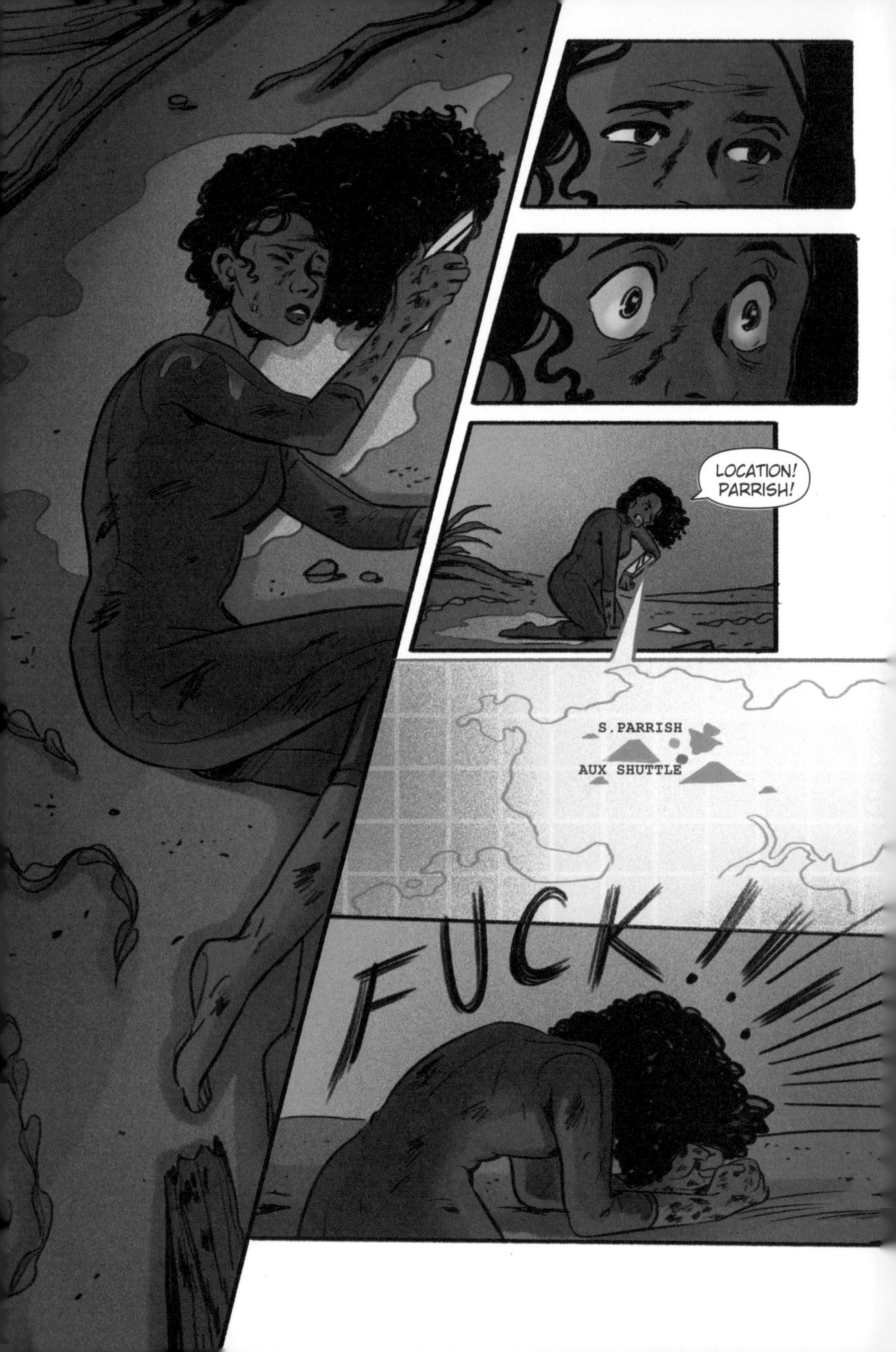
LOCATION!
PARRISH!
S.PARRISH
AUX SHUTTLE
FUCK!!!

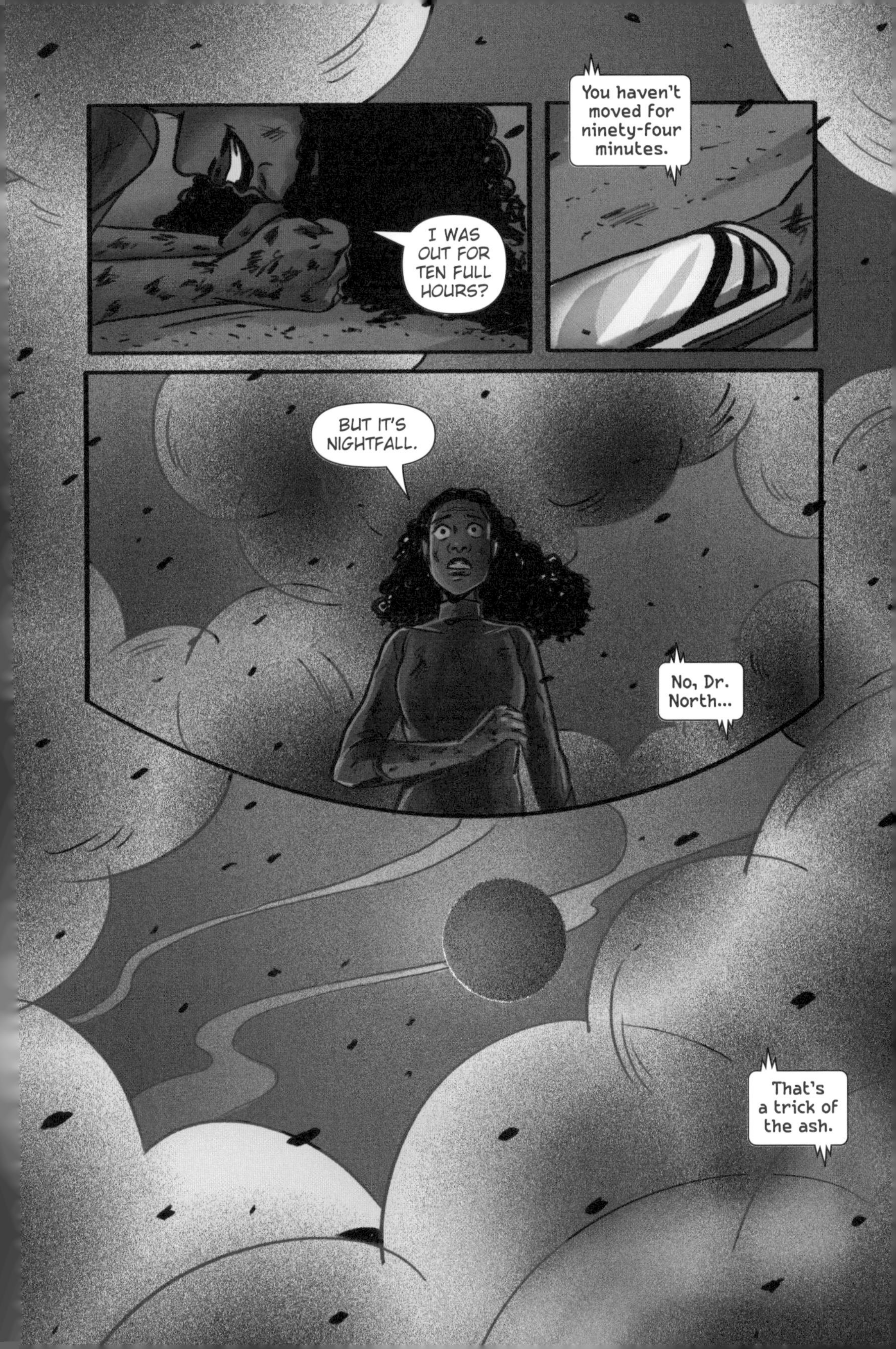
I WAS OUT FOR TEN FULL HOURS?
You haven't moved for ninety-four minutes.
BUT IT'S NIGHTFALL.
No, Dr. North...
That's a trick of the ash.

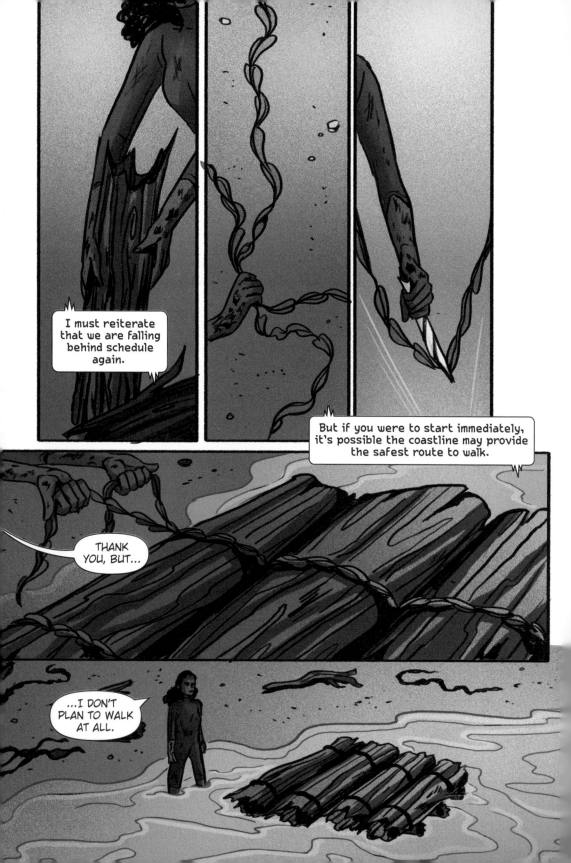

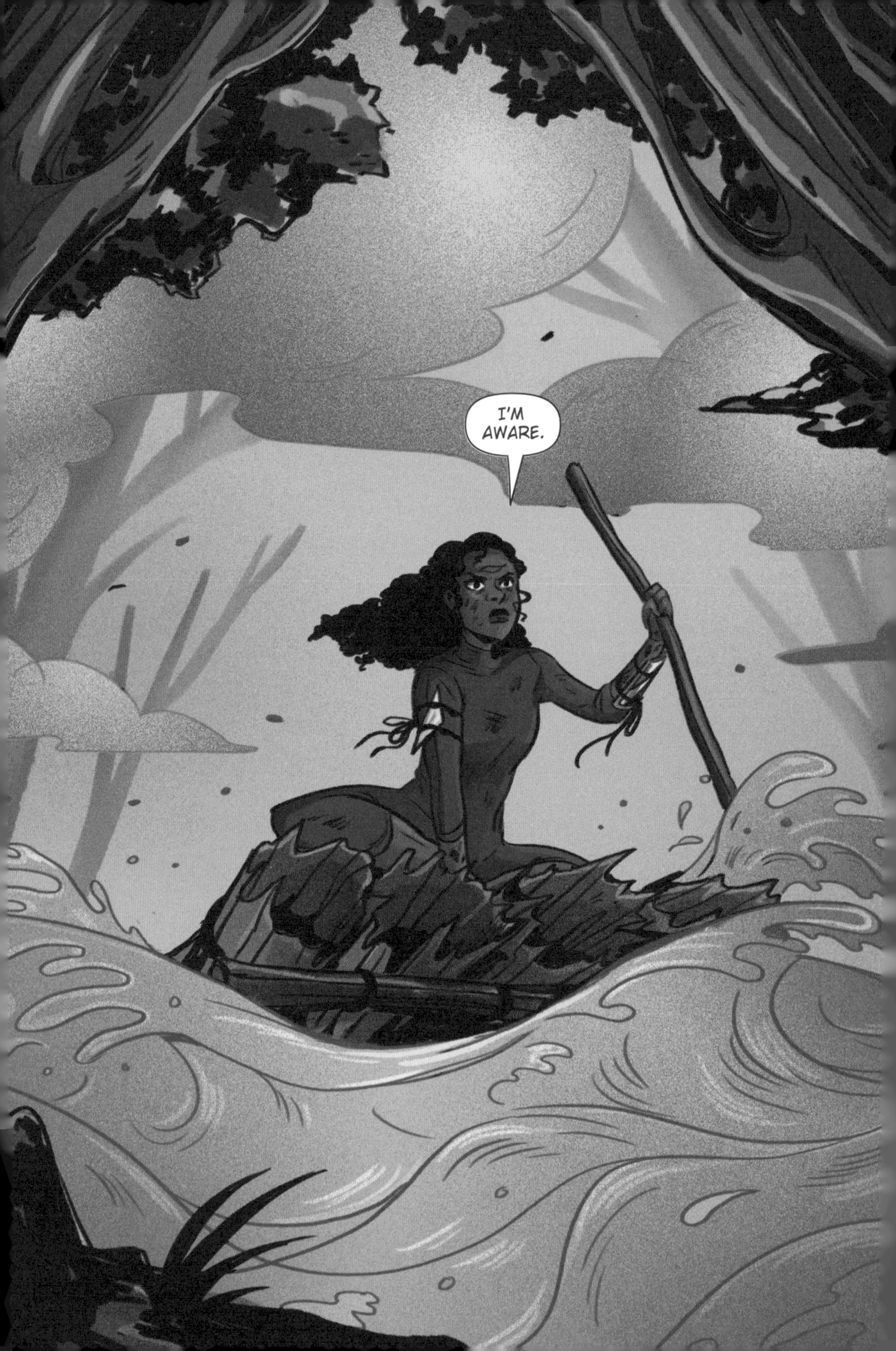
I'M AWARE.

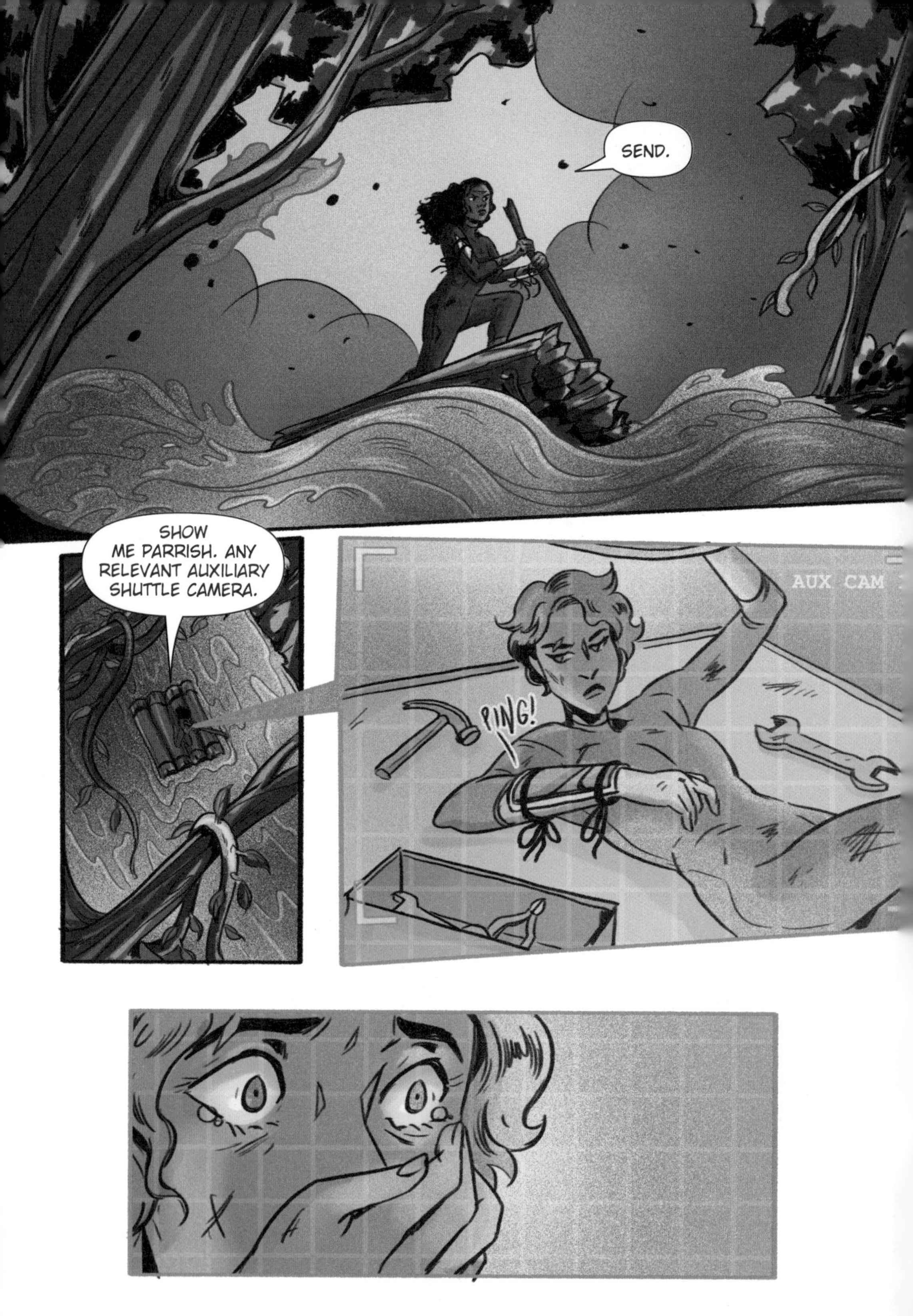
SEND.
SHOW ME PARRISH. ANY RELEVANT AUXILIARY SHUTTLE CAMERA.
AUX CAM
PING!

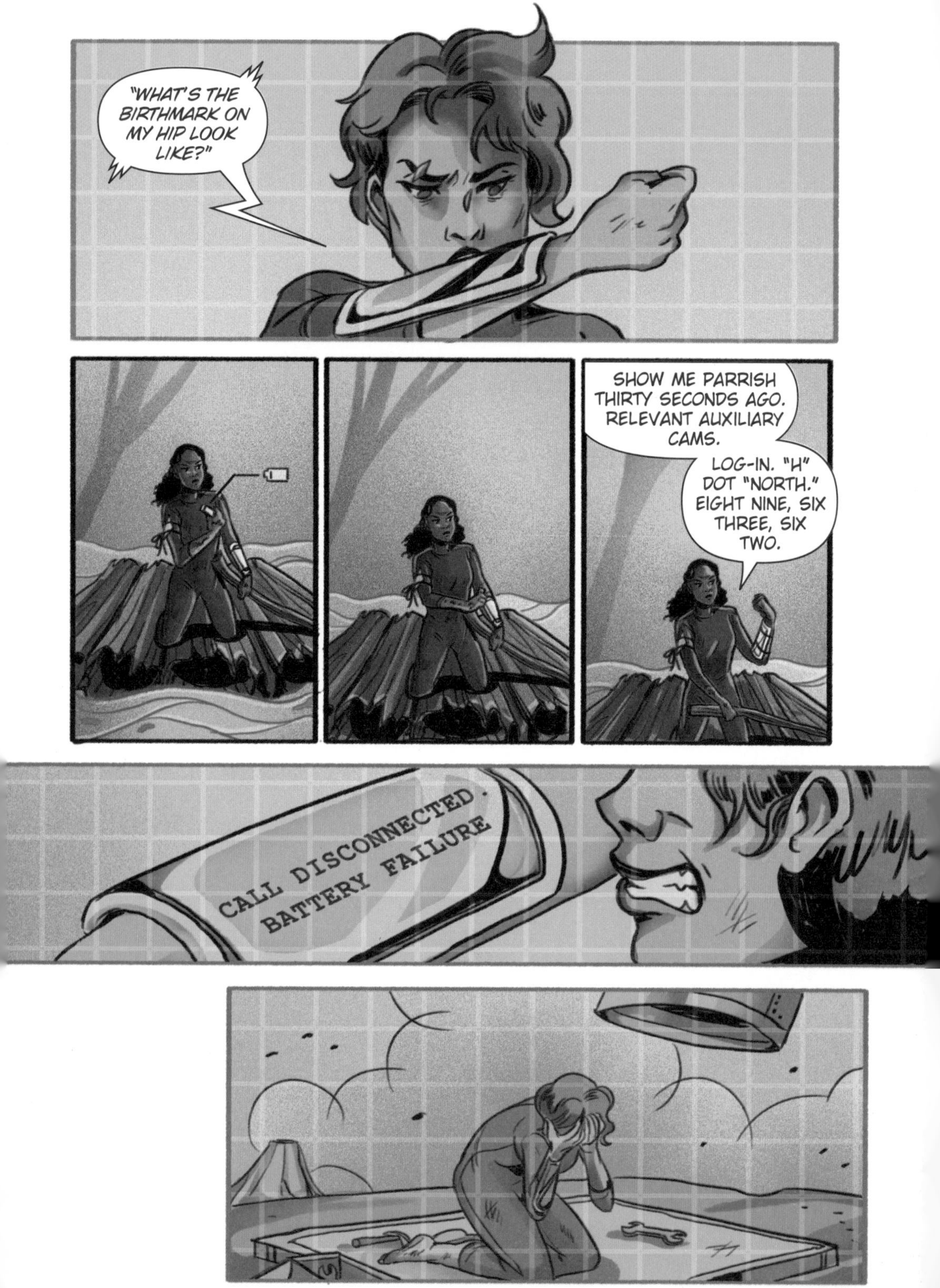
"WHAT'S THE BIRTHMARK ON MY HIP LOOK LIKE?"
SHOW ME PARRISH THIRTY SECONDS AGO. RELEVANT AUXILIARY CAMS.
LOG-IN. "H" DOT "NORTH." EIGHT NINE, SIX THREE, SIX TWO.
CALL DISCONNECTED.
BATTERY FAILURE

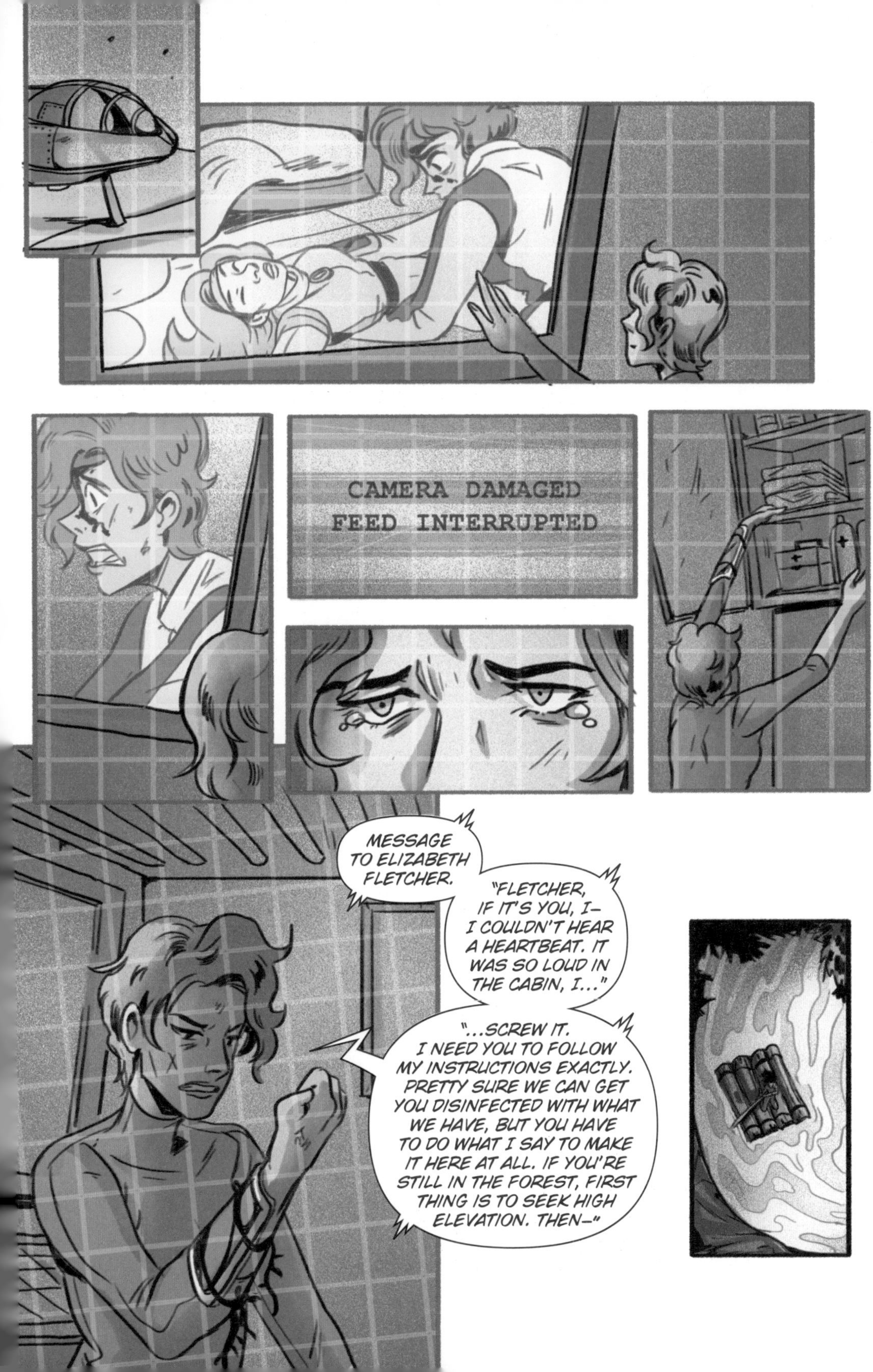
CAMERA DAMAGED
FEED INTERRUPTED
MESSAGE TO ELIZABETH FLETCHER.
"FLETCHER, IF IT'S YOU, I– I COULDN'T HEAR A HEARTBEAT. IT WAS SO LOUD IN THE CABIN, I..."
"...SCREW IT. I NEED YOU TO FOLLOW MY INSTRUCTIONS EXACTLY. PRETTY SURE WE CAN GET YOU DISINFECTED WITH WHAT WE HAVE, BUT YOU HAVE TO DO WHAT I SAY TO MAKE IT HERE AT ALL. IF YOU'RE STILL IN THE FOREST, FIRST THING IS TO SEEK HIGH ELEVATION. THEN–"

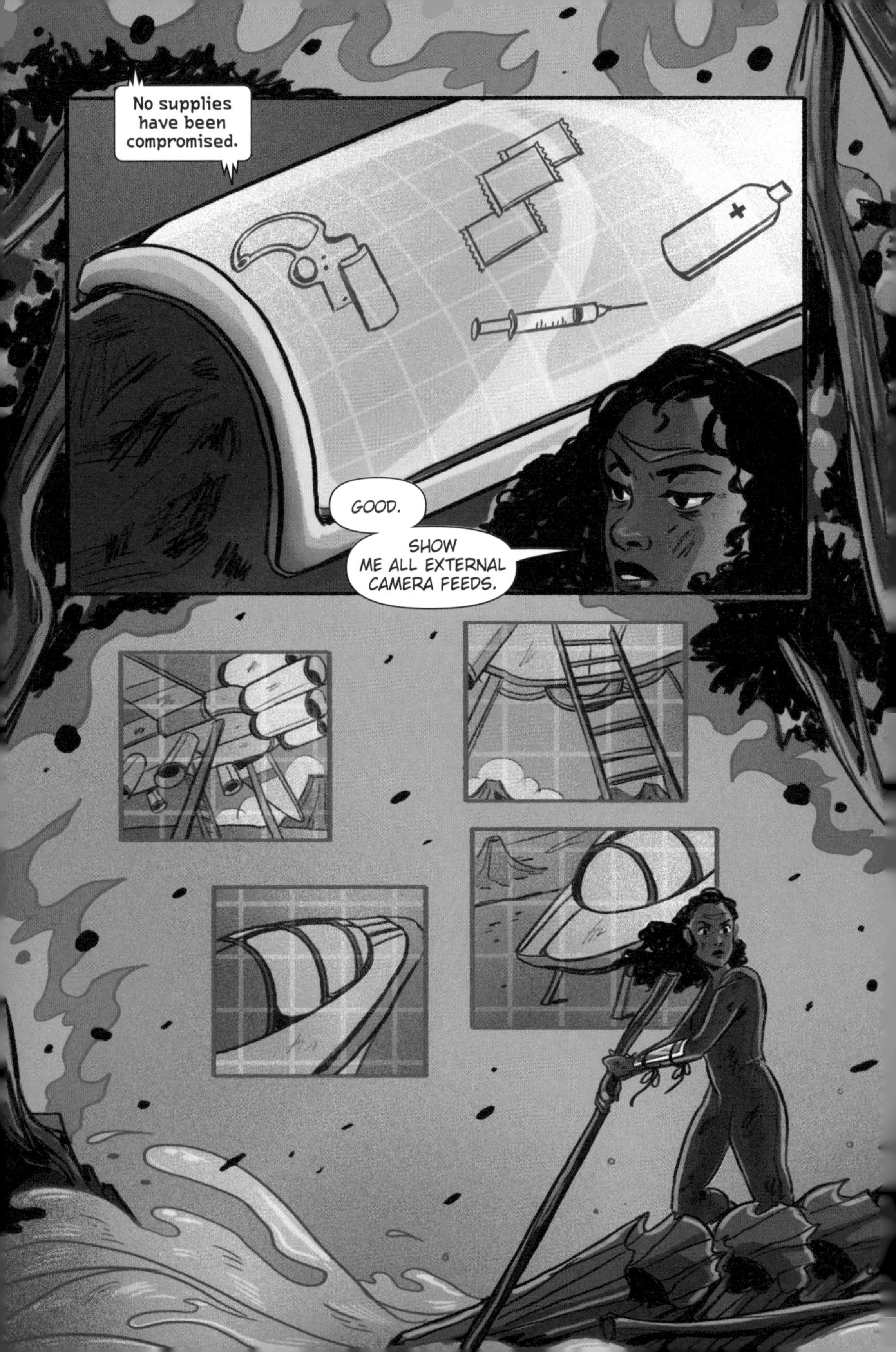
No supplies have been compromised.
GOOD.
SHOW ME ALL EXTERNAL CAMERA FEEDS.

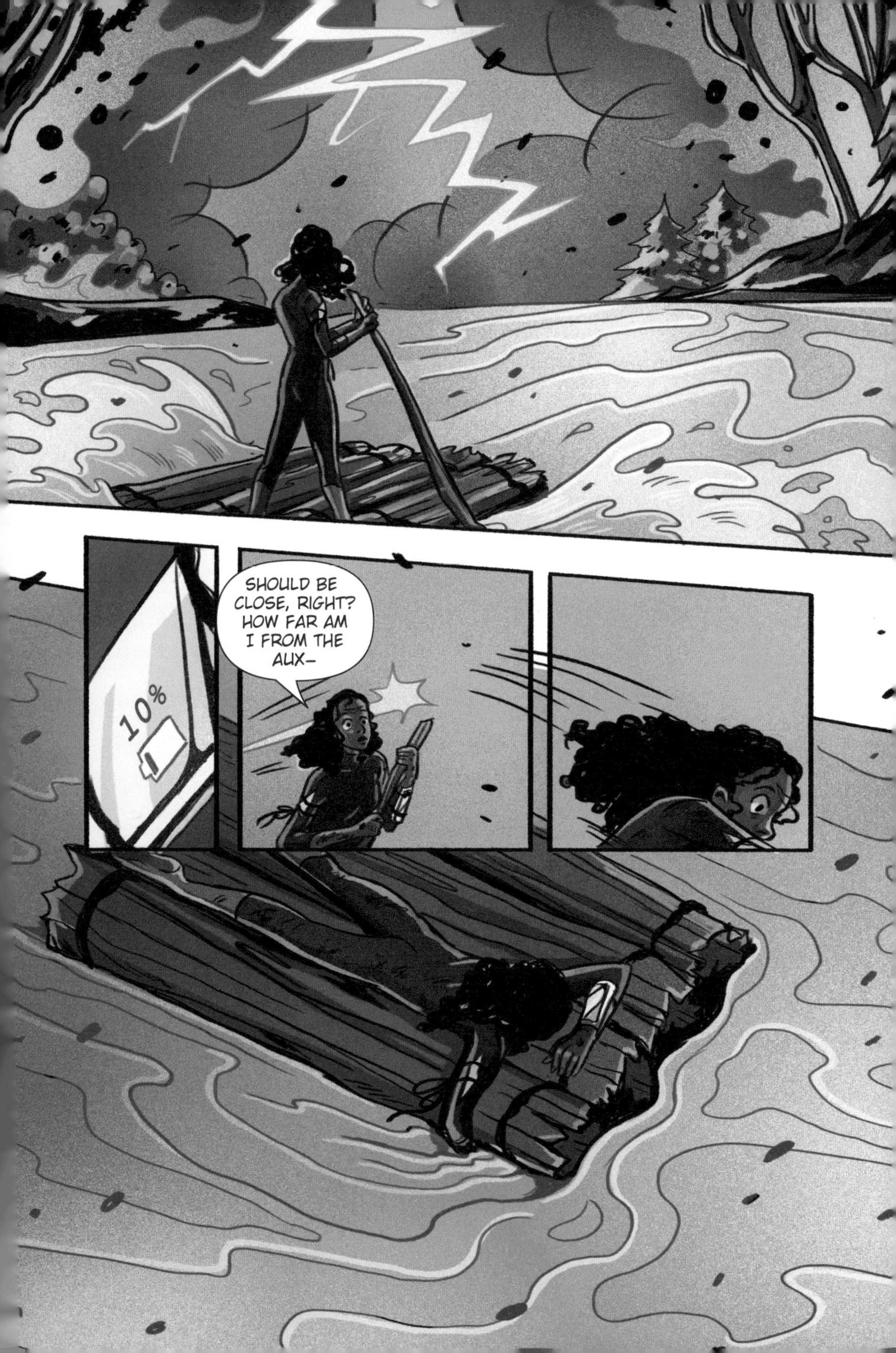
SHOULD BE CLOSE, RIGHT? HOW FAR AM I FROM THE AUX–
10%

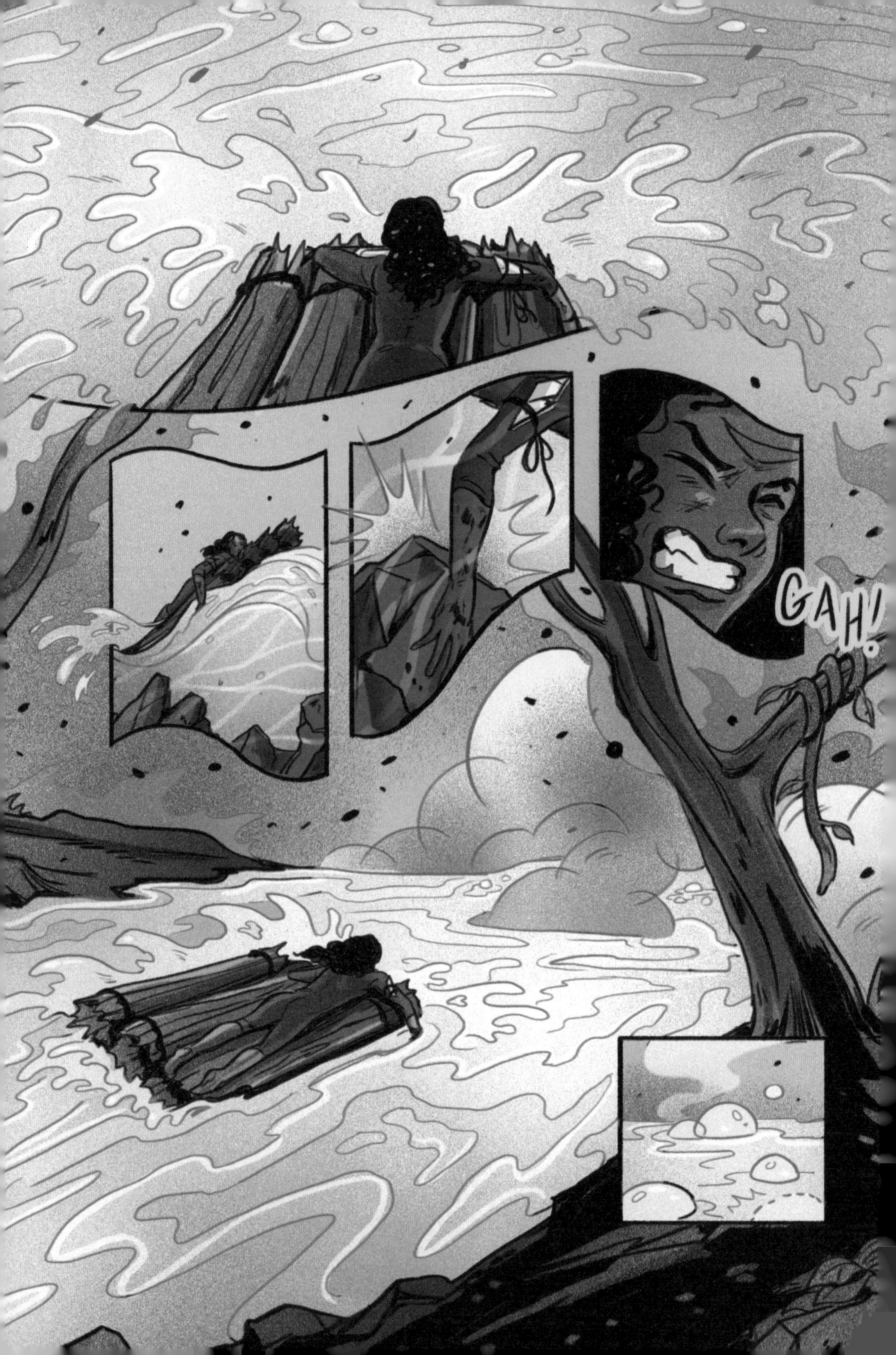
GAH!

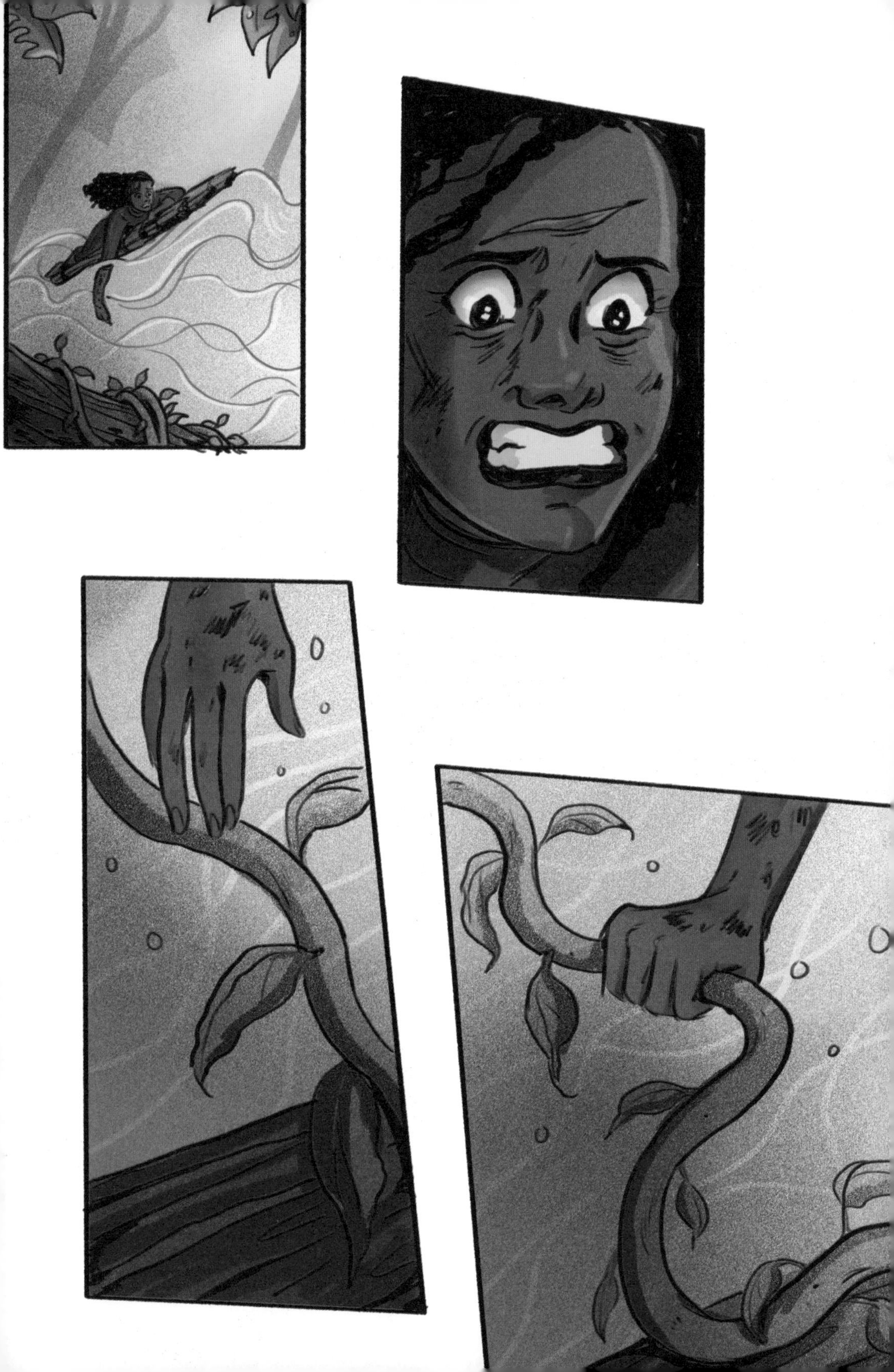

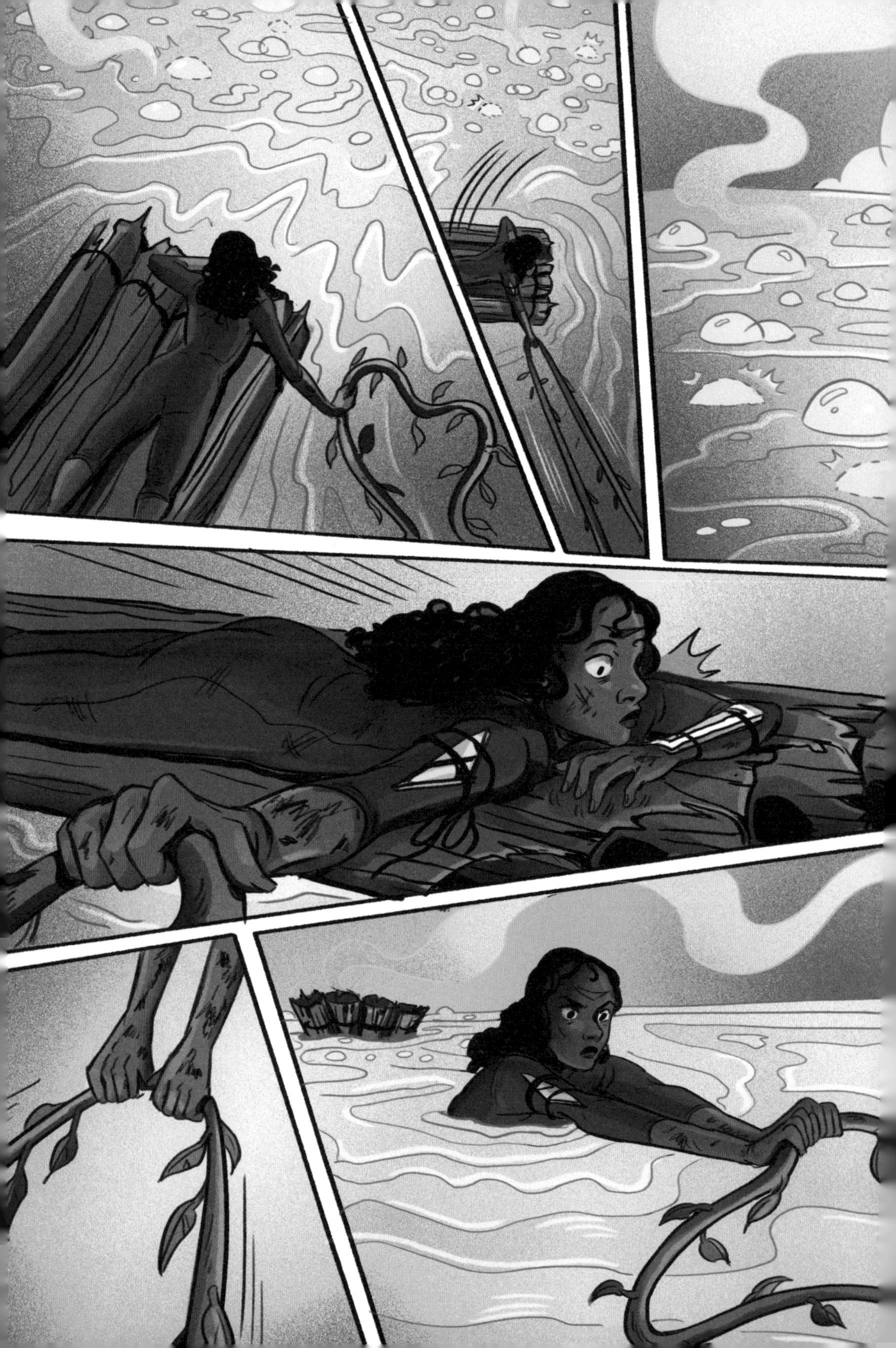

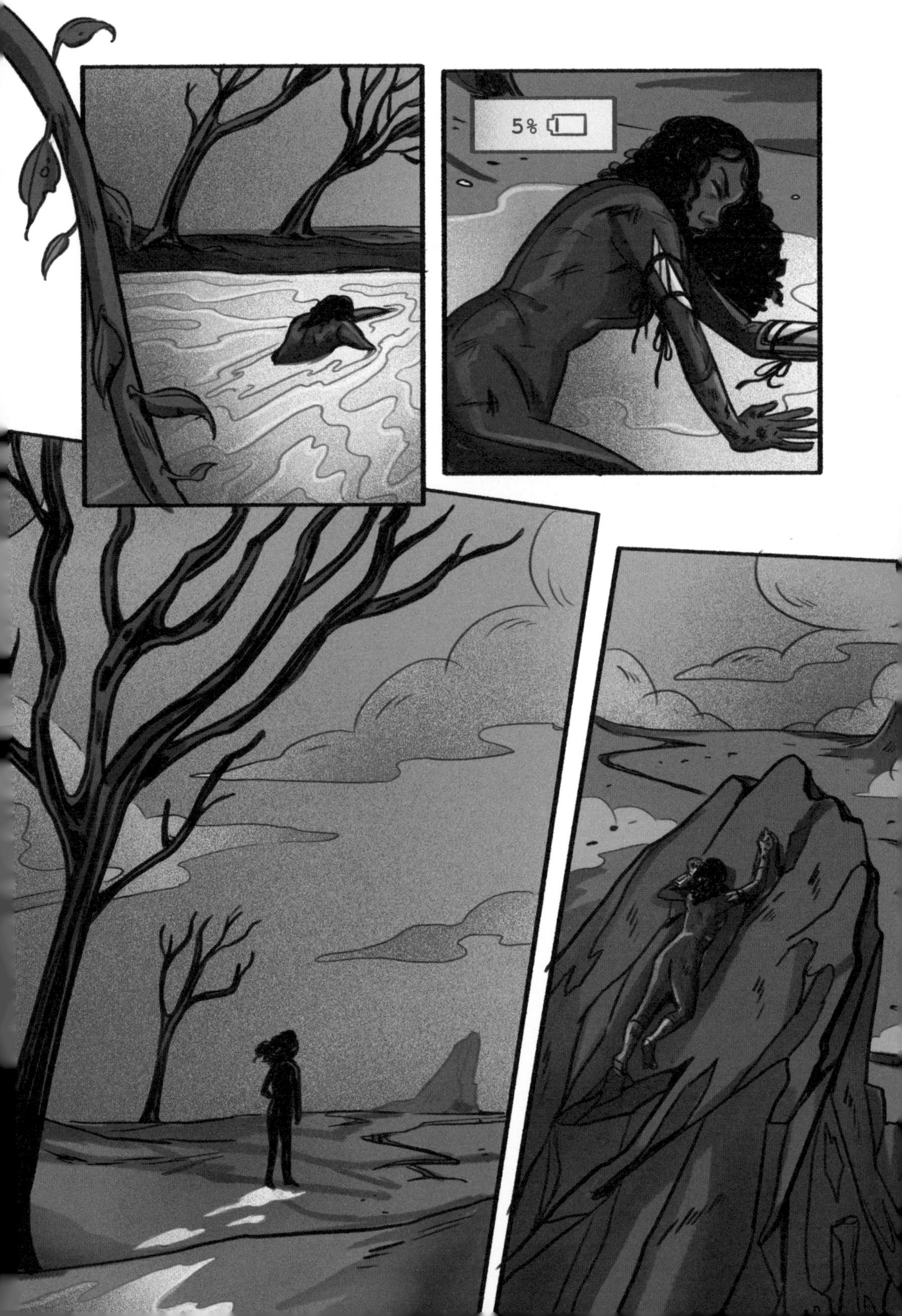
5%

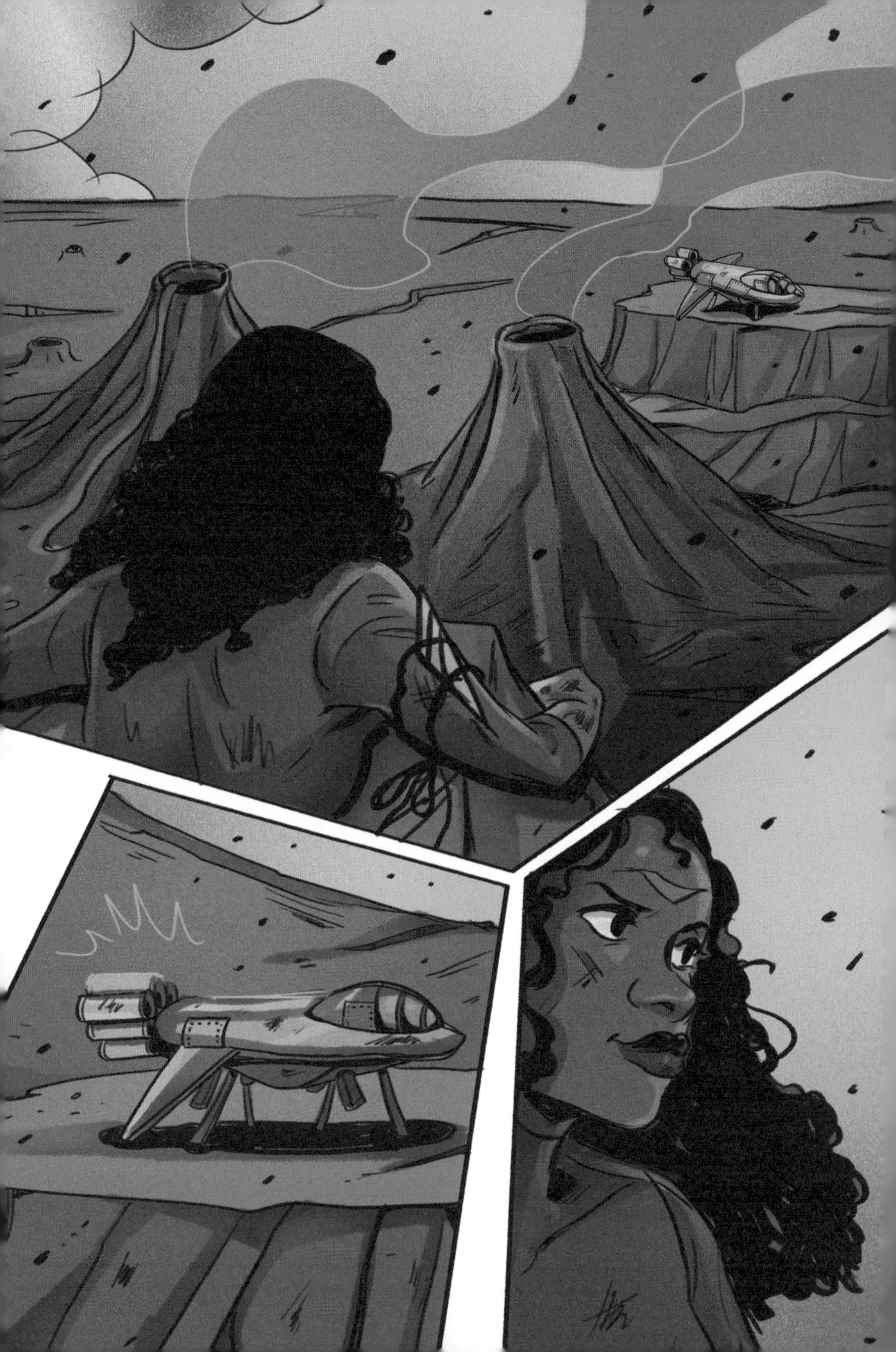

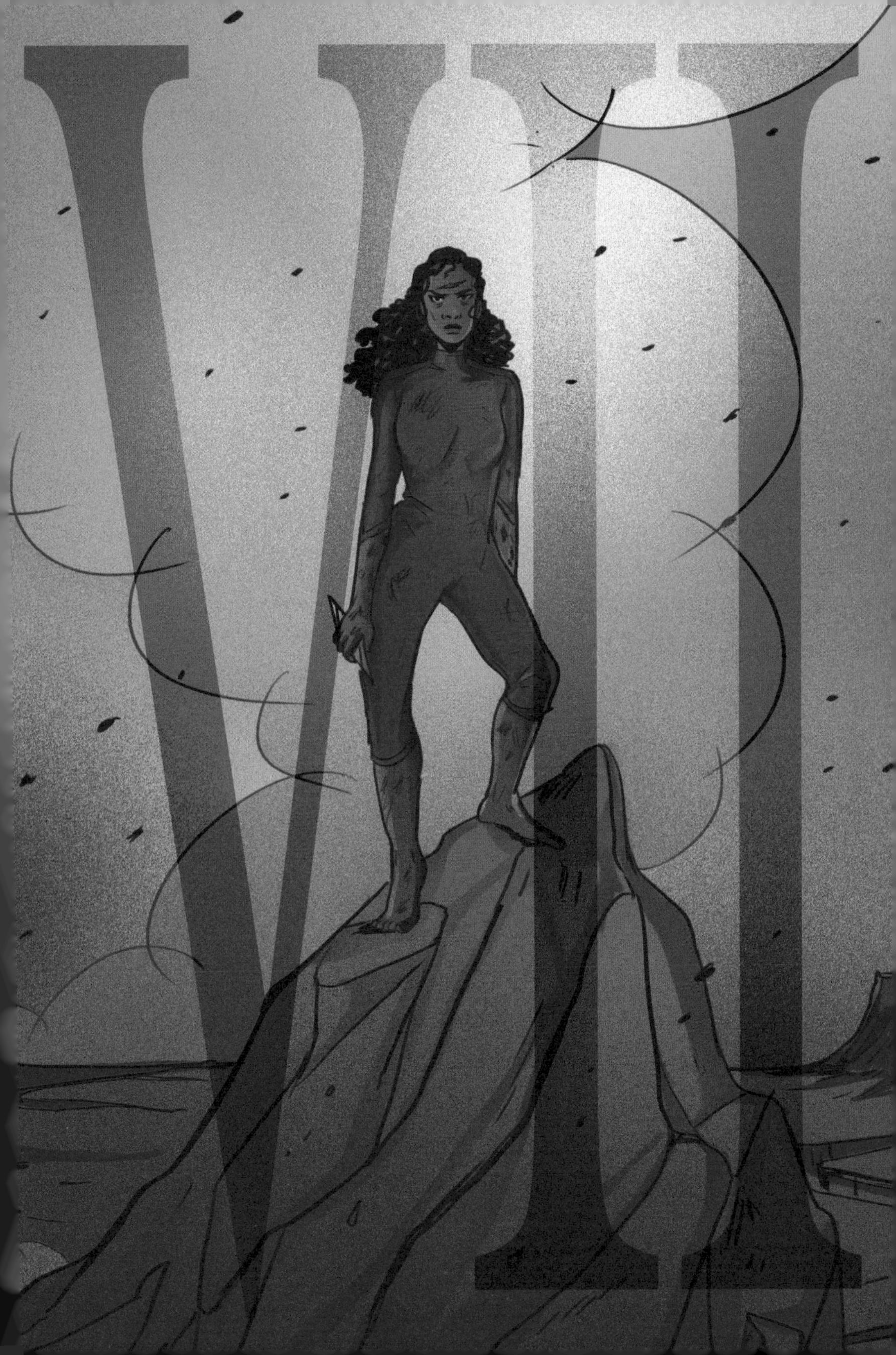
VII

FOLLOW SUBJECT PARRISH. ALL RELEVANT AUXILIARY CAMS.

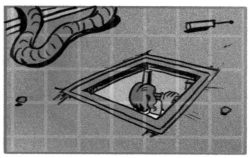

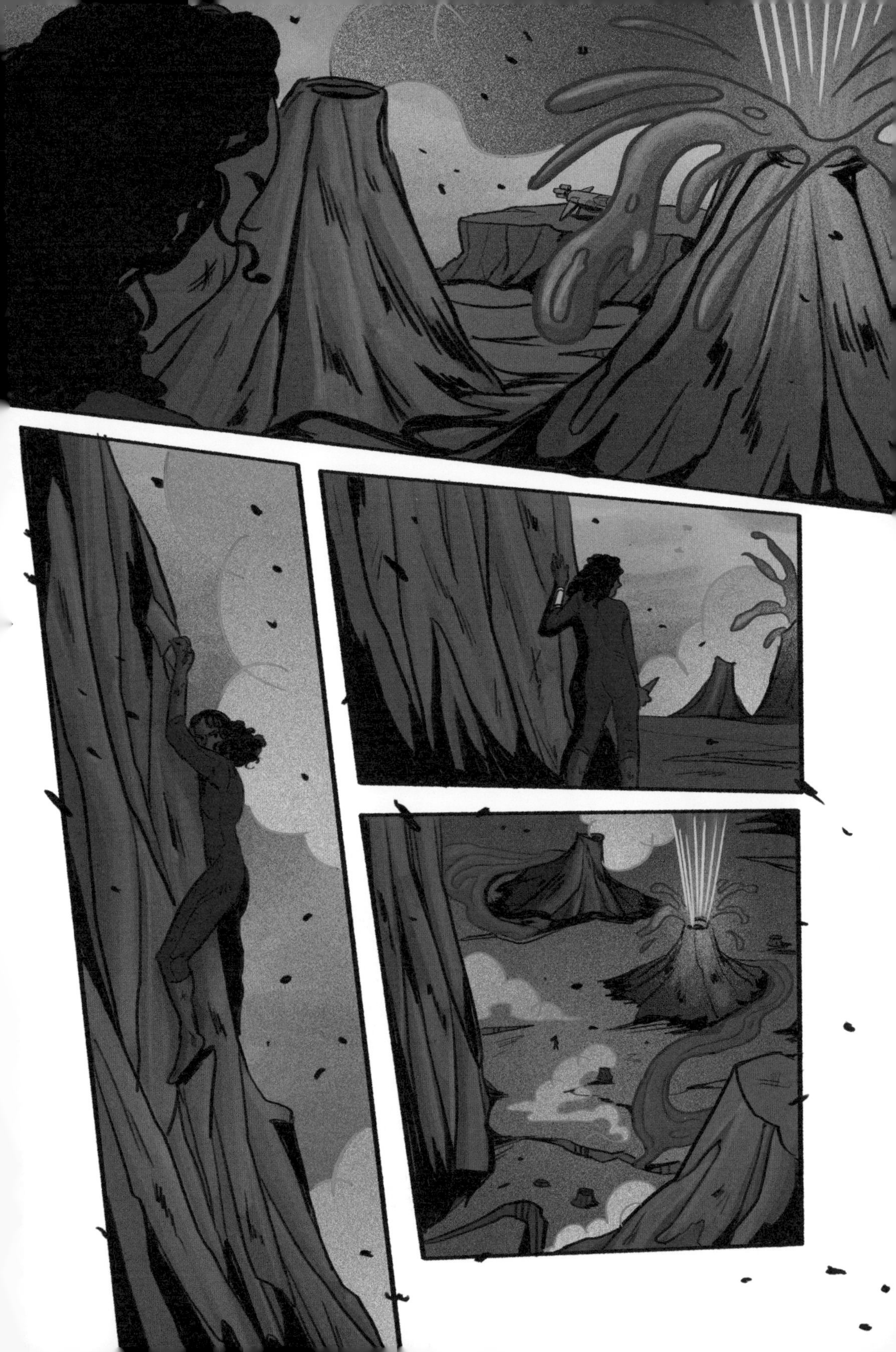

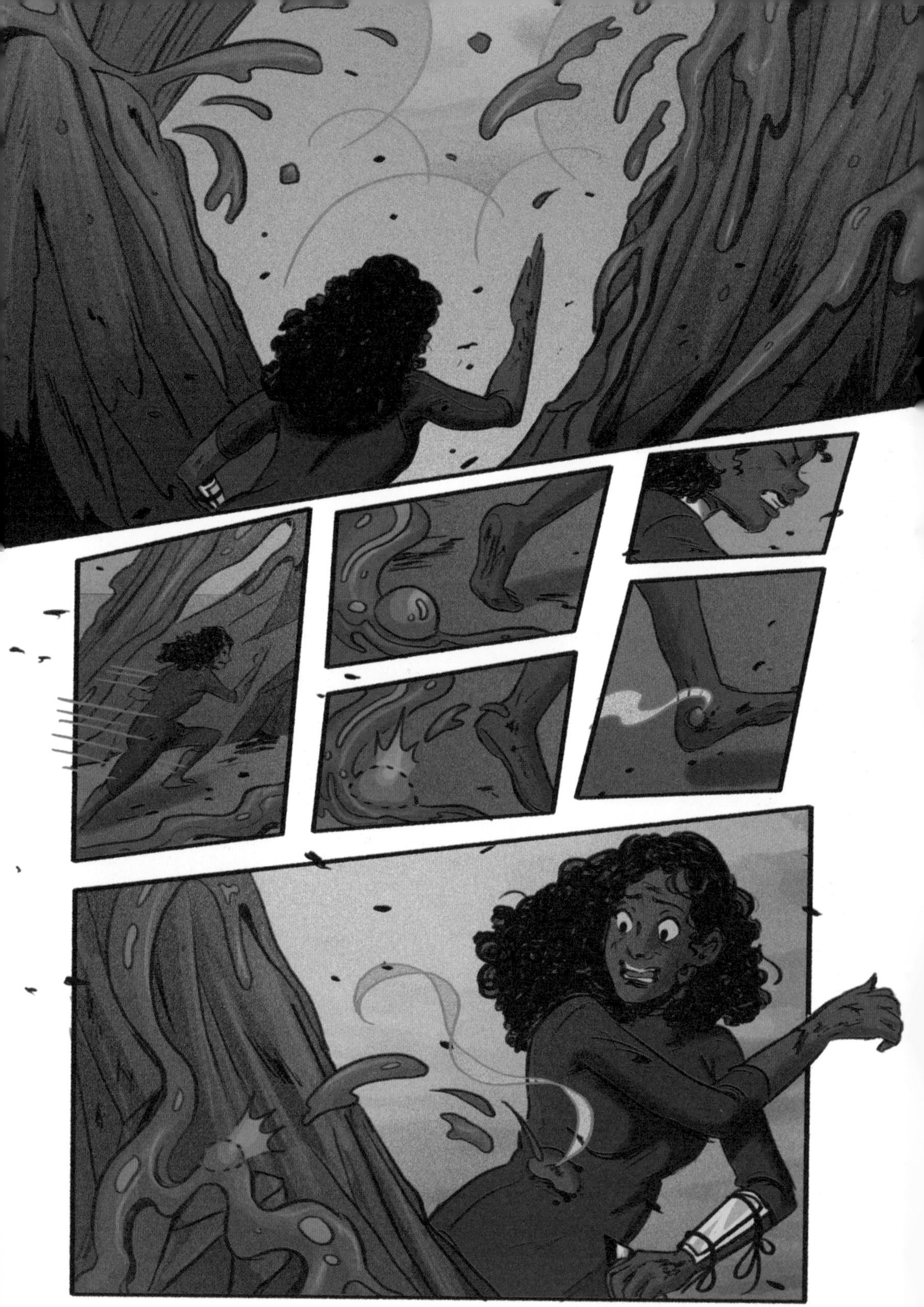

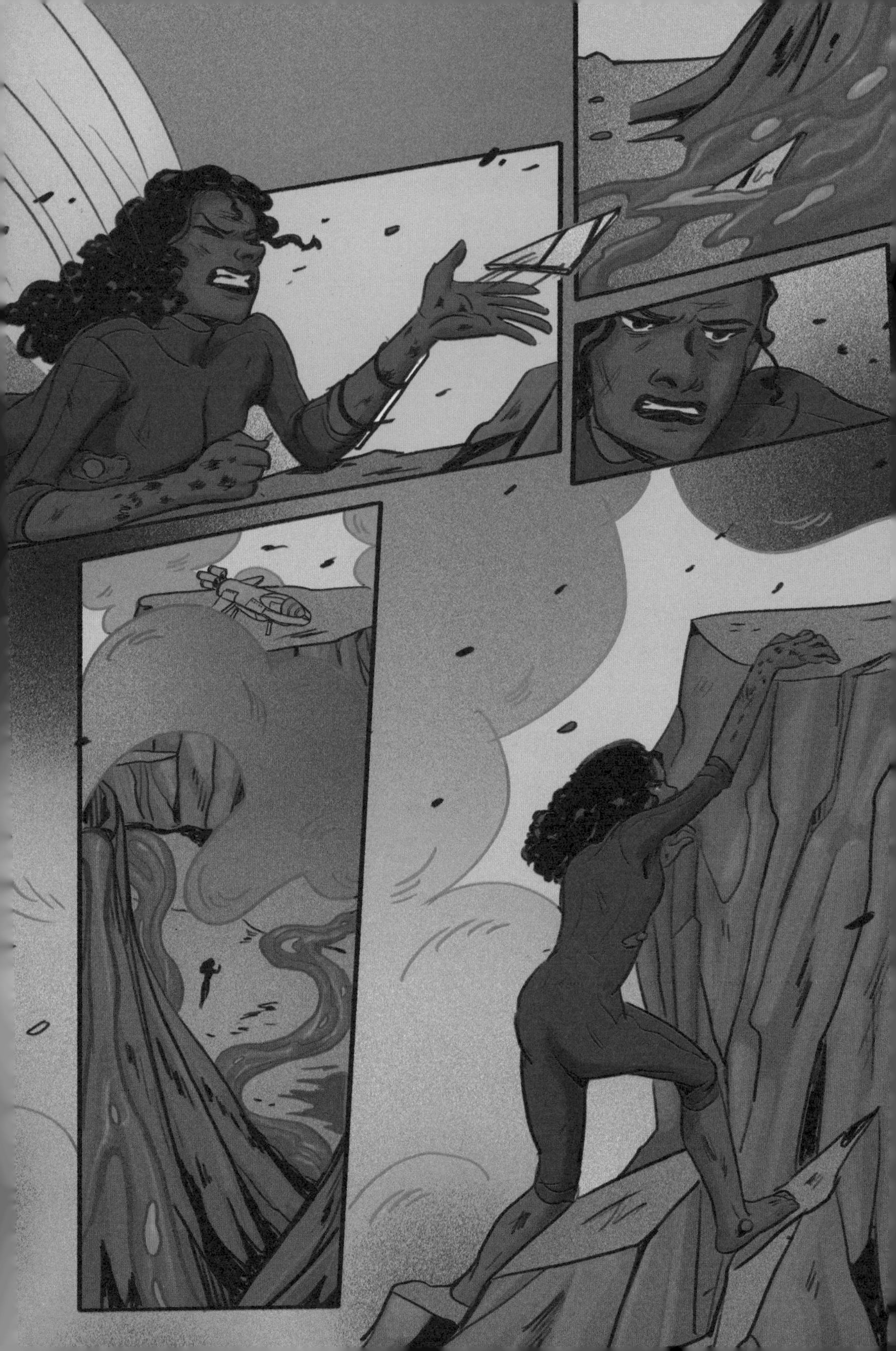

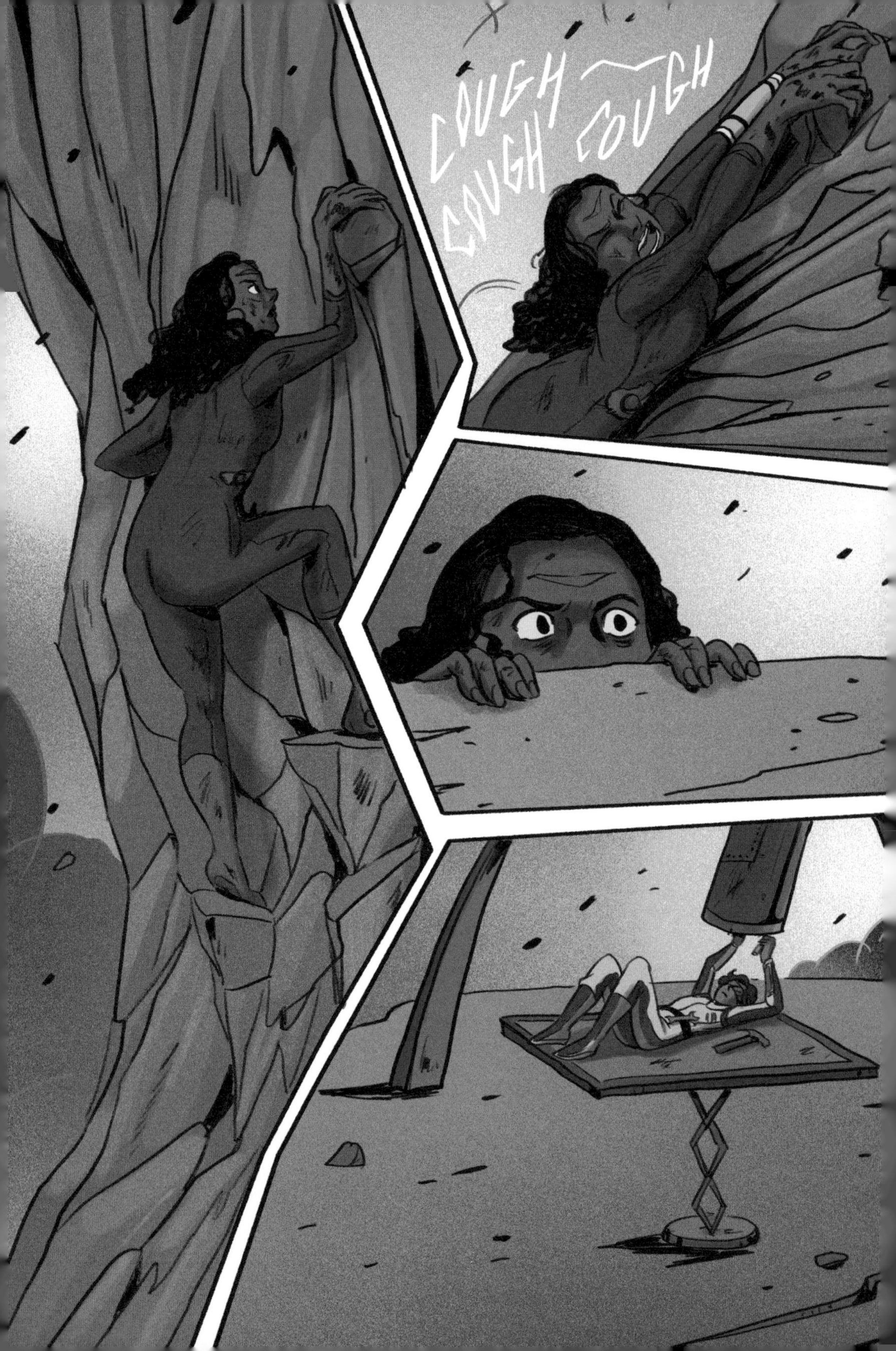
COUGH
COUGH
COUGH

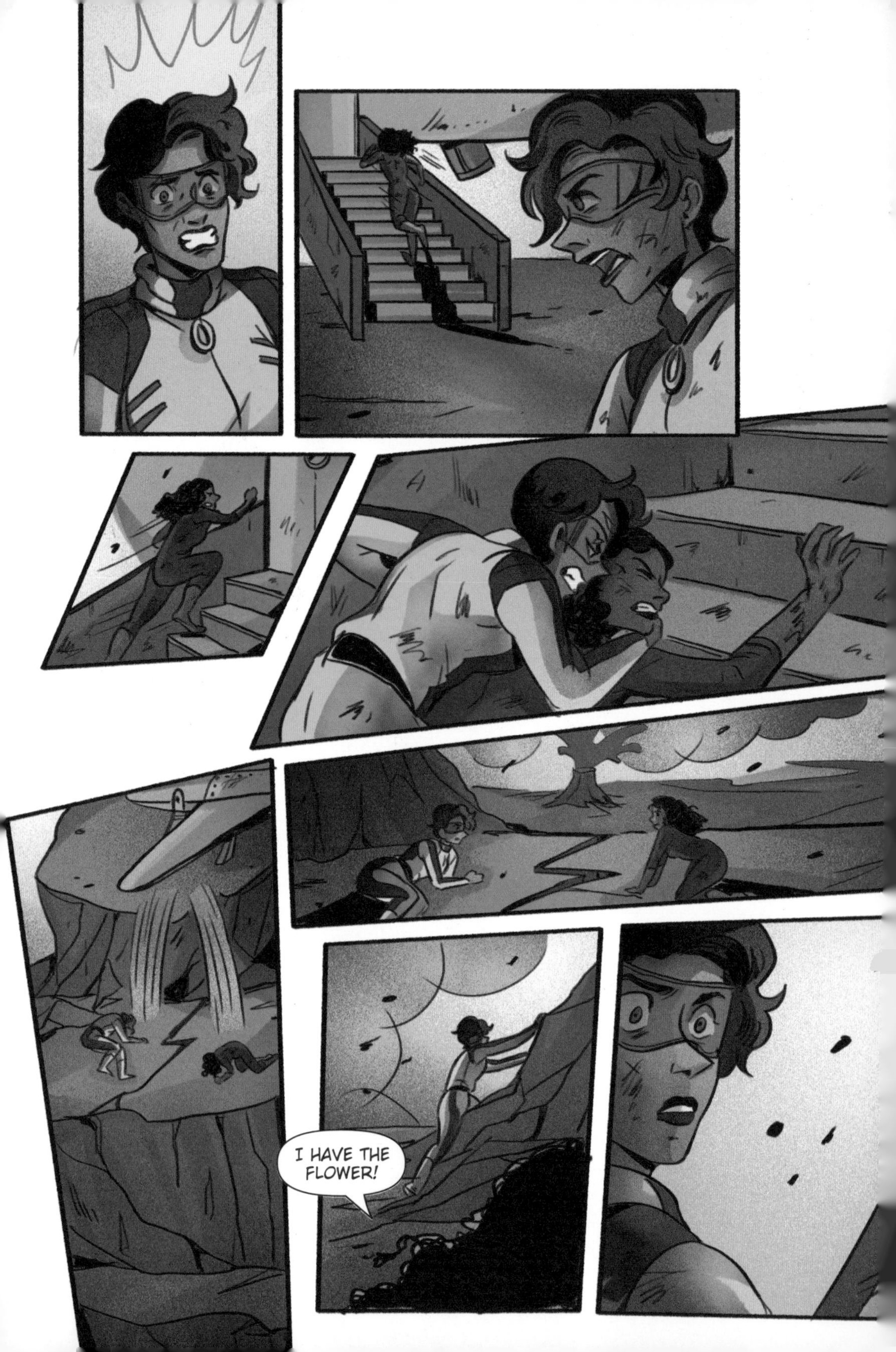
I HAVE THE FLOWER!

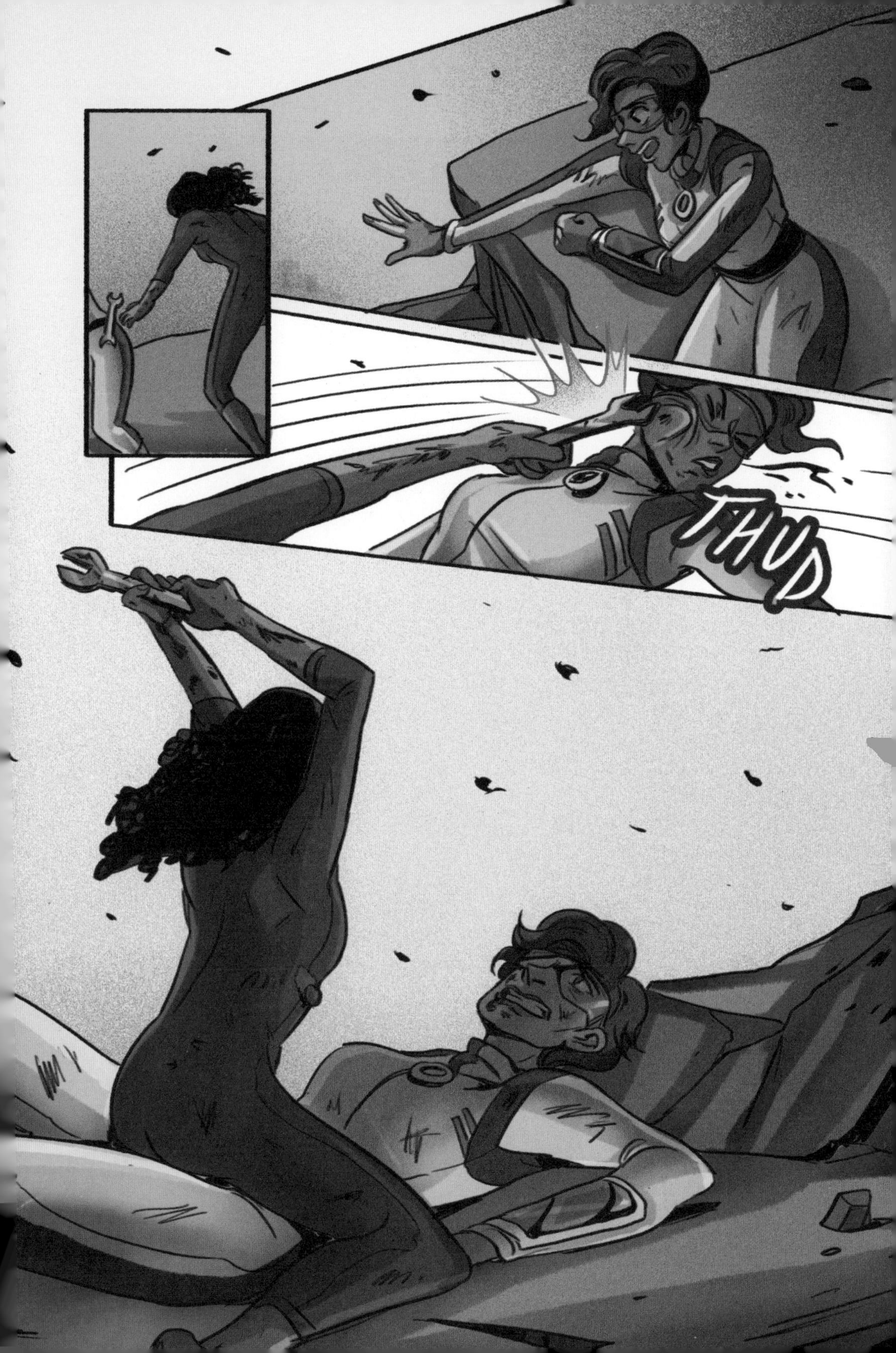
THUD

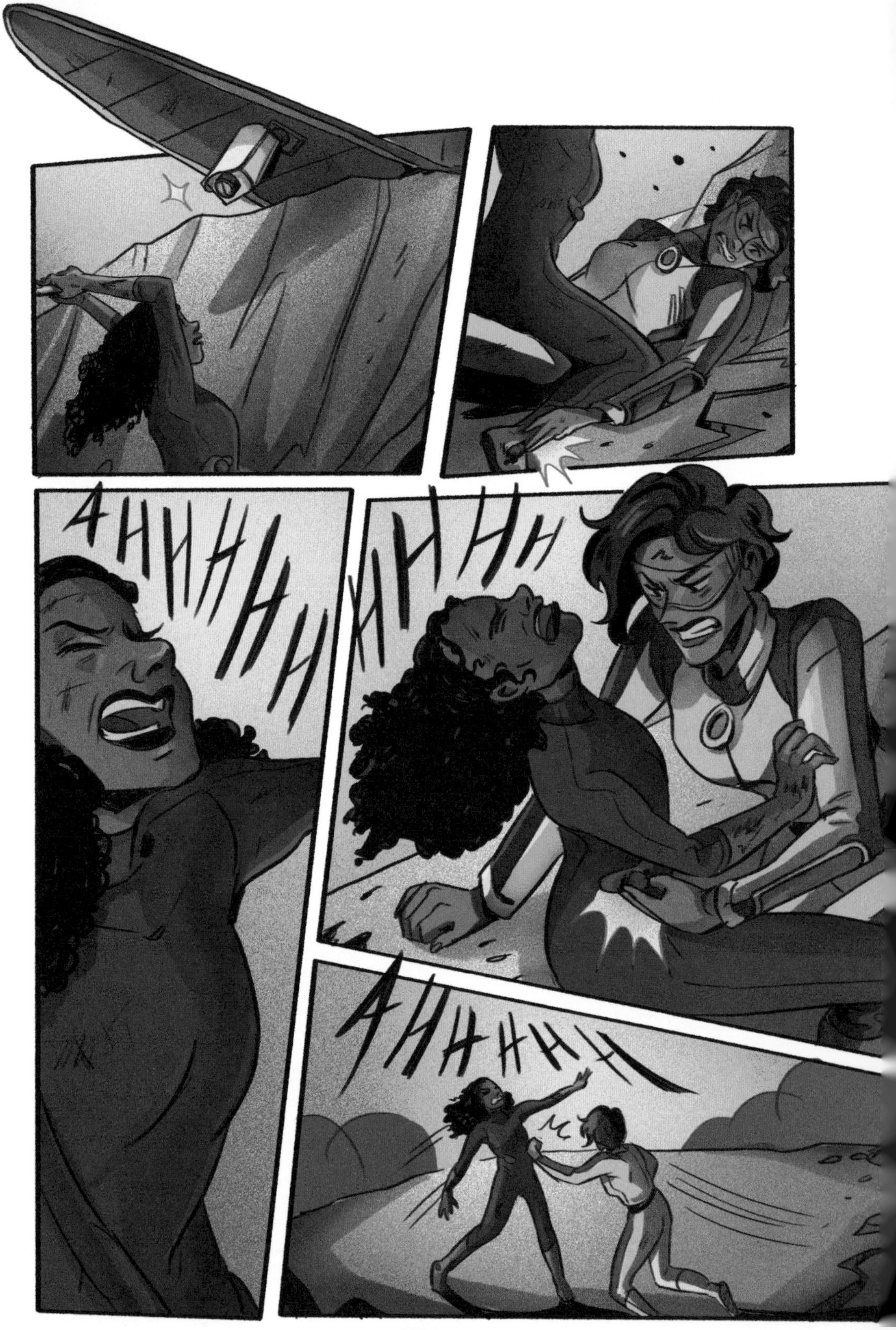
AHHHHHHH
HHHHHH
AHHHHHH

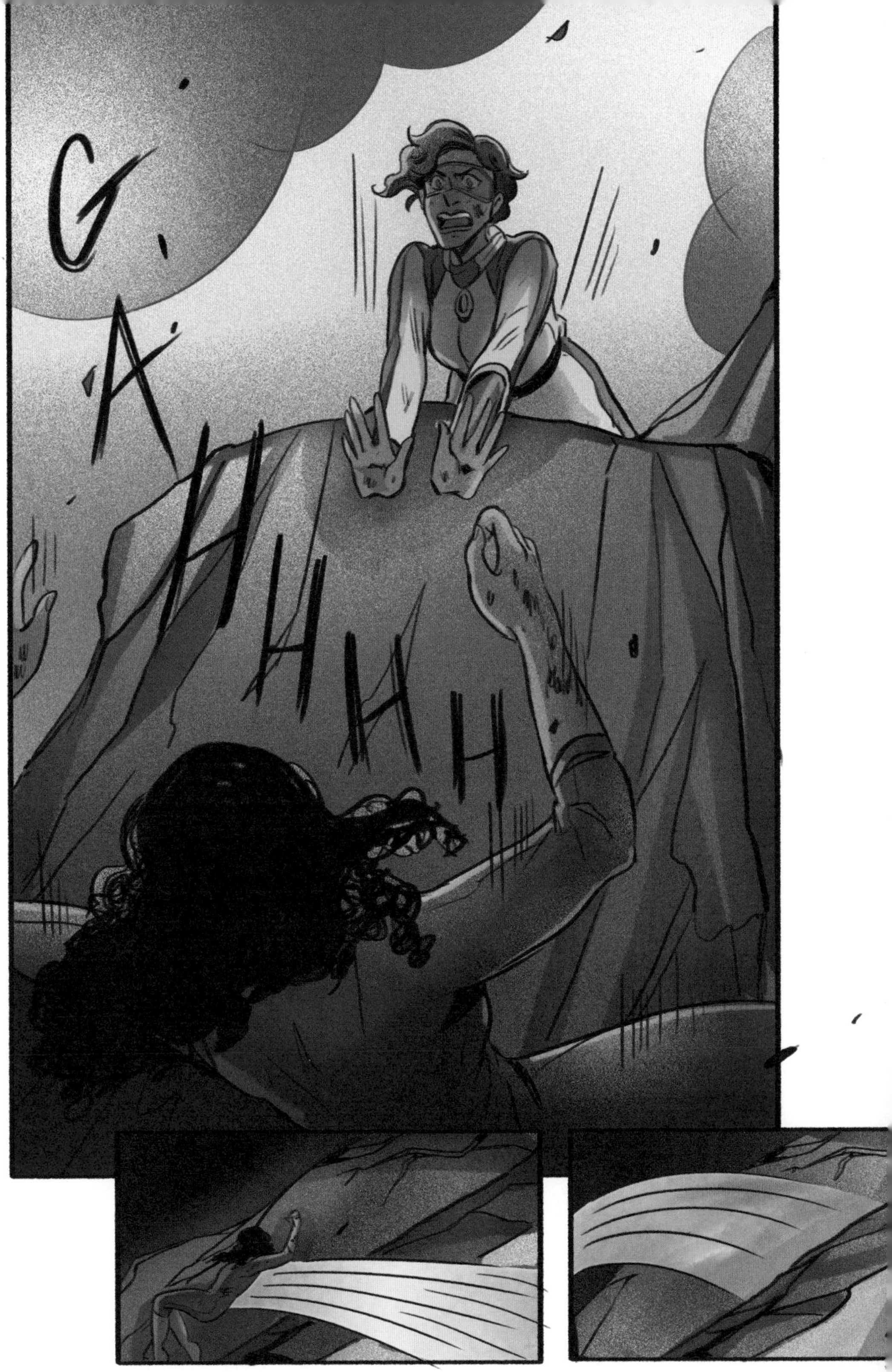
GAHHHHH

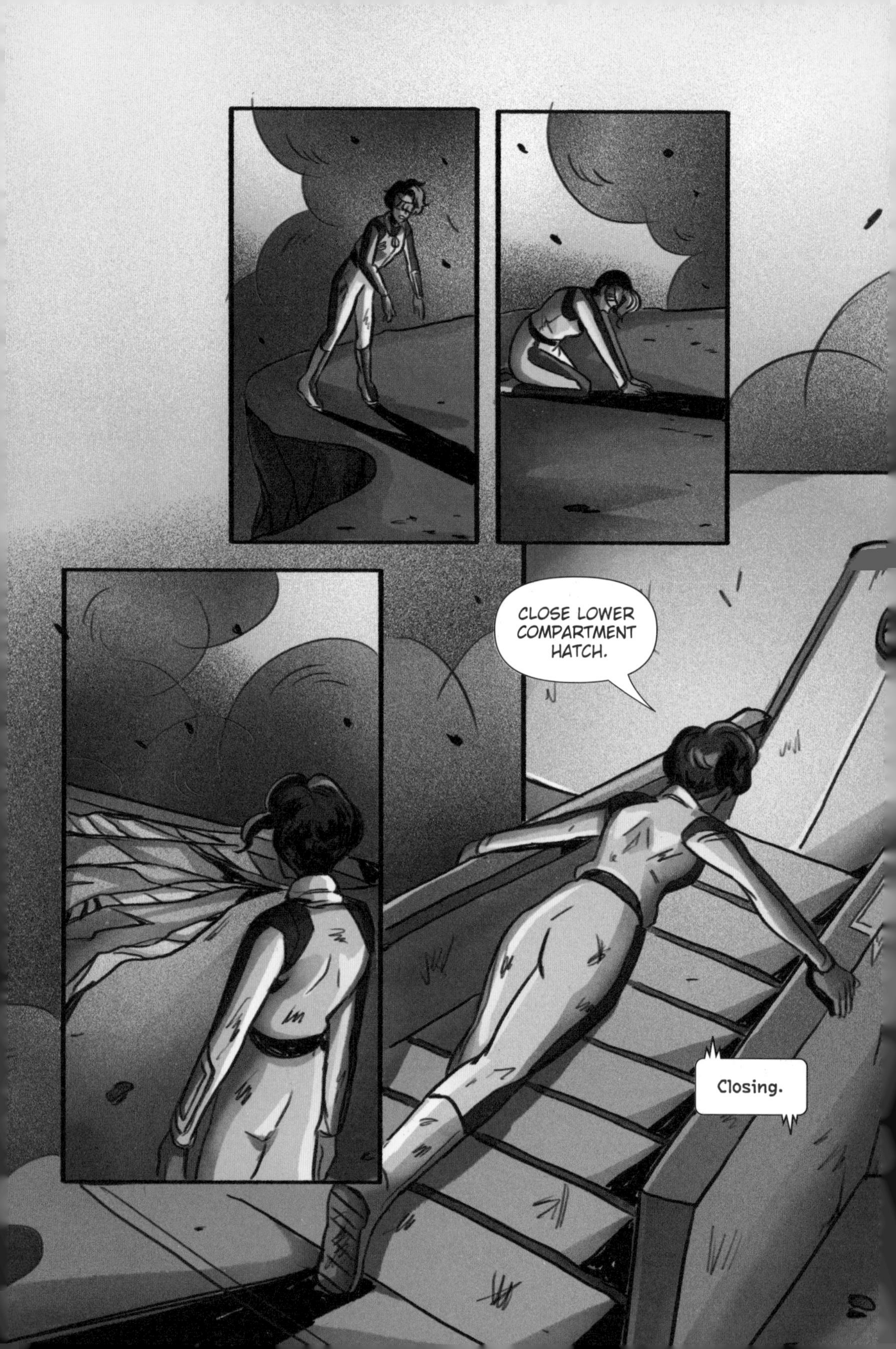
CLOSE LOWER COMPARTMENT HATCH.
Closing.

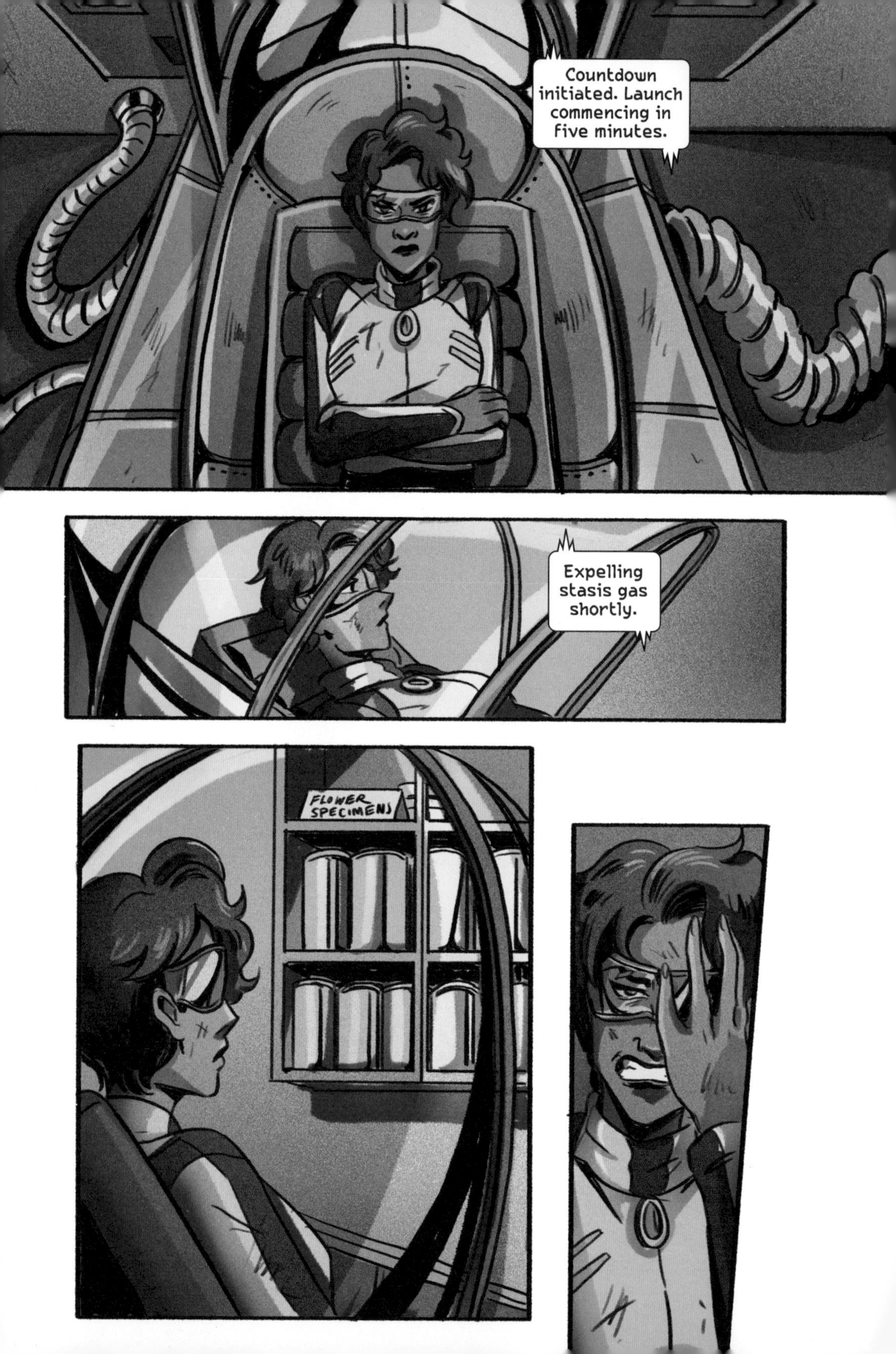
Countdown initiated. Launch commencing in five minutes.
Expelling stasis gas shortly.
FLOWER SPECIMENS

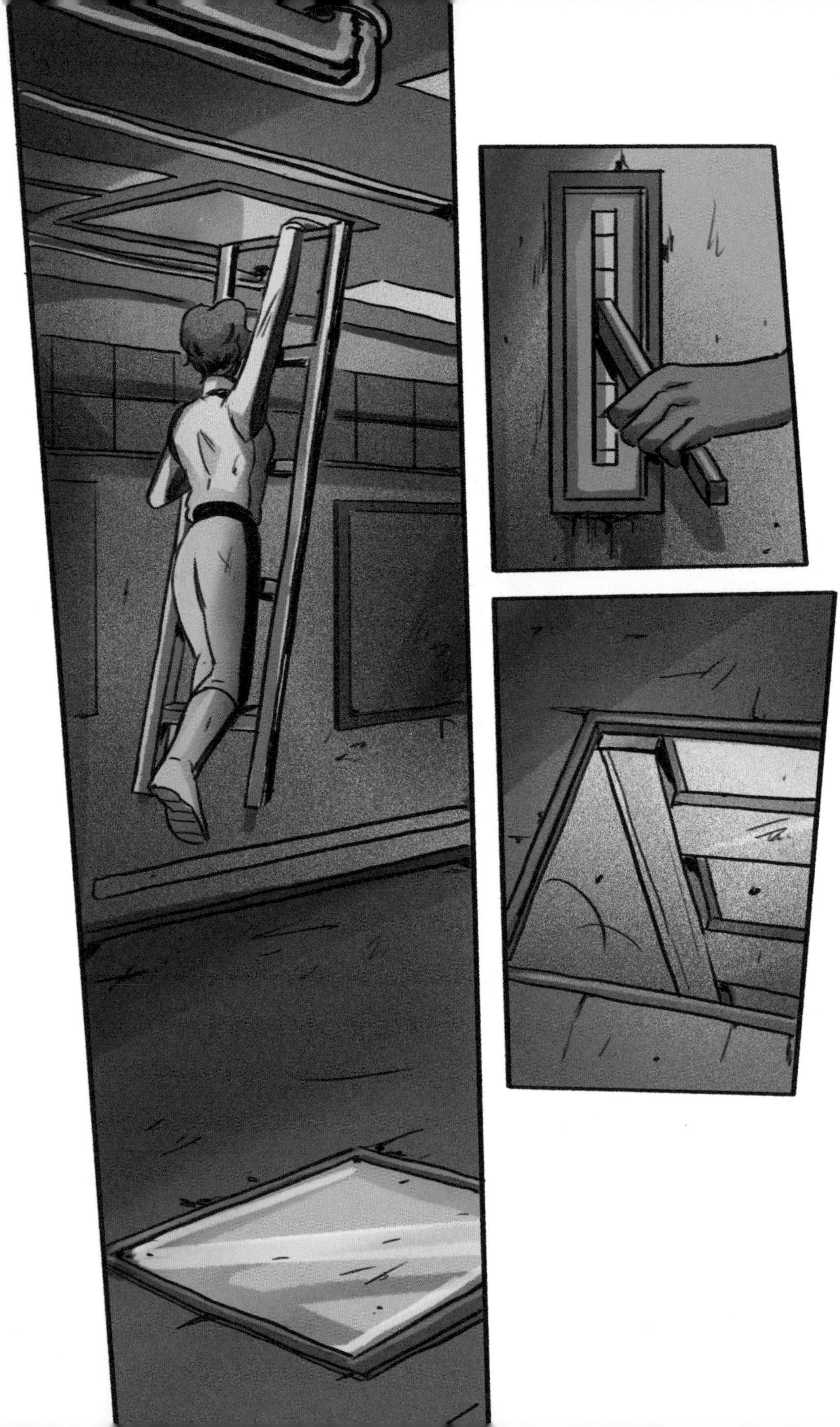

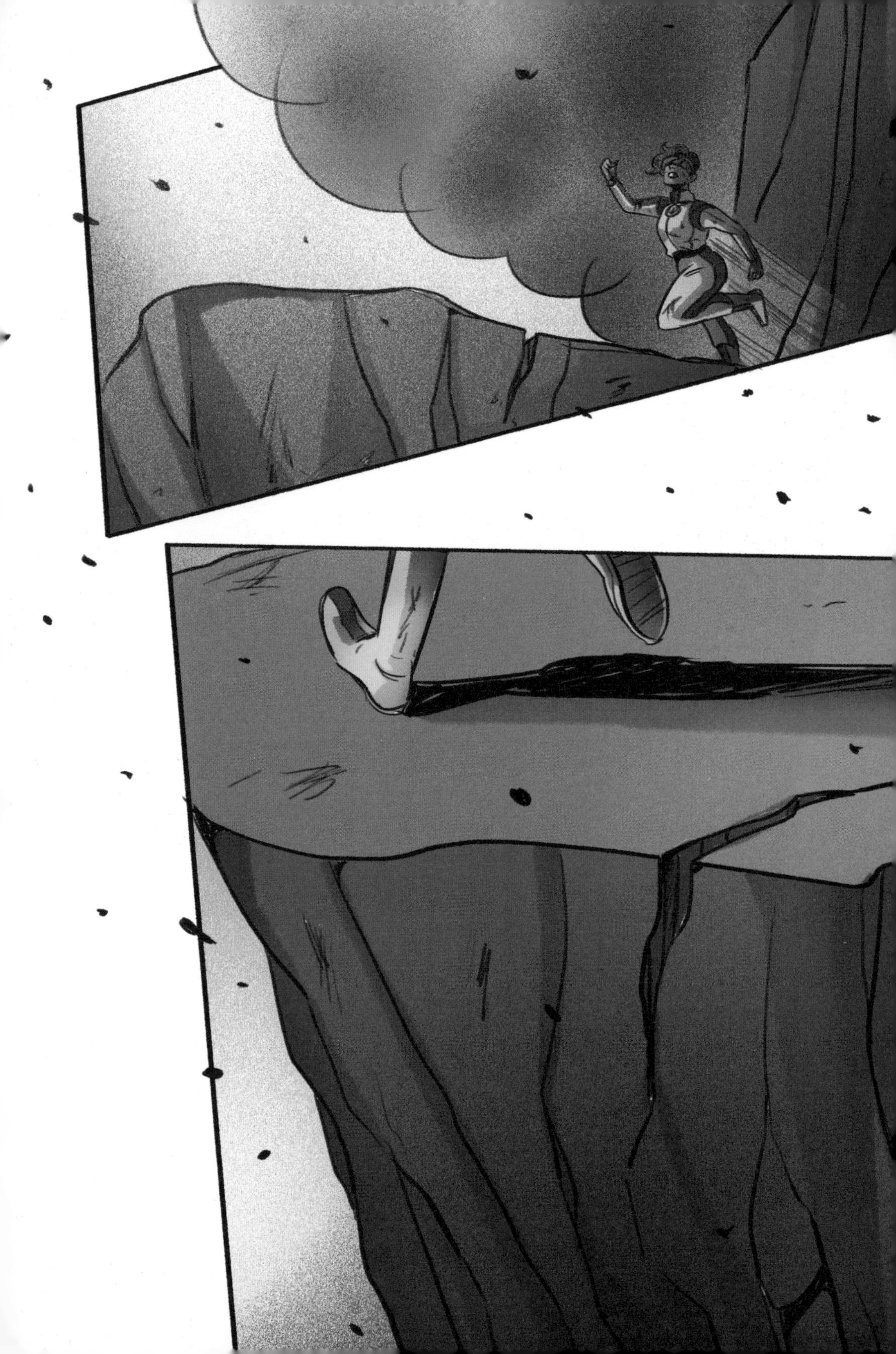

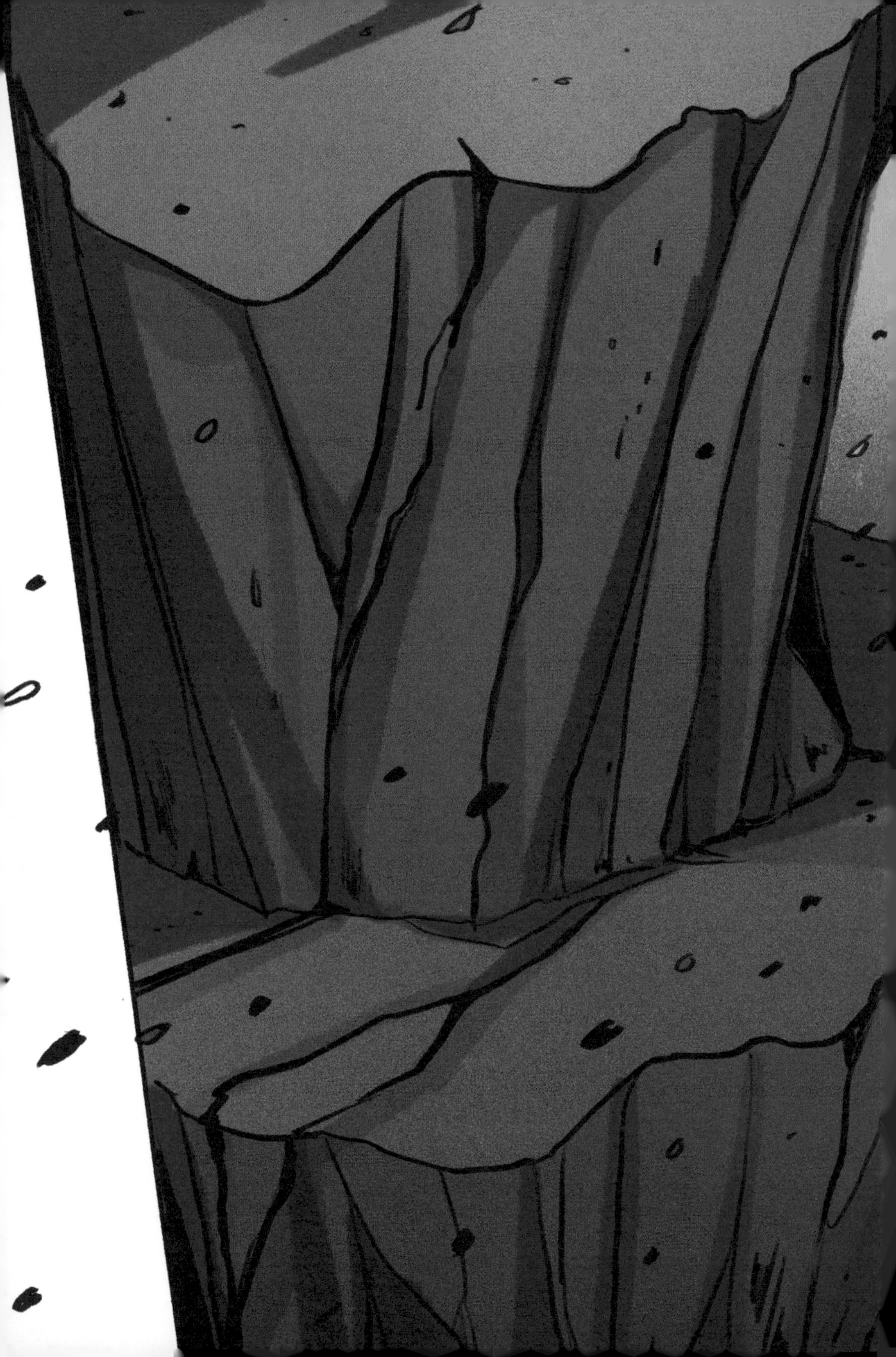

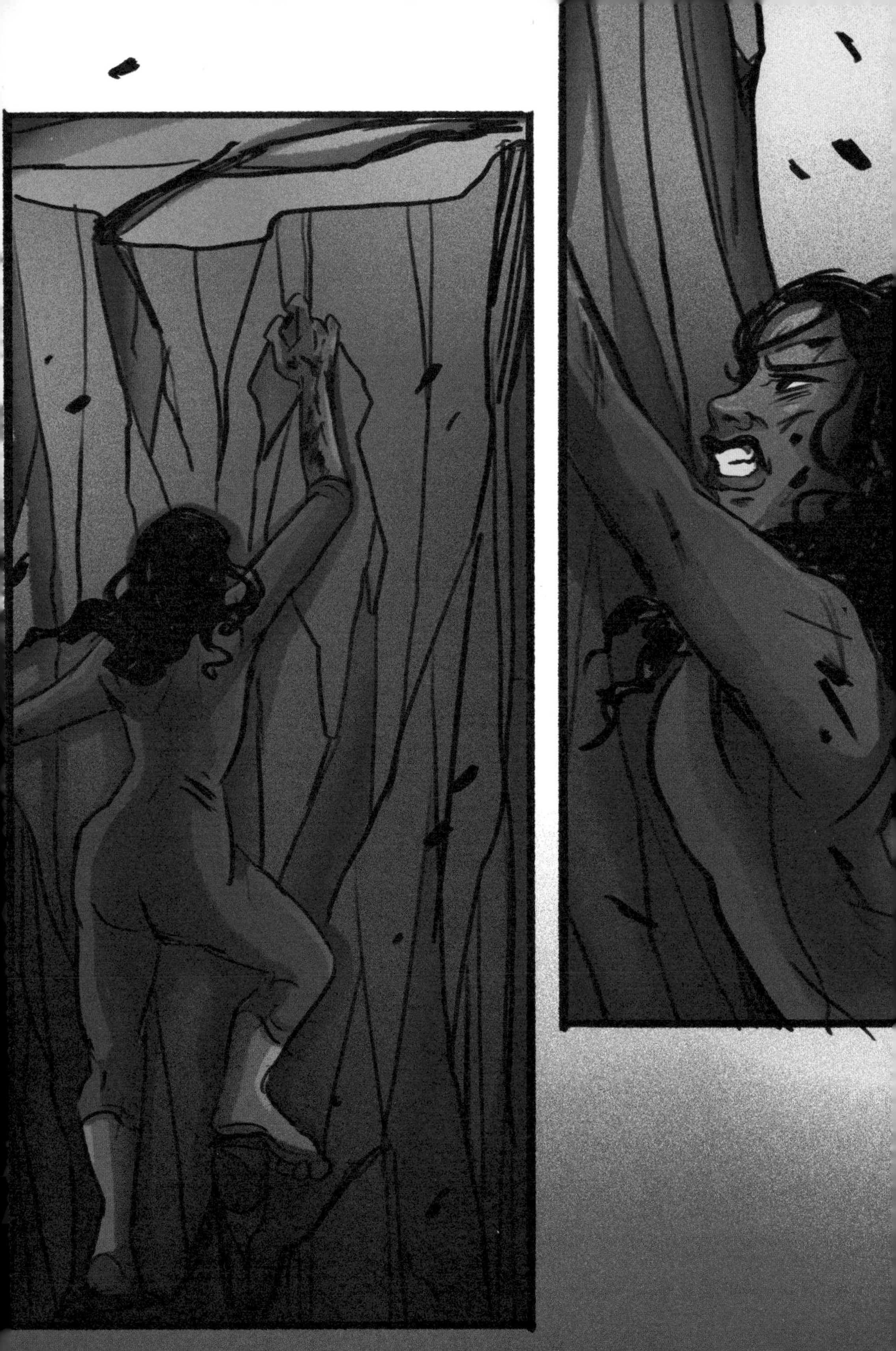

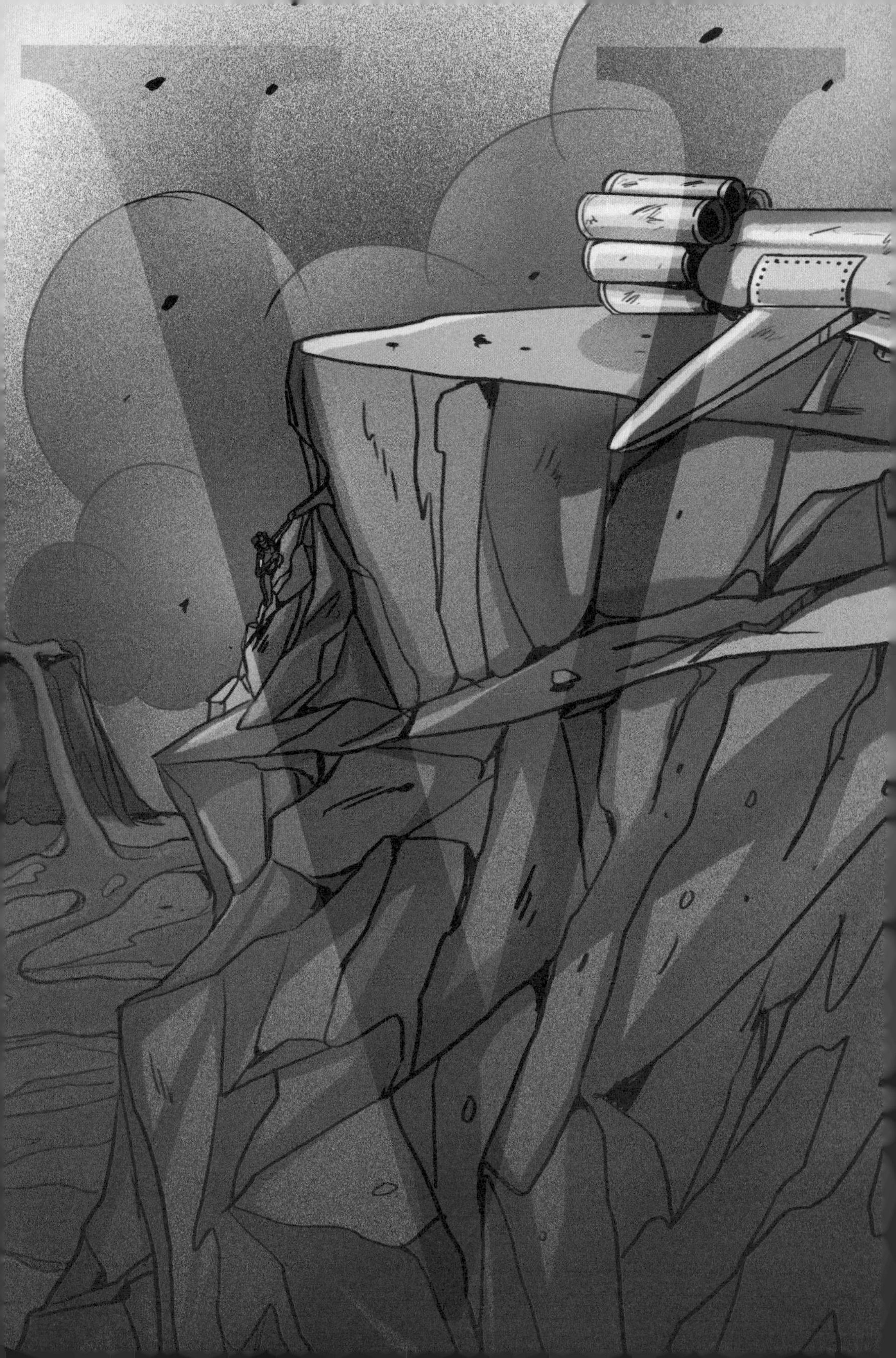

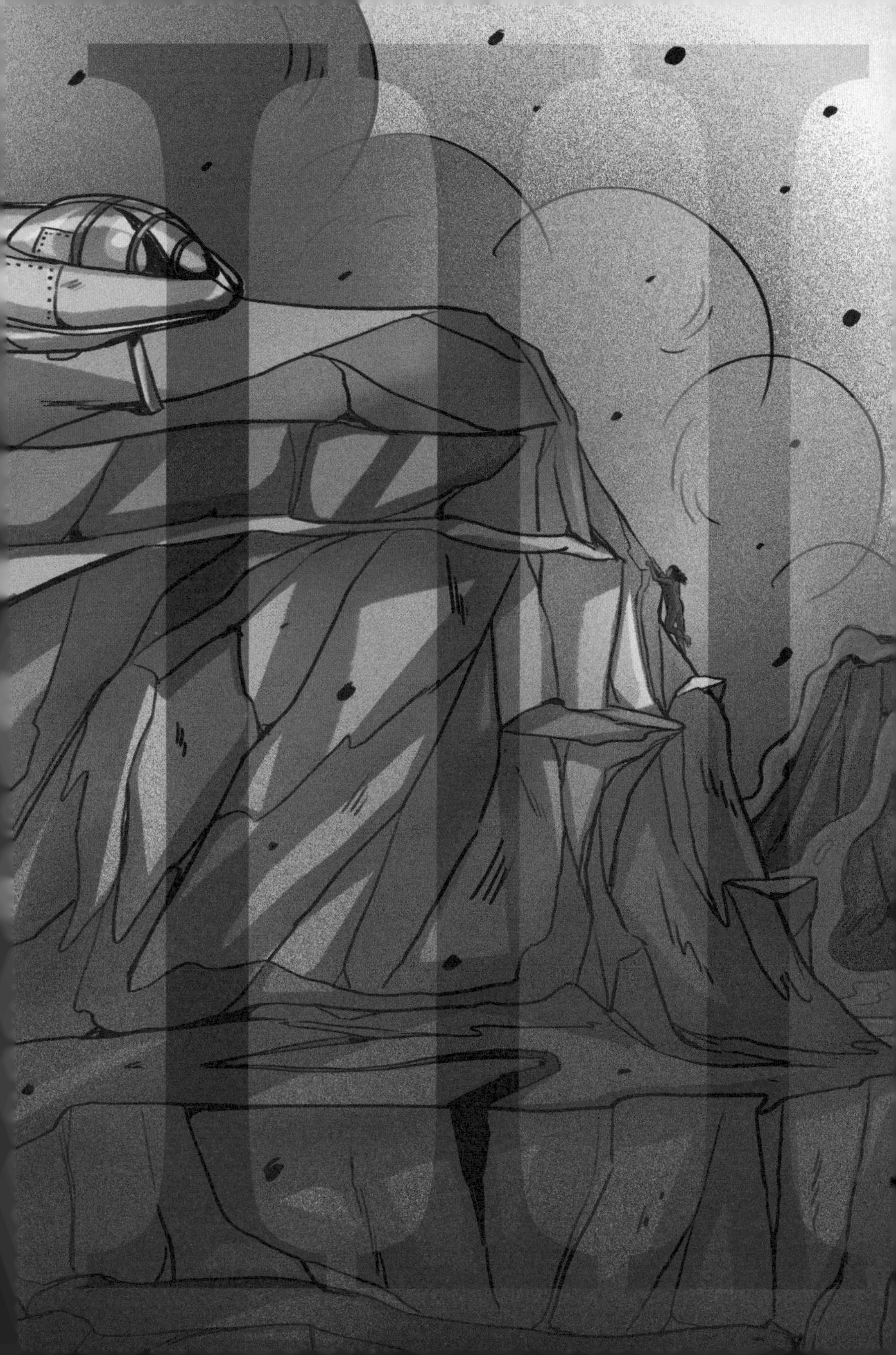
III

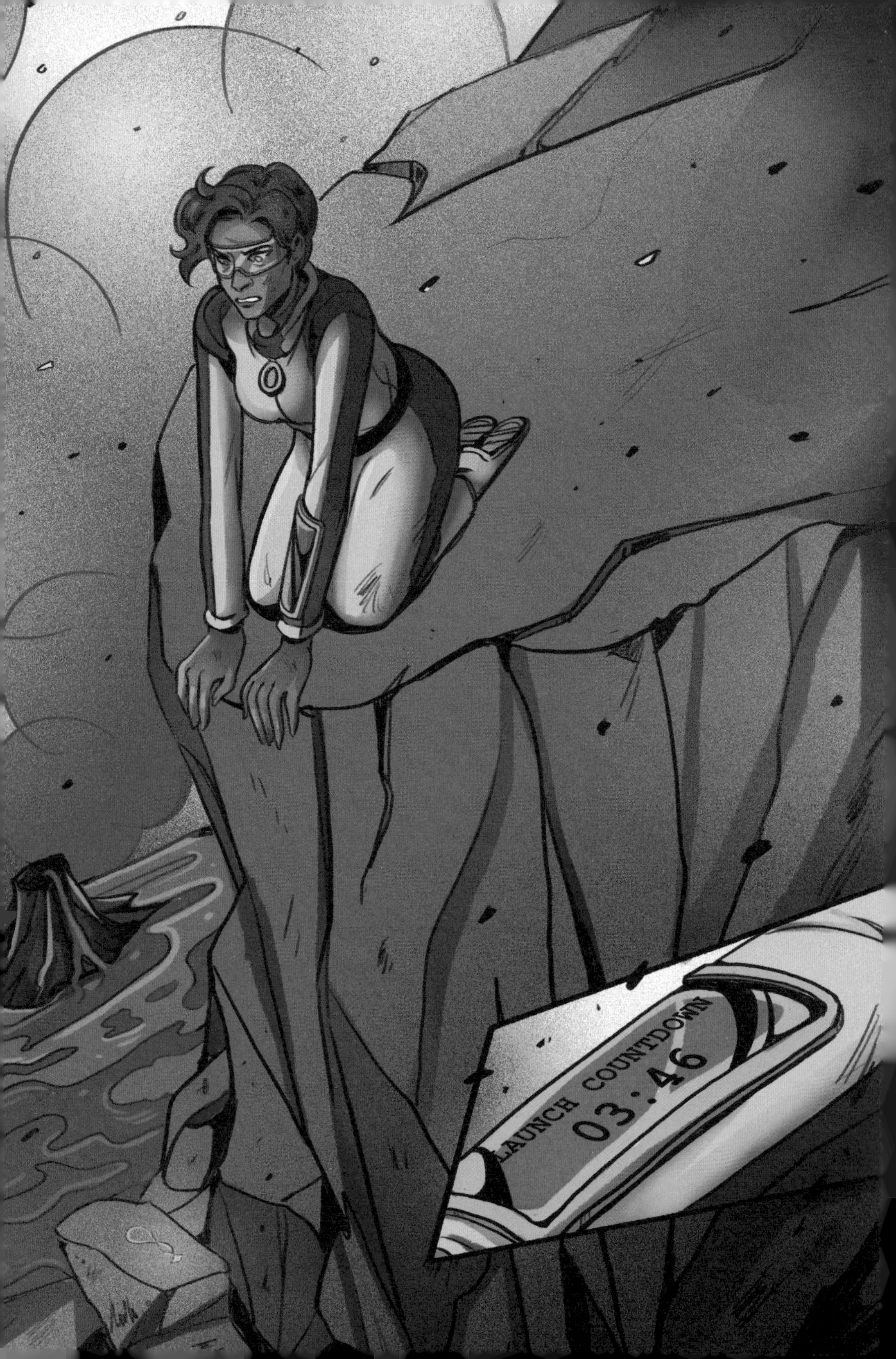
LAUNCH COUNTDOWN
03:46

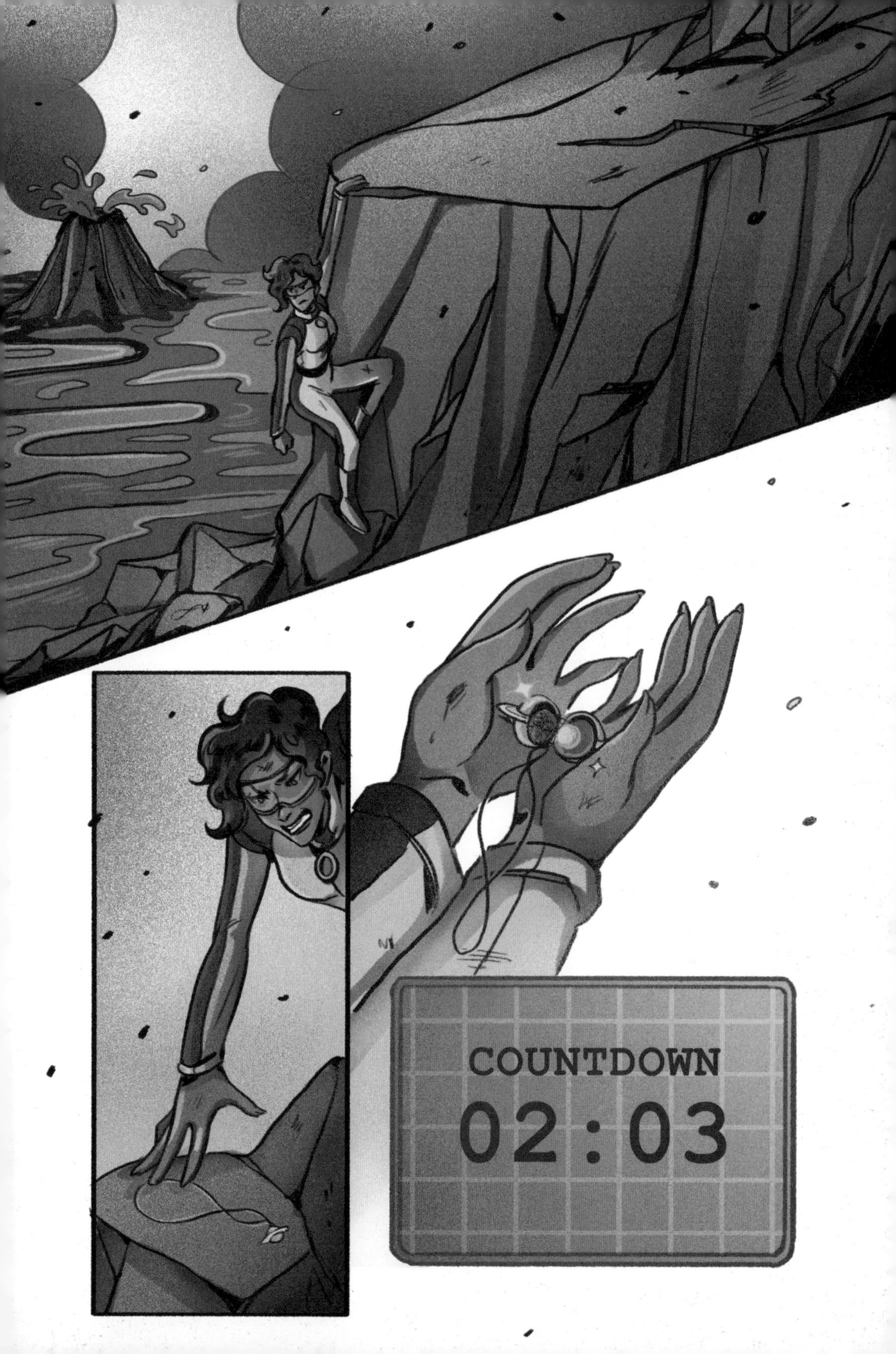
COUNTDOWN
02:03

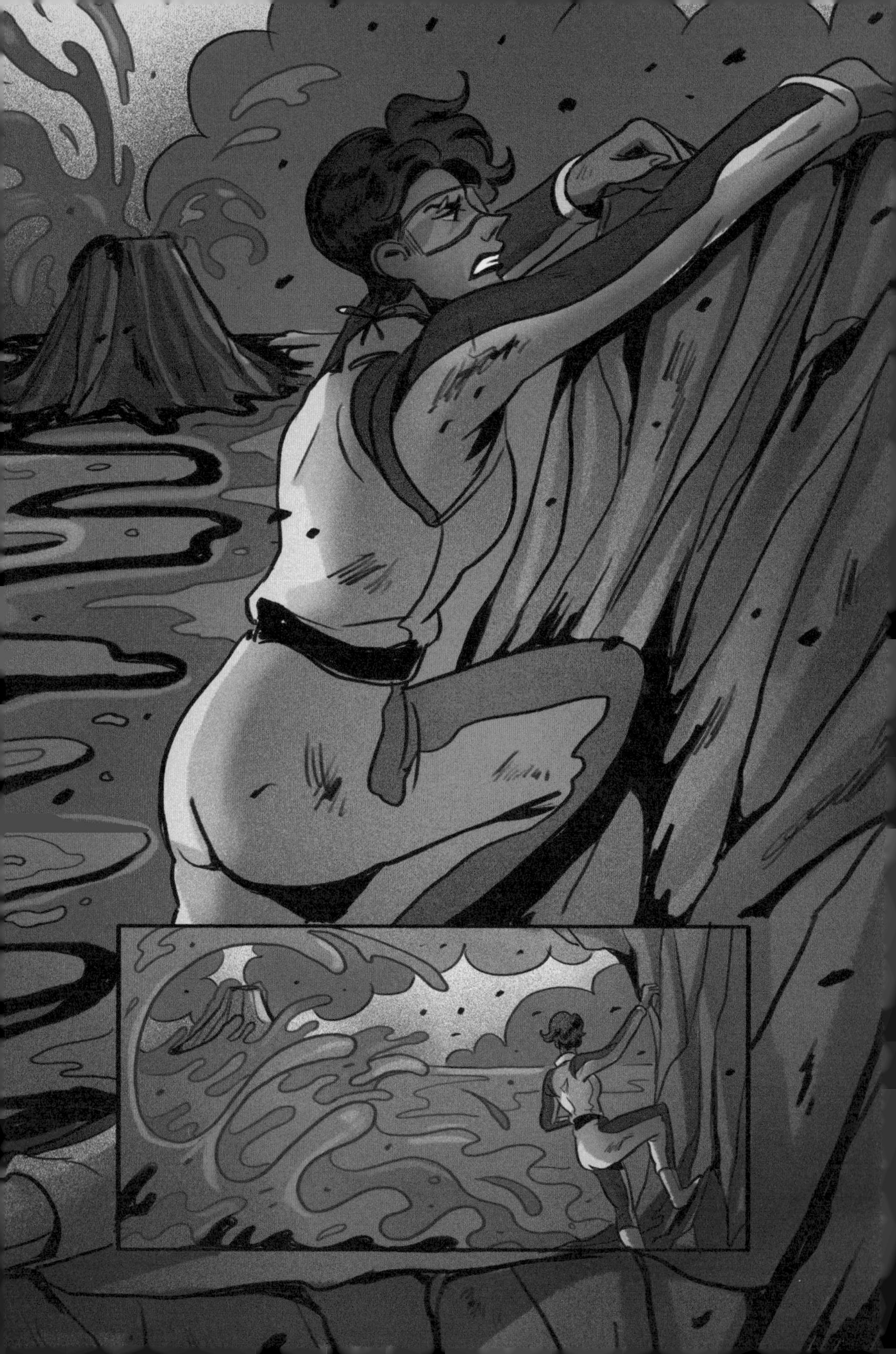

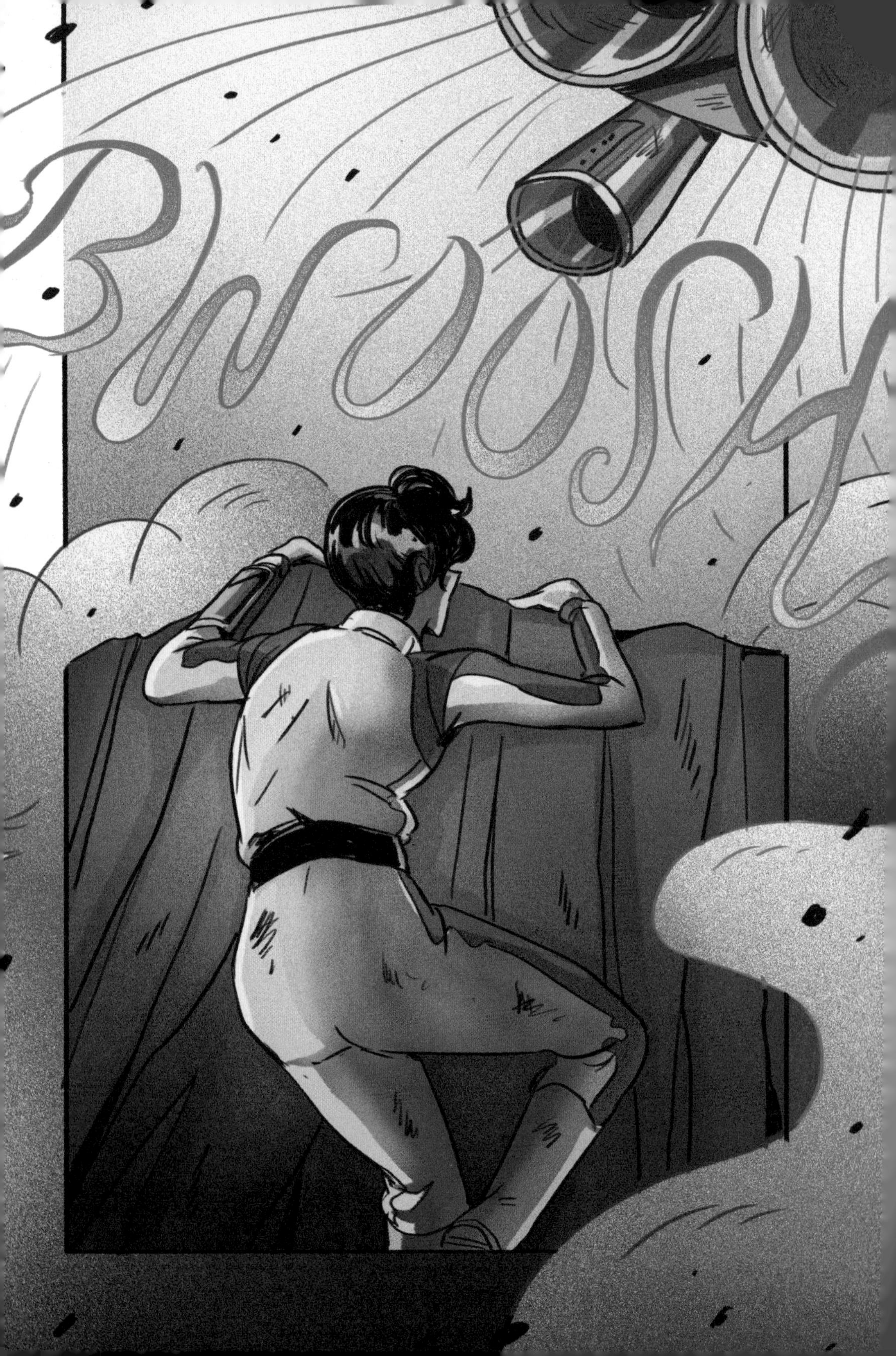
BWOOSH

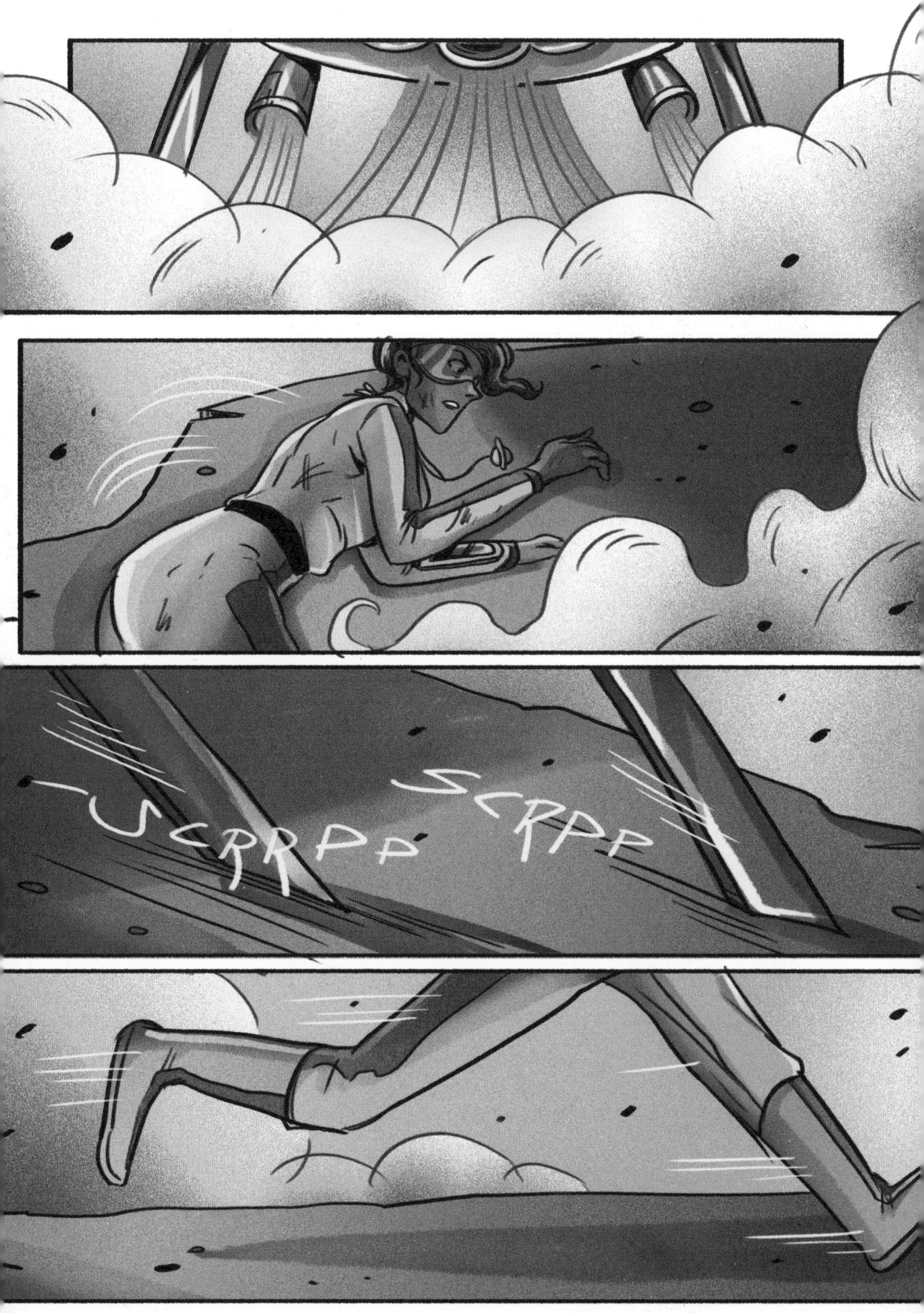
SCRPP
SCRPP

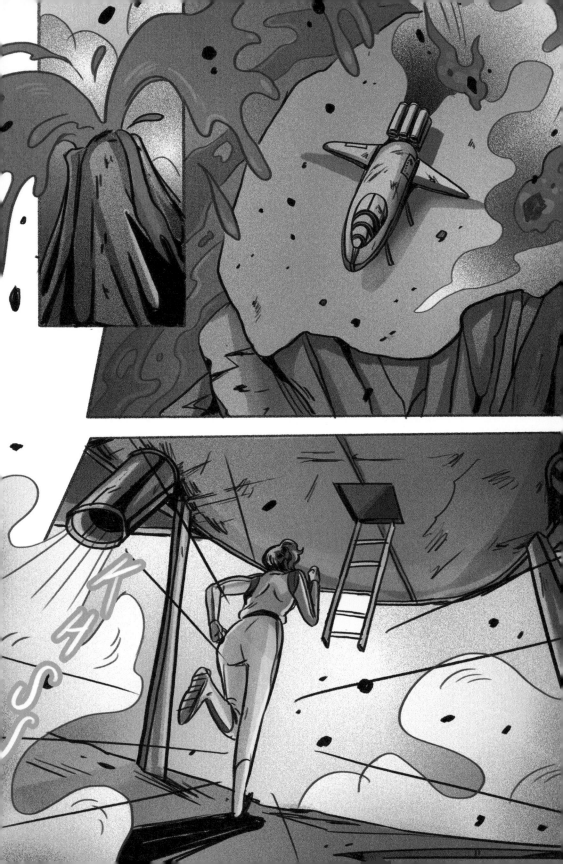

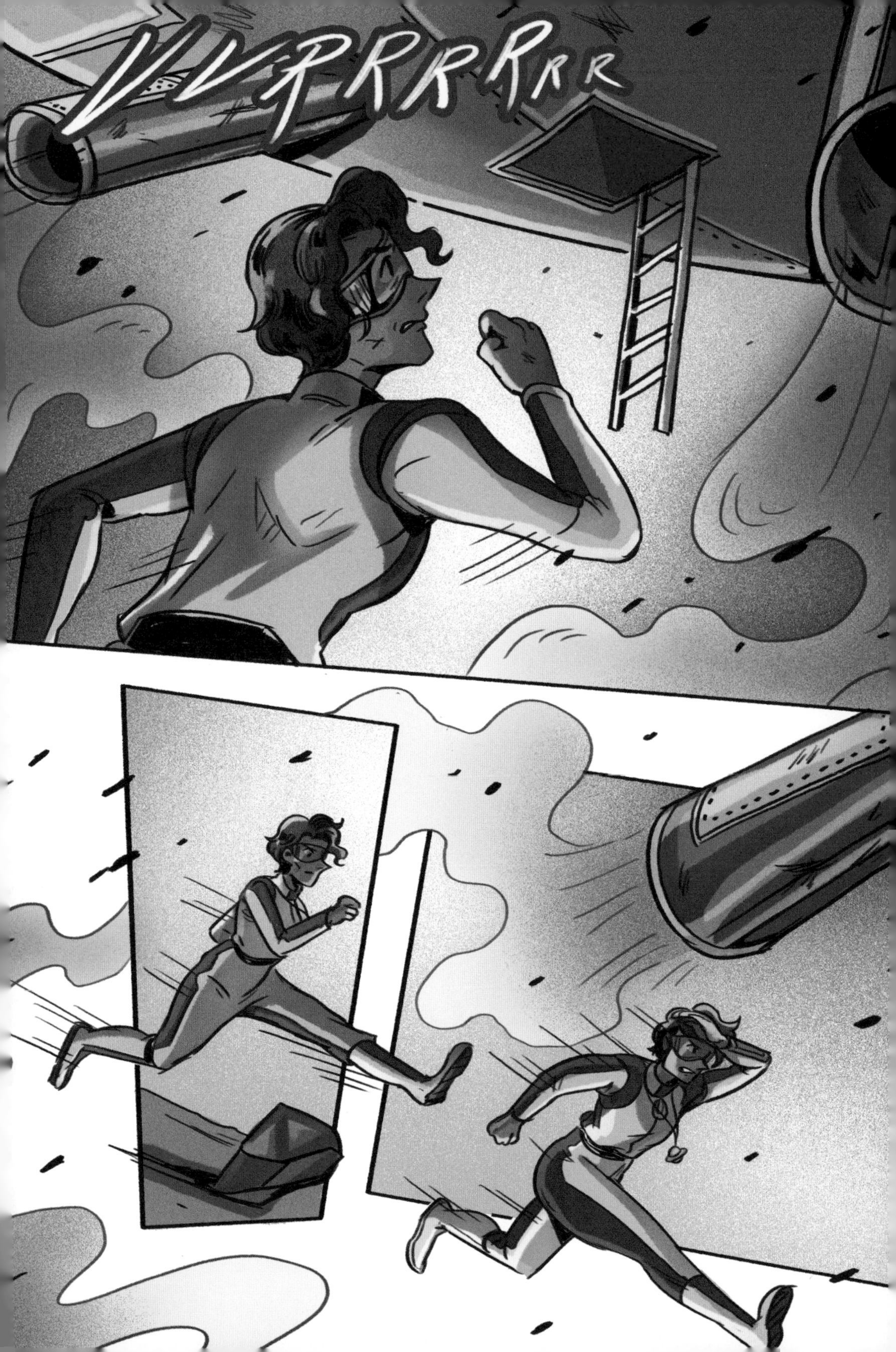
VVRRRRrr

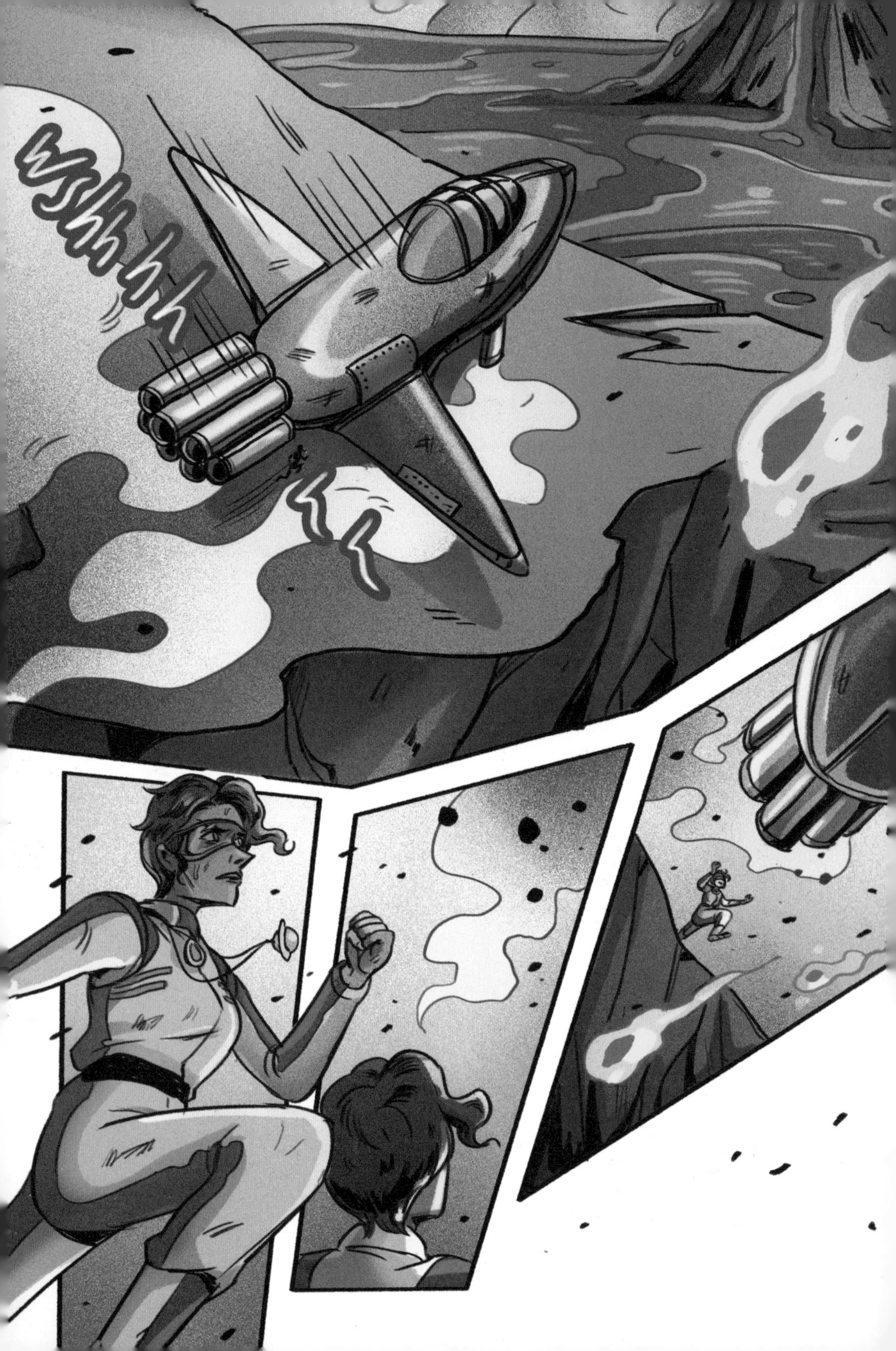
wshhhh

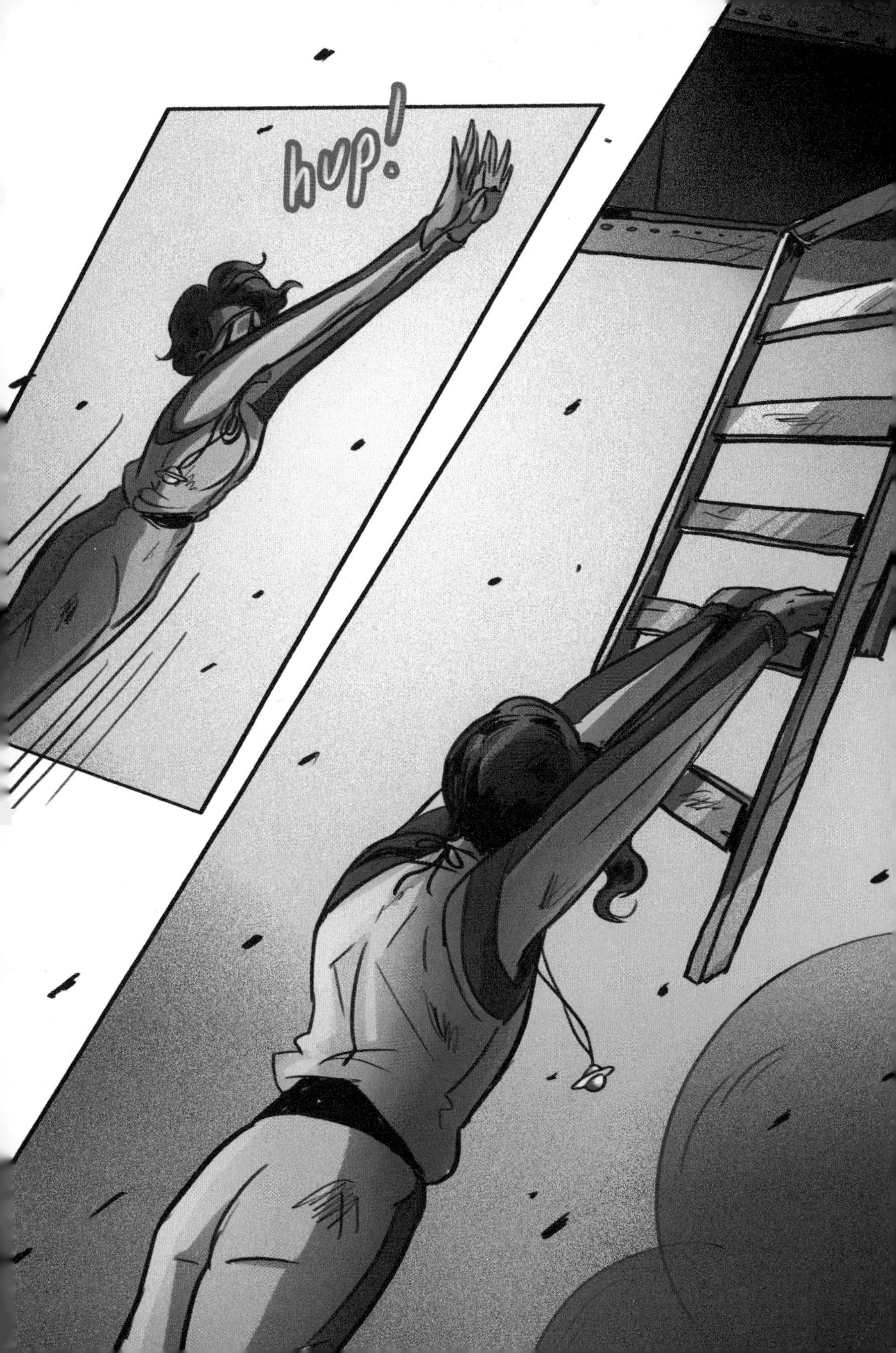
hup!

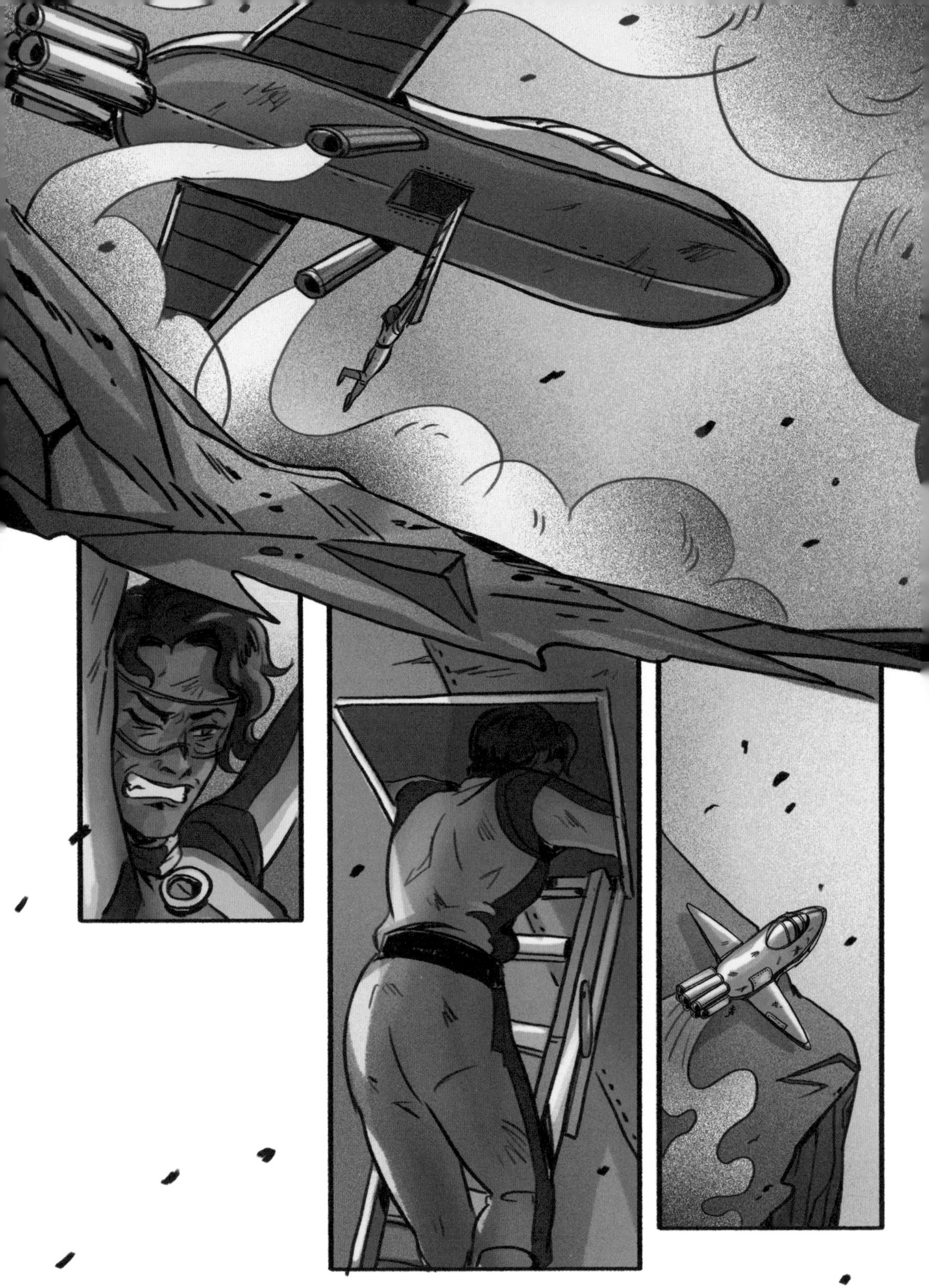

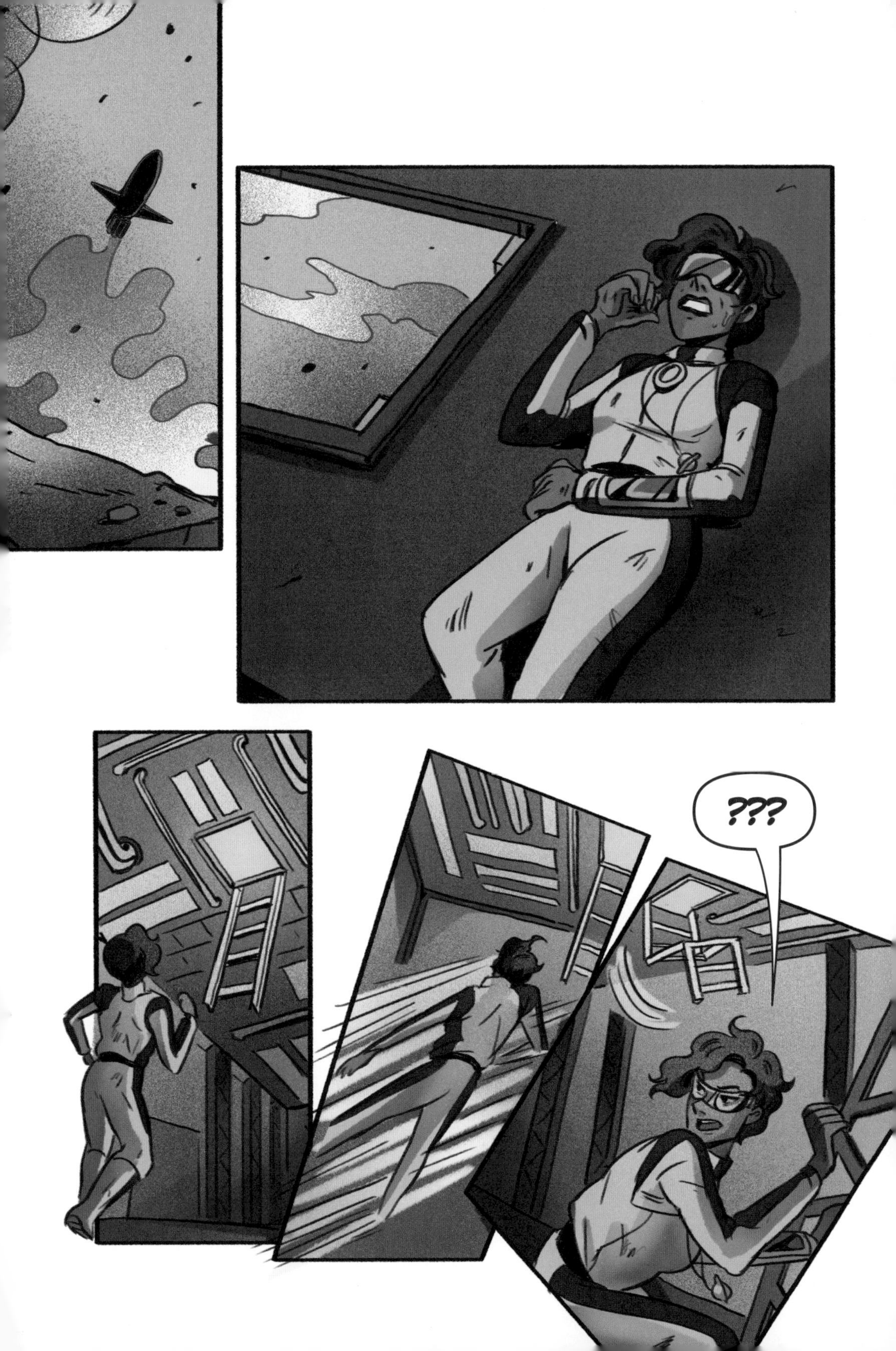
???

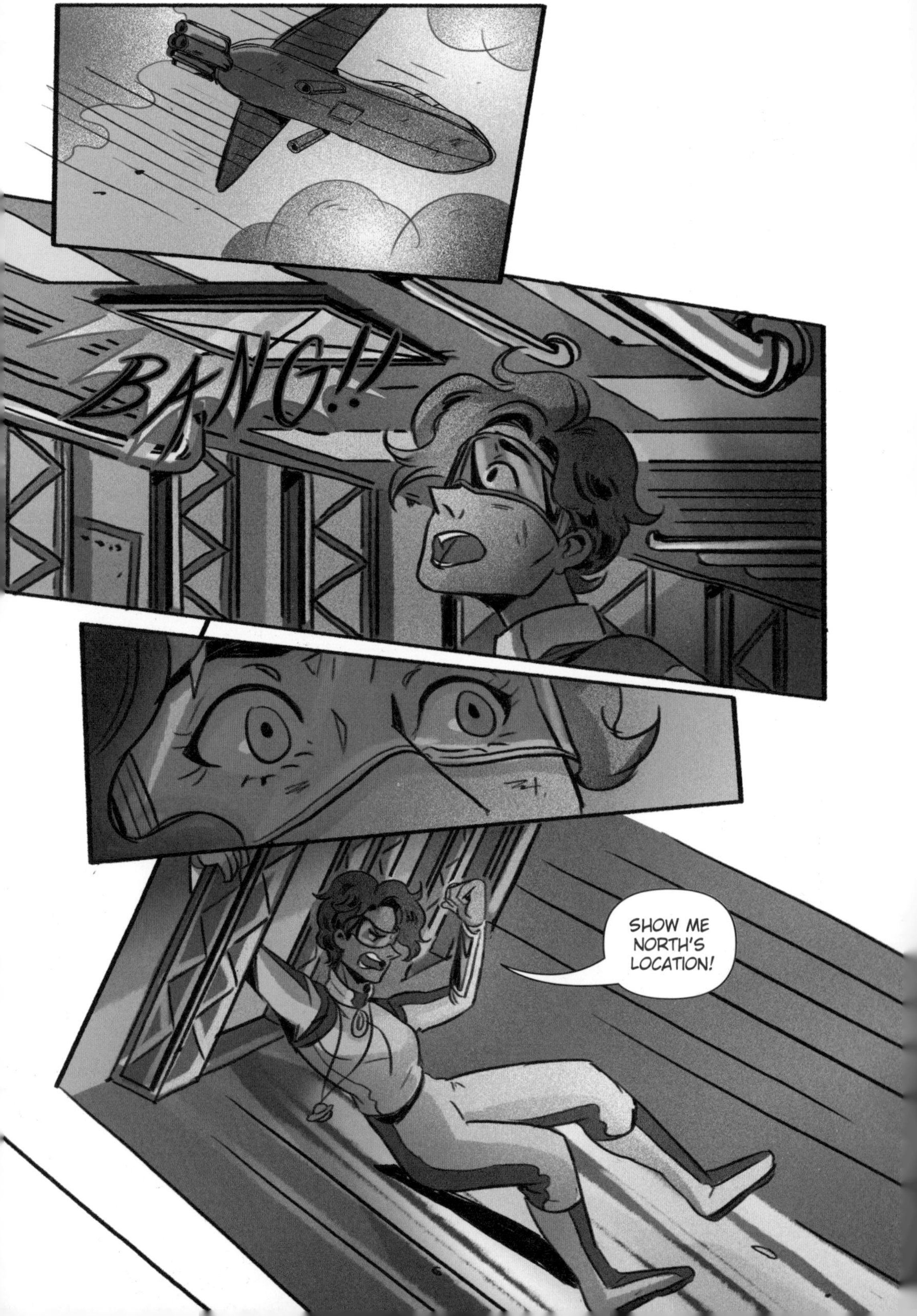
BANG!!
SHOW ME NORTH'S LOCATION!

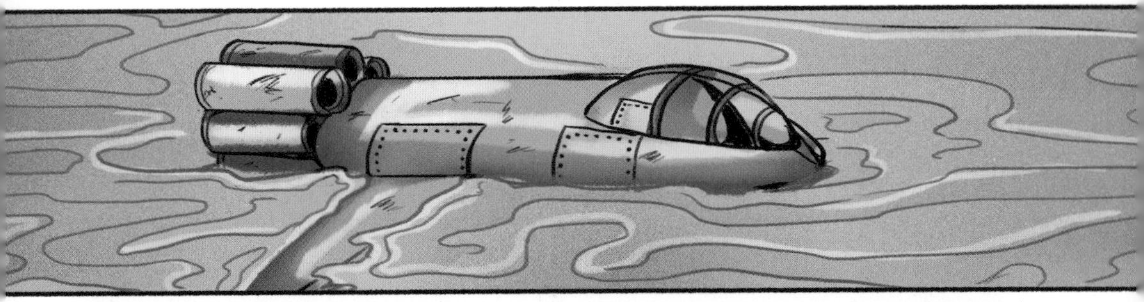

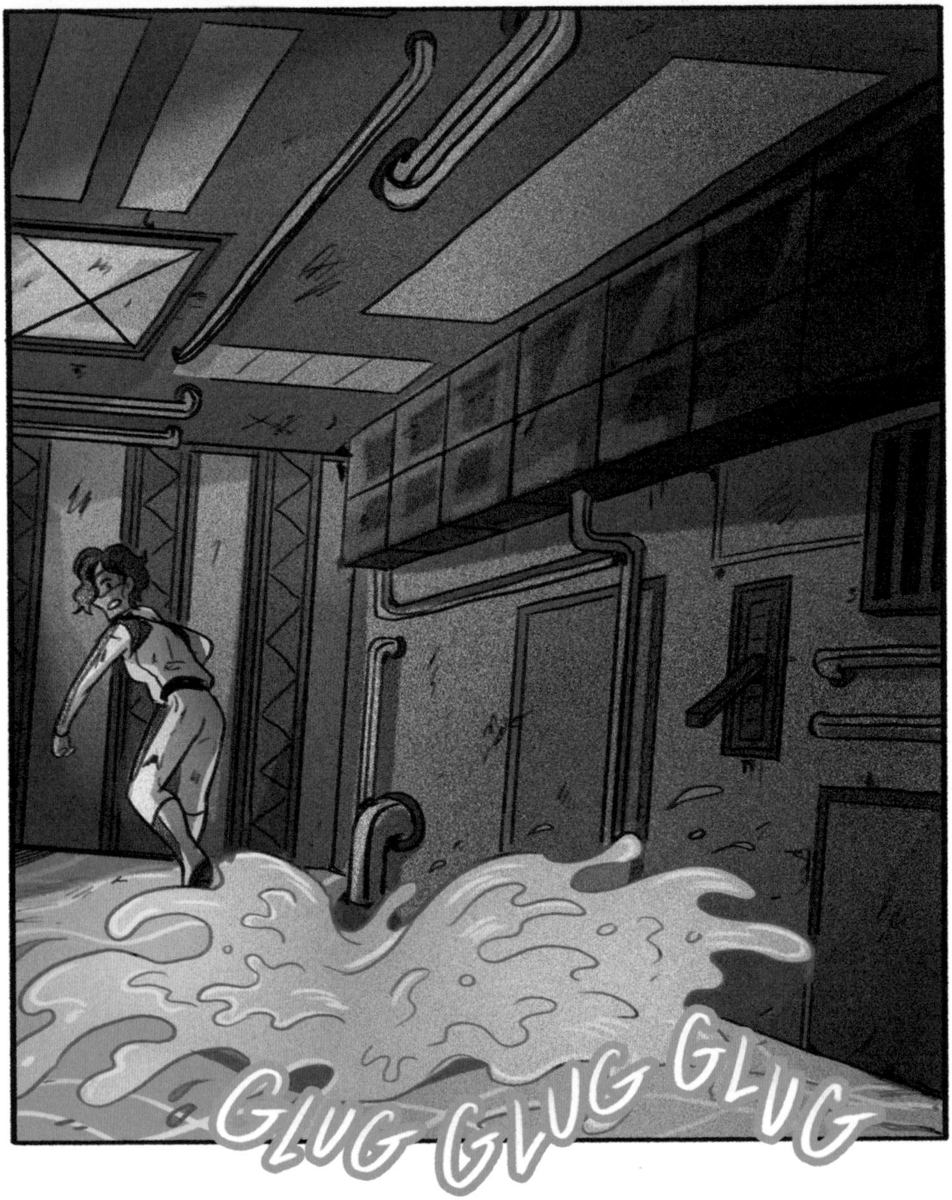
GLUG GLUG GLUG

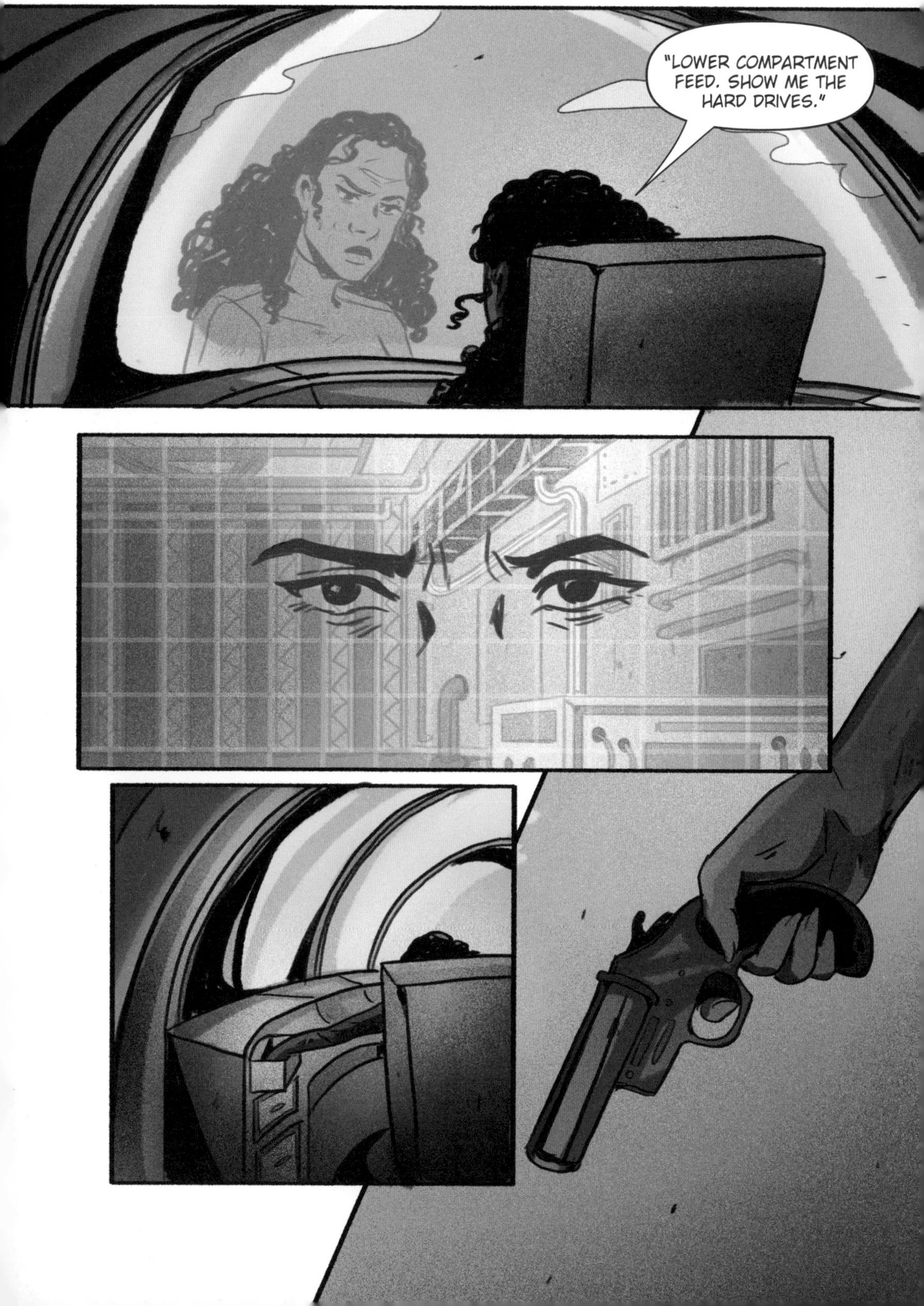
"LOWER COMPARTMENT FEED. SHOW ME THE HARD DRIVES."

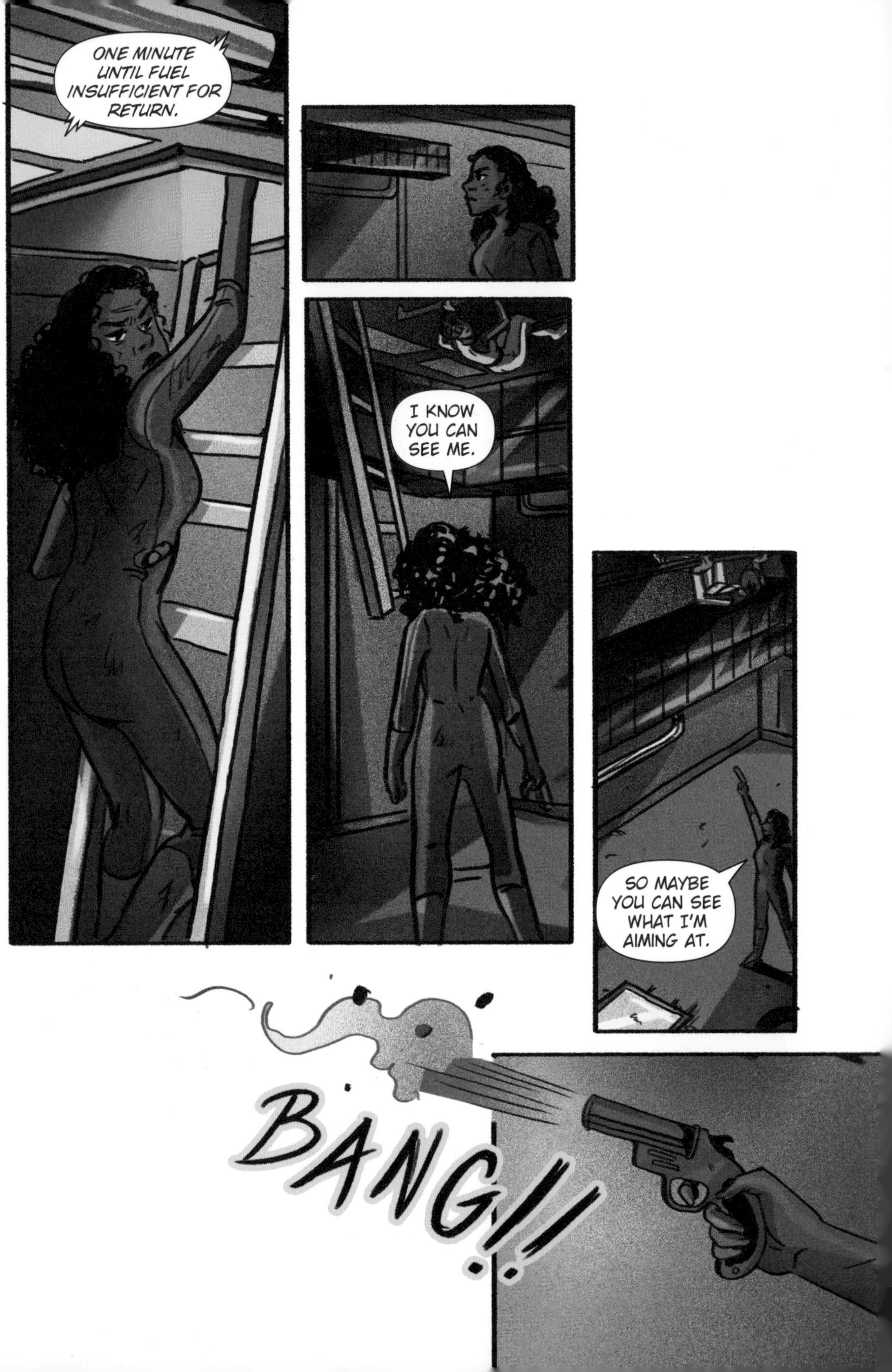
ONE MINUTE UNTIL FUEL INSUFFICIENT FOR RETURN.
I KNOW YOU CAN SEE ME.
SO MAYBE YOU CAN SEE WHAT I'M AIMING AT.
BANG!!

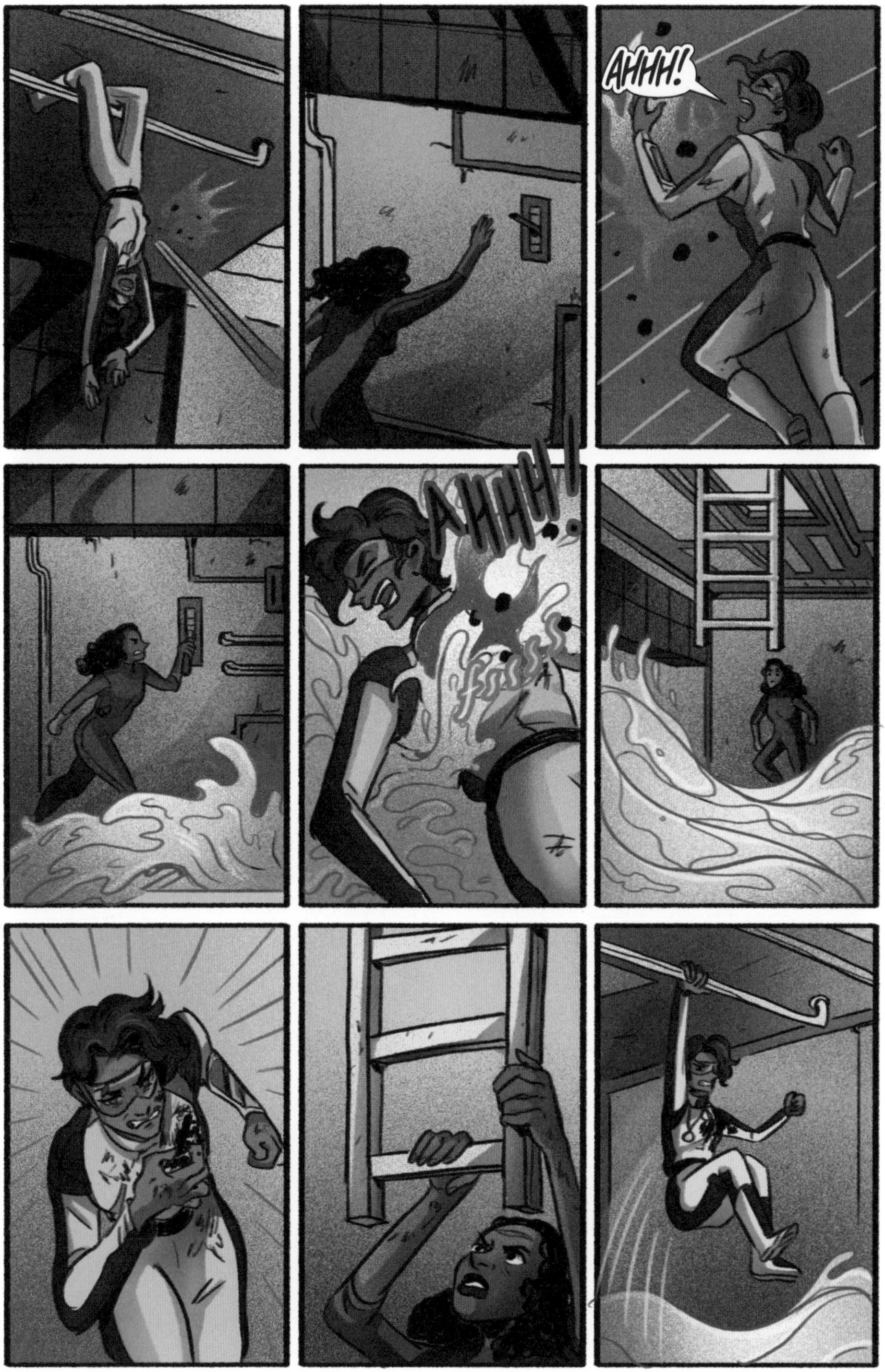
AHHH!
AHHH!

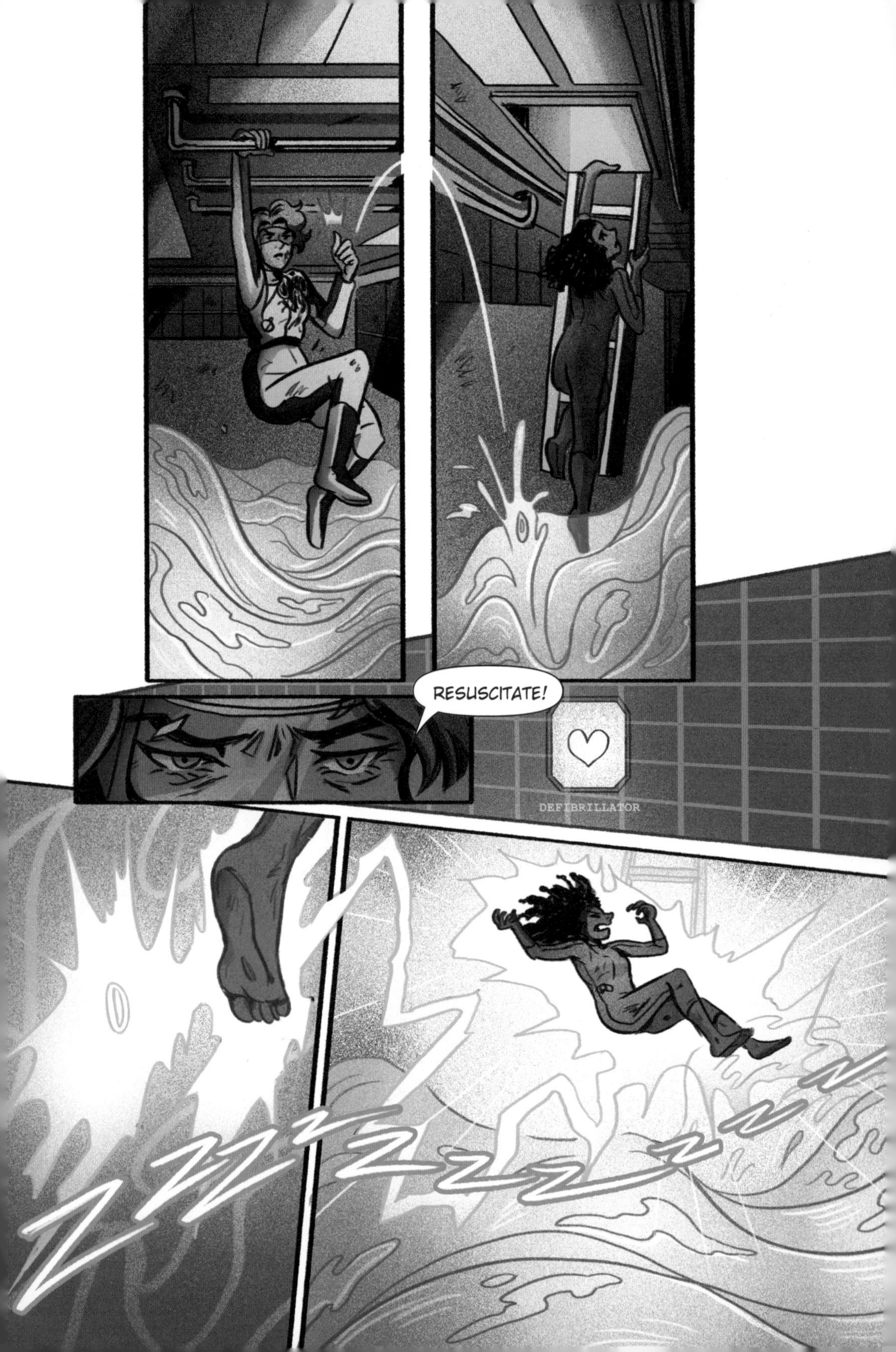

RESUSCITATE!
DEFIBRILLATOR
ZZZZZZZZZZZZ

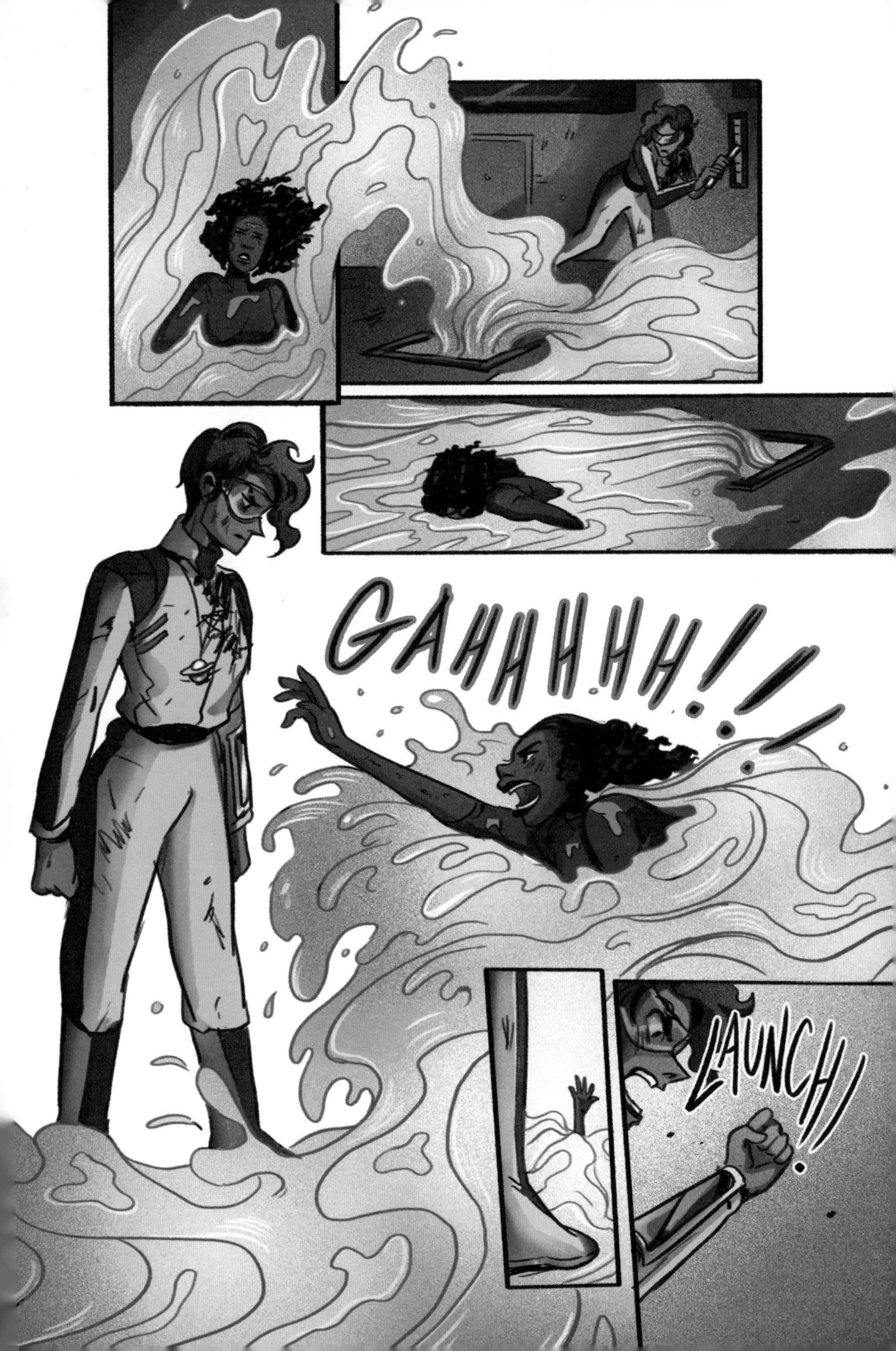
GAHHHHH!!!
LAUNCH!!

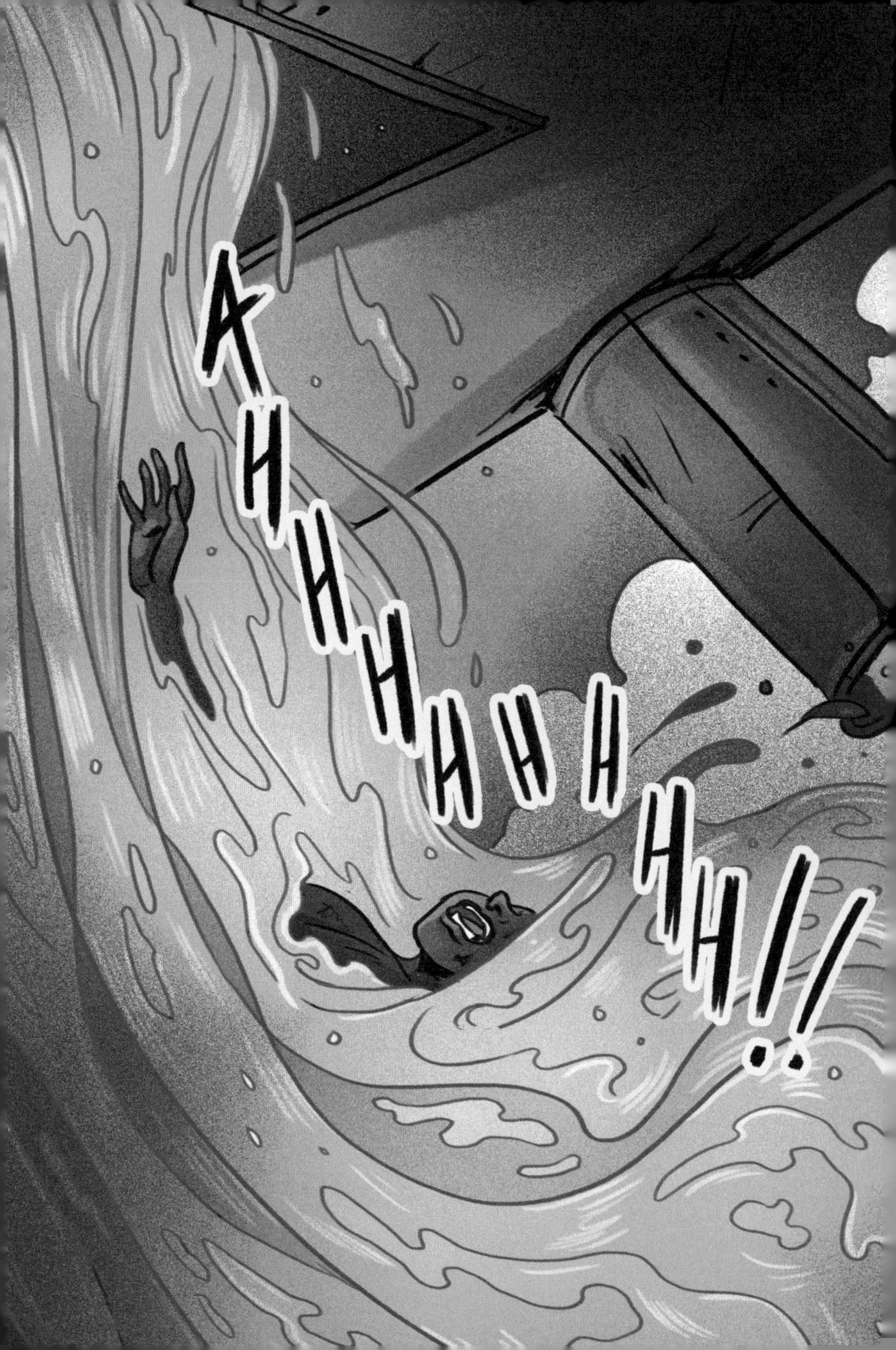
AHHHHHHHH!!

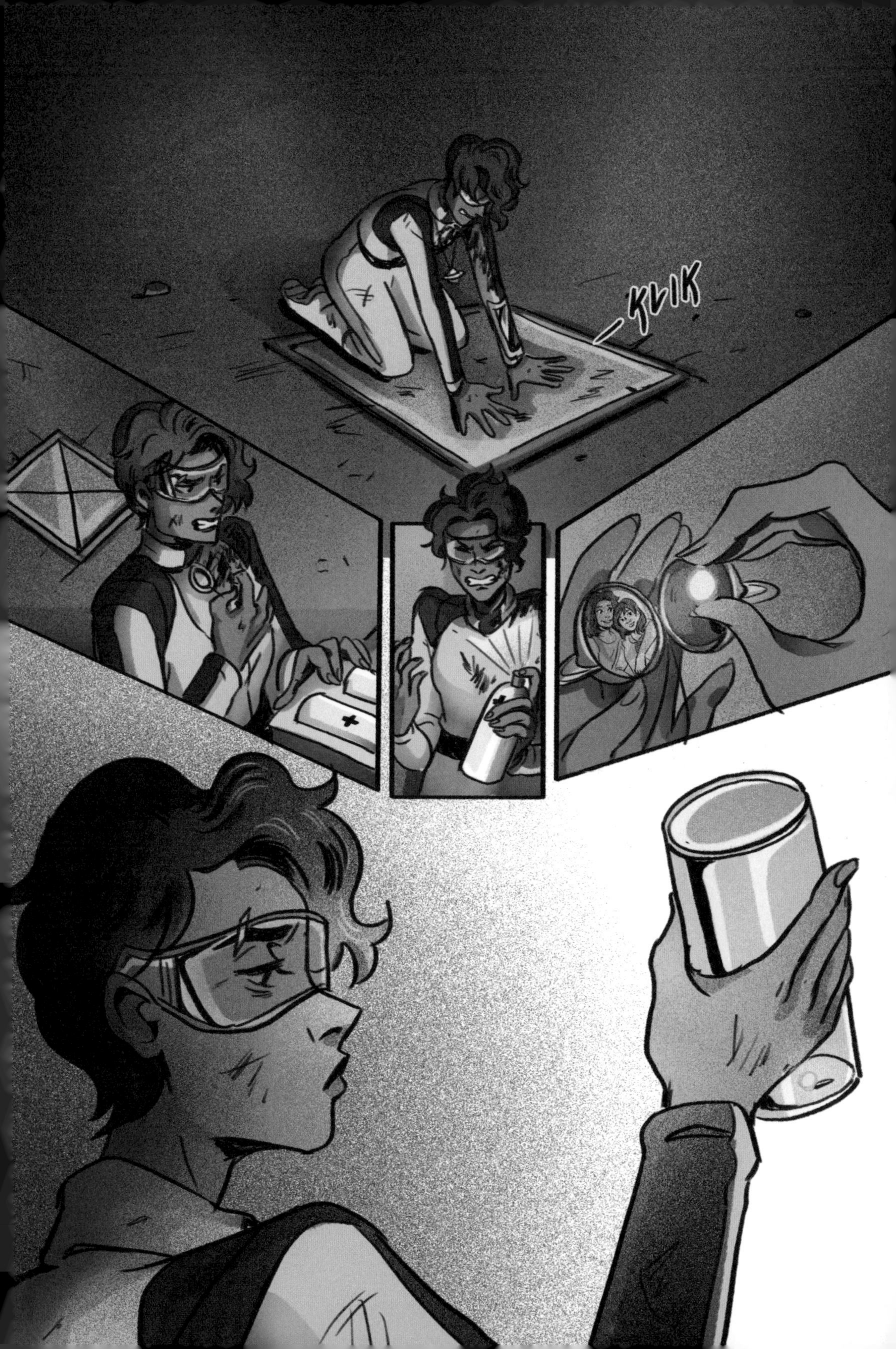
KLIK

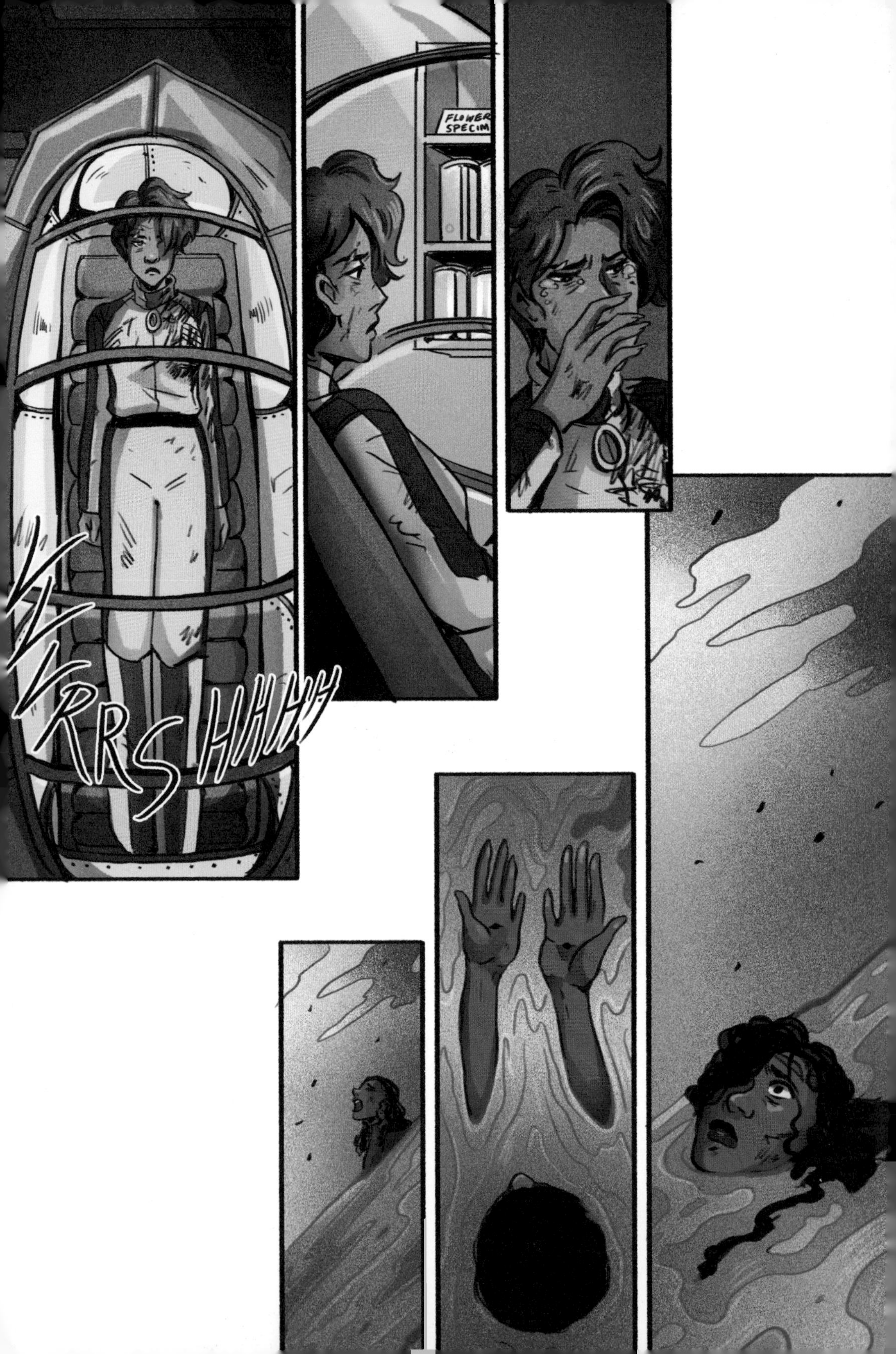
FLOWER SPECIM
VVVRRSHHHH

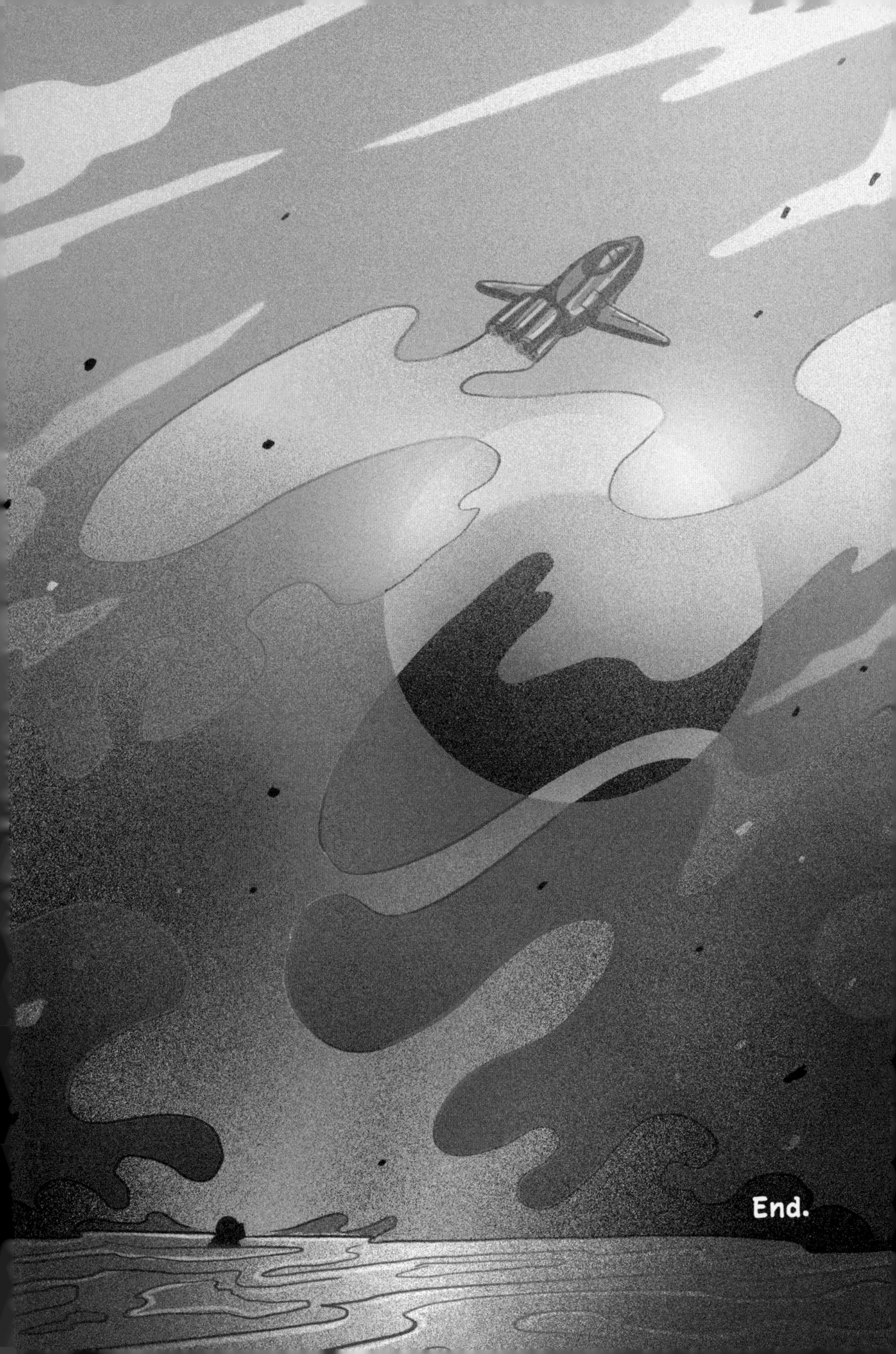
End.

MANY THANKS to my editor, Charlotte Greenbaum, who pushed the hardest of anyone to make this book a reality. I am also grateful to Maxwell Neely-Cohen, without whom this project would never have come about. Thank you to Arielle Jovellanos, whose art elevated my script in ways I couldn't have anticipated, and to my manager, Joe Riley, whose advocacy helped me breathe easier.

Additionally, I'd like to offer my eternal gratitude to Vicki Simons, who has enthusiastically supported my writing from the very beginning; Rob Rodems, for the comfort he provides between battles with my keyboard; as well as Dylan Morgan, Lukas Fauset, and Taylor Pavlik, whose early feedback on this story (and so many of my stories since) has made me a better writer.

—Eric Anthony Glover

TO MY mom and dad for everything.

To Charlotte for making sure I kept going.

To Eric who let me play in his world.

To my color assistants, Andrew, James, and Alexandra. I couldn't have done it without you.

To Ate, Jaemari, Emma, Nicole, Gail, Janet, Melva, and Tim for staying up and logging FaceTime hours with me on long work days.

Thank you, everyone!!

—Arielle Jovellanos

VISUAL DEVELOPMENT

by Arielle Jovellanos

CHARACTER DESIGNS

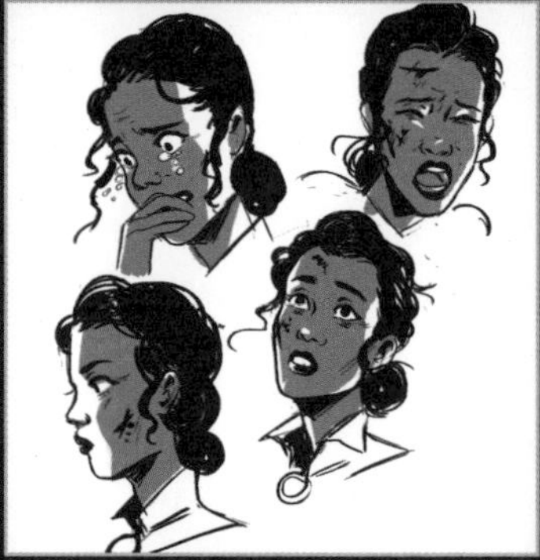

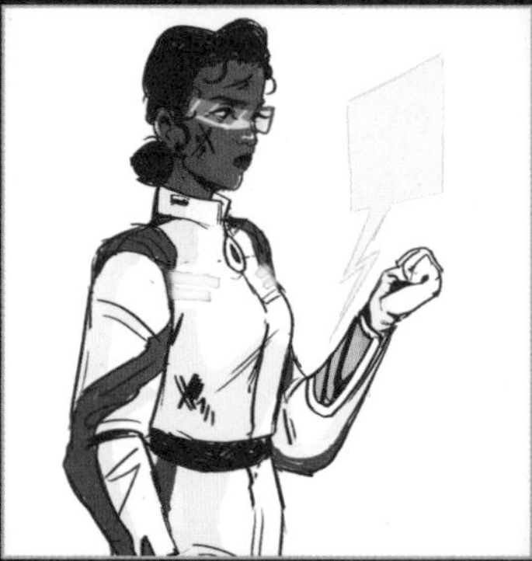

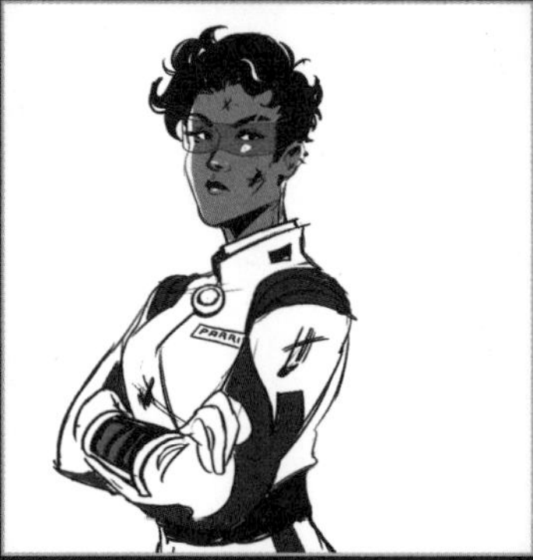

North was an interesting character to work with because I had to find ways to visually show how the planet wears her down as the story goes on. For example, putting her hair in a bun at the start allowed me to use the state of her hair as a marker dramatizing how she goes from a reclusive scientist on a mission to someone just desperately trying to survive.

When I was first designing the suit, I was mostly looking at Ripley from *Alien* and the plugsuits from *Neon Genesis Evangelion* as inspiration. In a couple pieces of concept art, I originally had the suit a darker color, but wound up going with an off-white because it would stand out more in most panel compositions and served as a better canvas for the rips and dirt stains North suffers on her journey.

The story is essentially a game of cat-and-mouse, so I clocked on using color to distinguish North and Parrish pretty early in the process. I think Parrish's red offsets North's blue in a very striking way, and the palette of the book generally contrasts between cool blues and warm reds, sometimes coalescing into purples when the two characters clash. I didn't plan for this, but the final page wound up a happy accident with the two characters' colors swapping: North is left behind in a reddish, fiery haze as Parrish flies out into a clear blue sky.

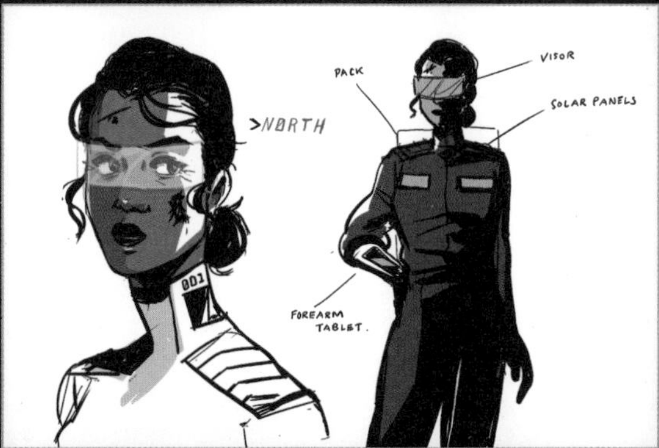
>NORTH
PACK
VISOR
SOLAR PANELS
FOREARM TABLET.

DIGITAL INTERFACE

When I first received Eric's manuscript, I noticed that so much of the story relies on North using her tablet, and I wanted to find a way to dramatize the visual language of something as simple as typing, receiving a notification, or watching a video. Here I was playing with various ways to make the Guardian interesting—really just finding ways to make its presence loom as its own character.

MOUNTAIN AND WASTELAND

I looked at Chesley Bonestell's space landscapes for inspiration and did a few concept sketches for the terrain of Eleos. While this didn't wind up being used in the book, I liked playing with the idea of a mountain that had ice rings around it, similar to the composition of Saturn's rings.

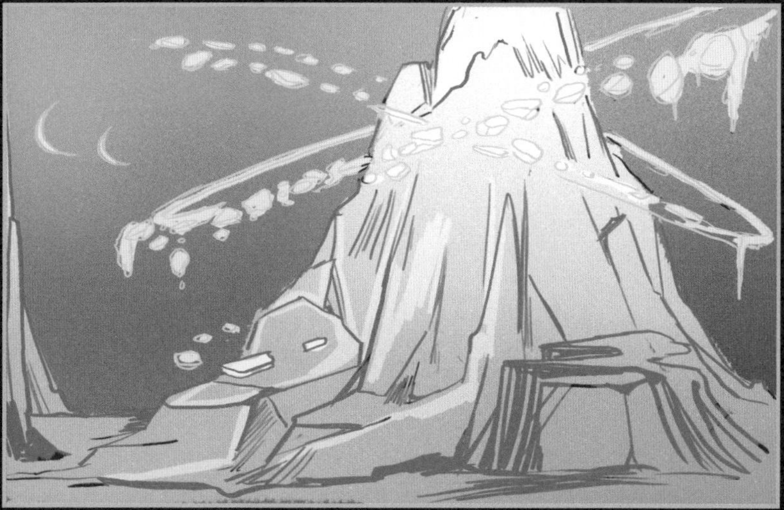

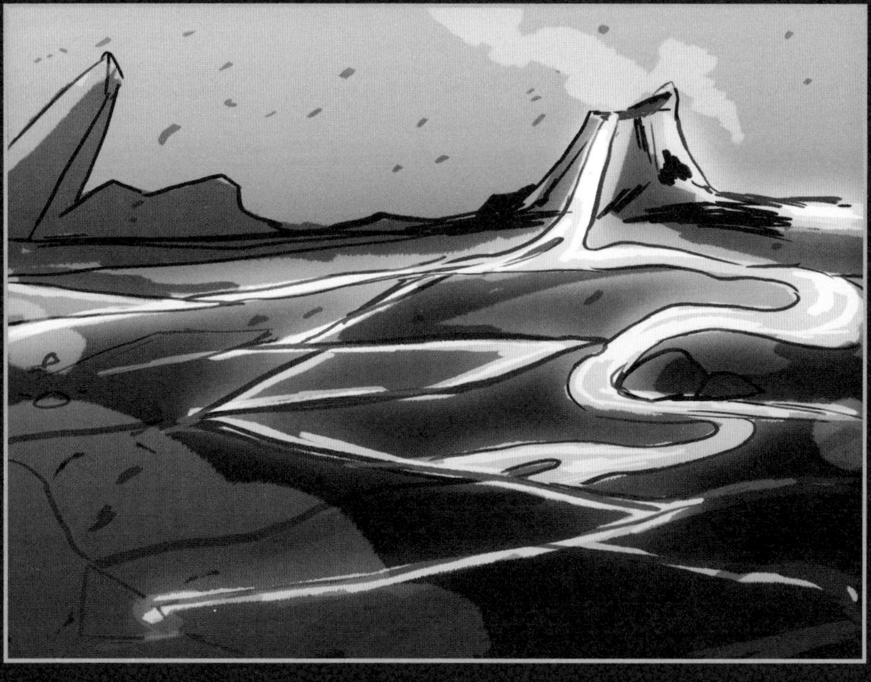

MEGASCOPE Curator: John Jennings
Editor: Charlotte Greenbaum
Designer: Kay Petronio
Managing Editor: Mary O'Mara
Production Manager: Alison Gervais
Lettering: Dave Sharpe
Additional Colors: Andrew Dalhouse

Cataloging-in-Publication Data has been
applied for and may be obtained from
the Library of Congress.

ISBN 978-1-4197-4228-6
eISBN 978-1-68335-778-0

Published in 2021 by Megascope, an imprint of
Abrams ComicArts ®, an imprint of ABRAMS

Printed and bound in China
10 9 8 7 6 5 4 3 2 1

ABRAMS The Art of Books
195 Broadway, New York, NY 10007
abramsbooks.com

ABRAMS COMIC ARTS
MEGASCOPE ✳

MEGASCOPE is dedicated to show-
casing speculative and non-fiction
works by and about people of color,
with a focus on science fiction,
fantasy, horror, history, and stories
of magical realism. The megascope
is a fictional device imagined by W.
E. B. Du Bois that can peer through
time and space into other realities.
This magical invention represents the
idea that so much of our collective
past has not seen the light of day, and
that there is so much history that we
have yet to discover. MEGASCOPE
will serve as a lens through which
we can broaden our view of history,
the present, and the future, and as a
method by which previously unheard
voices can find their way to an
ever-growing diverse audience.

MEGASCOPE ADVISORY BOARD

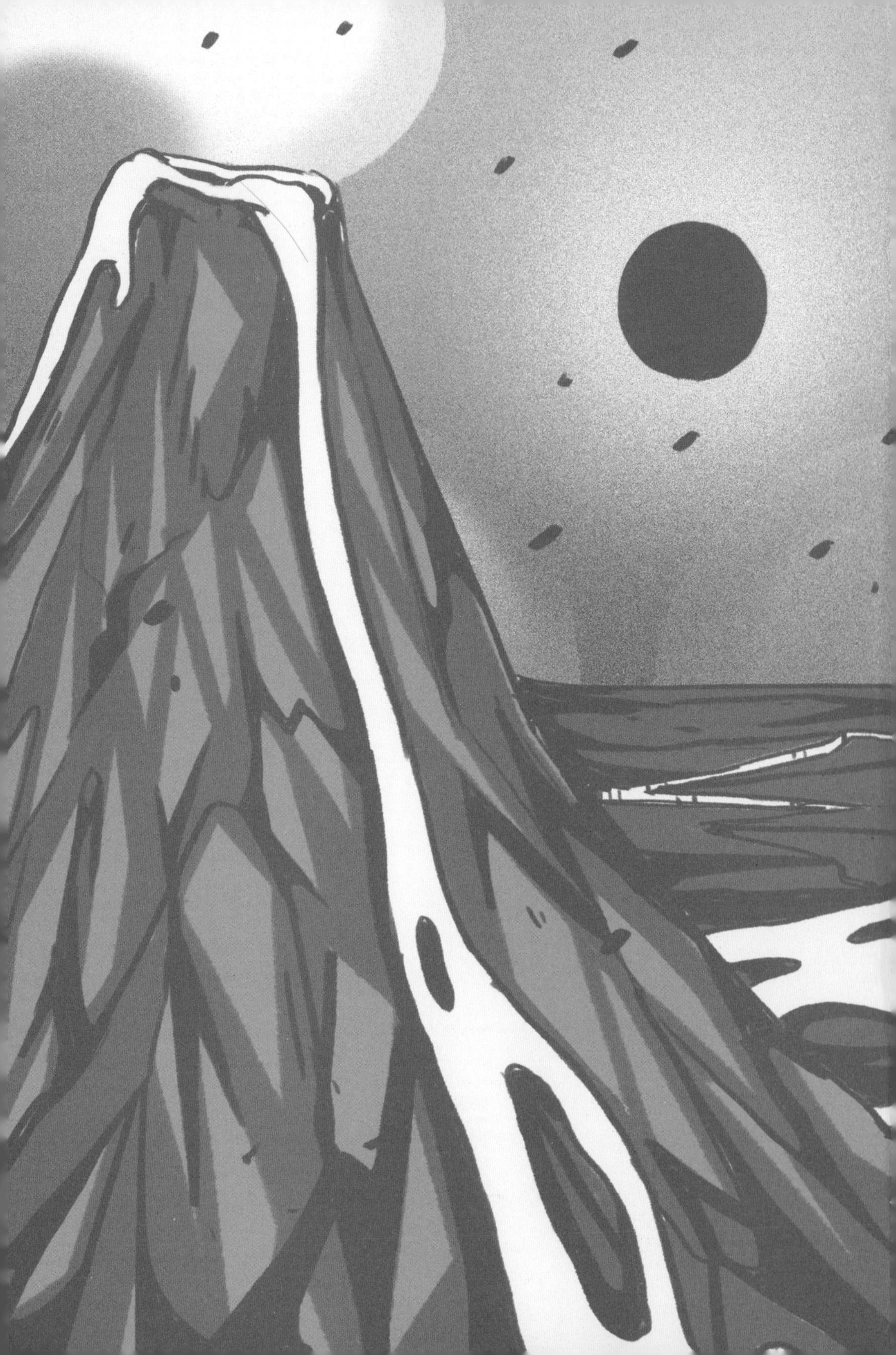